THE LIBERAL IMAGINATION

Lionel Trilling was born in New York City in 1905. He received his A.B., A.M., and Ph.D. degrees from Columbia University, where he is now professor of English.

He has written two critical studies—*Matthew Arnold* (1939) and *E. M. Forster* (1943)—and a novel, *The Middle of the Journey* (1947). He is the author of two widely reprinted stories, "The Other Margaret" and "Of This Time, Of That Place," and the editor of *The Portable Matthew Arnold* (1949) and a selection of the *Letters of John Keats* (1950).

The Liberal Imagination was published by the Viking Press in 1950.

THE LIBERAL
IMAGINATION

Essays on Literature
and Society

LIONEL TRILLING

Doubleday Anchor Books
Doubleday & Company, Inc.
Garden City, New York

The bibliographical note on pages xv-xvi records where the essays in this book, or earlier versions of them, originally appeared.

To Jacques Barzun

PREFACE

The essays of this volume were written over the last ten years, the greater number within the last three or four years. I have substantially revised almost all of them, but I have not changed the original intent of any. The bibliographical note indicates the circumstances of their first publication. For permission to reprint them here I am grateful to *The American Quarterly, Horizon, Kenyon Review, The Nation, The New Leader, The New York Times Book Review*, and *Partisan Review*, and the Columbia University Press, The Dial Press, The Macmillan Company, New Directions, and Rinehart and Company.

Although the essays are diverse in subject, they have, I believe, a certain unity. One way, perhaps the quickest way, of suggesting what this unity is might be to say that it derives from an abiding interest in the ideas of what we loosely call liberalism, especially the relation of these ideas to literature.

In the United States at this time liberalism is not only the dominant but even the sole intellectual tradition. For it is the plain fact that nowadays there are no conservative or reactionary ideas in general circulation. This does not mean, of course, that there is no impulse to conservatism or to reaction. Such impulses are certainly very strong, perhaps even stronger than most of us know. But the conservative impulse and the reactionary impulse do not, with some isolated and some ecclesiastical exceptions, express themselves in ideas but only in action or in irritable mental gestures which seek to resemble ideas.

This intellectual condition of conservatism and reaction will perhaps seem to some liberals a fortunate thing. When we say that a movement is "bankrupt of ideas" we are likely to suppose that it is at the end of its powers. But this is not so, and it is dangerous for us to suppose that it is so, as the experience of Europe in the last quarter-century suggests, for in the modern situation it is just when a movement despairs of having ideas that it turns to force, which it masks in ideology. What is more, it is not conducive to the real strength of liberalism that it should occupy the intellectual field alone. In the course of one of the essays of this book I refer to a remark of John Stuart Mill's in his famous article on Coleridge—Mill, at odds with Coleridge all down the intellectual and political line, nevertheless urged all liberals to become acquainted with this powerful conservative mind. He said that the prayer of every true partisan of liberalism should be, " 'Lord, enlighten thou our enemies . . .'; sharpen their wits, give acuteness to their perceptions and consecutiveness and clearness to their reasoning powers. We are in danger from their folly, not from their wisdom: their weakness is what fills us with apprehension, not their strength." What Mill meant, of course, was that the intellectual pressure which an opponent like Coleridge could exert would force liberals to examine their position for its weaknesses and complacencies.

We cannot very well set about to contrive opponents who will do us the service of forcing us to become more intelligent, who will require us to keep our ideas from becoming stale, habitual, and inert. This we will have to do for ourselves. It has for some time seemed to me that a criticism which has at heart the interests of liberalism might find its most useful work not in confirming liberalism in its sense of general rightness but rather in putting under some degree of pressure the liberal ideas and assumptions of the present time. If liberalism is, as I believe it to be, a large tendency rather than a concise body of doctrine, then, as that large tendency makes itself explicit, certain of its particular expressions are bound to be relatively weaker than others, and some even useless and mistaken. If this is so, then for liberalism to be aware of the weak or wrong expressions of itself would seem to be an advantage to the tendency as a whole.

Goethe says somewhere that there is no such thing as a liberal idea, that there are only liberal sentiments.

This is true. Yet it is also true that certain sentiments consort only with certain ideas and not with others. What is more, sentiments become ideas by a natural and imperceptible process. "Our continued influxes of feeling," said Wordsworth, "are modified and directed by our thoughts, which are indeed the representatives of all our past feelings." And Charles Péguy said, *"Tout commence en mystique et finit en politique"*—everything begins in sentiment and assumption and finds its issue in political action and institutions. The converse is also true: just as sentiments become ideas, ideas eventually establish themselves as sentiments.

If this is so, if between sentiments and ideas there is a natural connection so close as to amount to a kind of identity, then the connection between literature and politics will be seen as a very immediate one. And this will seem especially true if we do not intend the narrow but the wide sense of the word politics. It is the wide sense of the word that is nowadays forced upon us, for clearly it is no longer possible to think of politics except as the politics of culture, the organization of human life toward some end or other, toward the modification of sentiments, which is to say the quality of human life. The word liberal is a word primarily of political import, but its political meaning defines itself by the quality of life it envisages, by the sentiments it desires to affirm. This will begin to explain why a writer of literary criticism involves himself with political considerations. These are not political essays, they are essays in literary criticism. But they assume the inevitable intimate, if not always obvious, connection between literature and politics.

The making of the connection requires, as I have implied, no great ingenuity, nor any extravagant manipulation of the word literature or, beyond taking it in the large sense specified, of the word politics. It is a connection which is quickly understood and as quickly made and acted upon by certain governments. And although it is often resisted by many very good literary critics, it has for some time been accepted with enthusiasm by the most interesting of our creative writers; the literature of the modern period, of the last century and a half, has been characteristically political. Of the writers of the last hundred and fifty years who command our continuing attention, the very large majority have in one way or another turned their passions, their adverse, critical, and very intense passions, upon the condition of the polity. The preoccupation with the research into the self that has marked this literature, and the revival of the concepts of religion that has marked a notable part of it, do not controvert but rather support the statement about its essential commitment to politics.

When Mill urged liberals to read Coleridge, he had in mind not merely Coleridge's general power of intellect as it stood in critical opposition to the liberalism of the day; he had also in mind certain particular attitudes and views that sprang, as he believed, from Coleridge's nature and power as a poet. Mill had learned through direct and rather terrible experience what the tendency of liberalism was in regard to the sentiments and the imagination. From the famous "crisis" of his youth he had learned, although I believe he never put it in just this way, that liberalism stood in a paradoxical relation to the emotions. The paradox is that liberalism is concerned with the emotions above all else, as proof of which the word happiness stands at the very center of its thought, but in its effort to establish the emotions, or certain among them, in some sort of freedom, liberalism somehow tends to deny them in their full possibility. Dickens' *Hard Times* serves to remind us that the liberal principles upon which Mill was brought up, although extreme, were not isolated and unique, and the principles of Mill's rearing very nearly destroyed him, as in fact they did destroy the Louisa Gradgrind of Dickens' novel. And nothing is more touching than the passionate gratitude which Mill gave to poetry for having restored him to the possibility of an emotional life after he had lived in a despairing apathy which brought him to the verge of suicide. That is why, although his political and metaphysical disagreement with Coleridge was extreme, he so highly valued Coleridge's politics and metaphysics—he valued them because they were a poet's, and he hoped that they might modify liberalism's tendency to envisage the world in what he called a "prosaic" way and recall liberals to a sense of variousness and possibility. Nor did he think that there was only a private emotional advantage to be gained from the sense of variousness and possibility—he believed it to be an intellectual and political necessity.

Contemporary liberalism does not depreciate emotion in the abstract, and in the abstract it sets great store by variousness and possibility. Yet, as is true of any other human entity, the conscious and the unconscious life of liberalism are not always in accord. So far as liberalism is active and positive, so far, that is, as it moves toward organization, it tends to select the emotions and qualities that are most susceptible of organization. As it carries out its active and positive ends it unconsciously limits its view of the world to what it can deal with, and it unconsciously tends to develop theories and principles, particularly in relation to the nature of the human mind, that justify its limitation. Its characteristic paradox appears again, and in another form, for in the very interests of its great primal act of imagination by which it establishes its essence and existence—in the interests, that is, of its vision of a general enlargement and freedom and rational direction of human life—it drifts toward a denial of the emotions and the imagination. And in the very interest of affirming its confidence in the power of the mind, it inclines to constrict and make mechanical its conception of the nature of mind. Mill, to refer to him a last time, understood from his own experience that the imagination was properly the joint possession of the emotions and the intellect, that it was fed by the emotions, and that without it the intellect withers and dies, that without it the mind cannot work and cannot properly conceive itself. I do not know whether or not Mill had particularly in mind a sentence from the passage from Thomas Burnet's *Archaeologiae Philosophicae* which Coleridge quotes as the epigraph to *The Ancient Mariner*, the sentence in which Burnet says that a judicious belief in the existence of demons has the effect of keeping the mind from becoming "narrow, and lapsed entirely into mean thoughts," but he surely understood what Coleridge, who believed in demons as little as Mill did, intended by his citation of the passage. Coleridge wanted to enforce by that quaint sentence from Burnet what is the general import of *The Ancient Mariner* apart from any more particular doctrine that exegesis may discover —that the world is a complex and unexpected and terrible place which is not always to be understood by the mind as we use it in our everyday tasks.

It is one of the tendencies of liberalism to simplify, and this tendency is natural in view of the effort which liberalism makes to organize the elements of life in a rational way. And when we approach liberalism in a critical spirit, we shall fail in critical completeness if we do not take into account the value and necessity of its organizational impulse. But at the same time we must understand that organization means delegation, and agencies, and bureaus, and technicians, and that the ideas that can survive delegation, that can be passed on to agencies and bureaus and technicians, incline to be ideas of a certain kind and of a certain simplicity: they give up something of their largeness and modulation and complexity in order to survive. The lively sense of contingency and possibility, and of those exceptions to the rule which may be the beginning of the end of the rule— this sense does not suit well with the impulse to organization. So that when we come to look at liberalism in a critical spirit, we have to expect that there will be a discrepancy between what I have called the primal imagination of liberalism and its present particular manifestations.

The job of criticism would seem to be, then, to recall liberalism to its first essential imagination of variousness and possibility, which implies the awareness of complexity and difficulty. To the carrying out of the job of criticizing the liberal imagination, literature has a unique relevance, not merely because so much of modern literature has explicitly directed itself upon politics, but more importantly because literature is the human activity that takes the fullest and most precise account of variousness, possibility, complexity, and difficulty.

L. T.

New York
December, 1949

BIBLIOGRAPHICAL NOTE

"Reality in America," part i was first published in *Partisan Review*, January–February 1940; part ii was first published in *The Nation*, April 20, 1946.

"Sherwood Anderson" was first published in *The Kenyon Review*, Summer, 1941; some of the added matter appeared in *The New York Times Book Review*, November 9, 1947.

"Freud and Literature" was first published in *The Kenyon Review*, Spring, 1940, and in revised form in *Horizon*, September 1947.

"The Princess Casamassima" was first published as the introduction to Henry James, *The Princess Casamassima*, New York, The Macmillan Company, 1948.

"The Function of the Little Magazine" was first published as the introduction to *The Partisan Reader: Ten Years of Partisan Review, 1933–1944: An Anthology*, edited by William Phillips and Philip Rahv, New York, The Dial Press, 1946.

"Huckleberry Finn" was first published as the introduction to Mark Twain, *The Adventures of Huckleberry Finn*, New York, Rinehart and Company, 1948.

"Kipling" was first published in *The Nation*, October 16, 1943.

"The Immortality Ode" was read before the English Institute, September 1941, and first published in *The English Institute Annual*, 1941, New York, Columbia University Press, 1942.

"Art and Neurosis" was first published in *Partisan Review*, Winter, 1945; some of the material added in the present version appeared in *The New Leader*, December 13, 1947.

"The Sense of the Past" was read before the English Graduate Union of Columbia University in February 1942, and first published in *Partisan Review*, May–June 1942.

"Tacitus Now" was first published in *The Nation*, August 22, 1942.

"Manners, Morals, and the Novel" was read at the Conference on the Heritage of the English-Speaking Peoples and Their Responsibilities, at Kenyon College, September 1947, and first published in *The Kenyon Review*, Winter, 1948.

"The Kinsey Report" was first published in *Partisan Review*, April 1948.

"F. Scott Fitzgerald" was first published in *The Nation*, April 25, 1945; some of the material added in the present version first appeared in the introduction to *The Great Gatsby*, New York, New Directions, 1945.

"Art and Fortune" was read before the English Institute, September 1948, and first published in *Partisan Review*, December 1948.

"The Meaning of a Literary Idea" was read at the Conference in American Literature at the University of Rochester, February 1949, and first published in *The American Quarterly*, Fall, 1949.

CONTENTS

THE LIBERAL IMAGINATION

Reality in America

I

It is possible to say of V. L. Parrington that with his *Main Currents in American Thought* he has had an influence on our conception of American culture which is not equaled by that of any other writer of the last two decades. His ideas are now the accepted ones wherever the college course in American literature is given by a teacher who conceives himself to be opposed to the genteel and the academic and in alliance with the vigorous and the actual. And whenever the liberal historian of America finds occasion to take account of the national literature, as nowadays he feels it proper to do, it is Parrington who is his standard and guide. Parrington's ideas are the more firmly established because they do not have to be imposed—the teacher or the critic who presents them is likely to find that his task is merely to make articulate for his audience what it has always believed, for Parrington formulated in a classic way the suppositions about our culture which are held by the American middle class so far as that class is at all liberal in its social thought and so far as it begins to understand that literature has anything to do with society.

Parrington was not a great mind; he was not a precise thinker or, except when measured by the low eminences that were about him, an impressive one. Separate Parrington from his informing idea of the economic and social determination of thought and what is left is a simple intelligence, notable for its generosity and enthusiasm but certainly not for its accuracy or originality.

Take him even with his idea and he is, once its direction is established, rather too predictable to be continuously interesting; and, indeed, what we dignify with the name of economic and social determinism amounts in his use of it to not much more than the demonstration that most writers incline to stick to their own social class. But his best virtue was real and important—he had what we like to think of as the saving salt of the American mind, the lively sense of the practical, workaday world, of the welter of ordinary undistinguished things and people, of the tangible, quirky, unrefined elements of life. He knew what so many literary historians do not know, that emotions and ideas are the sparks that fly when the mind meets difficulties.

Yet he had after all but a limited sense of what constitutes a difficulty. Whenever he was confronted with a work of art that was complex, personal and not literal, that was not, as it were, a public document, Parrington was at a loss. Difficulties that were complicated by personality or that were expressed in the language of successful art did not seem quite real to him and he was inclined to treat them as aberrations, which is one way of saying what everybody admits, that the weakest part of Parrington's talent was his aesthetic judgment. His admirers and disciples like to imply that his errors of aesthetic judgment are merely lapses of taste, but this is not so. Despite such mistakes as his notorious praise of Cabell, to whom in a remarkable passage he compares Melville, Parrington's taste was by no means bad. His errors are the errors of understanding which arise from his assumptions about the nature of reality.

Parrington does not often deal with abstract philosophical ideas, but whenever he approaches a work of art we are made aware of the metaphysics on which his aesthetics is based. There exists, he believes, a thing called *reality;* it is one and immutable, it is wholly external, it is irreducible. Men's minds may waver, but reality is always reliable, always the same, always easily to be known. And the artist's relation to reality he conceives as a simply one. Reality being fixed and given,

the artist has but to let it pass through him, he is the
lens in the first diagram of an elementary book on optics:
Fig. 1, Reality; Fig. 2, Artist; Fig. 1′, Work of Art. Figs.
1 and 1′ are normally in virtual correspondence with each
other. Sometimes the artist spoils this ideal relation by
"turning away from" reality. This results in certain fantastic works, unreal and ultimately useless. It does not
occur to Parrington that there is any other relation
possible between the artist and reality than this passage
of reality through the transparent artist; he meets evidence of imagination and creativeness with a settled
hostility, the expression of which suggests that he regards
them as the natural enemies of democracy.

In this view of things, reality, although it is always reliable, is always rather sober-sided, even grim. Parrington, a genial and enthusiastic man, can understand how
the generosity of man's hopes and desires may leap beyond reality; he admires will in the degree that he suspects mind. To an excess of desire and energy which
blinds a man to the limitations of reality he can indeed
be very tender. This is one of the many meanings he
gives to *romance* or *romanticism,* and in spite of himself
it appeals to something in his own nature. The praise
of Cabell is Parrington's response not only to Cabell's
elegance—for Parrington loved elegance—but also to
Cabell's insistence on the part which a beneficent self-
deception may and even should play in the disappoint-
ing fact-bound life of man, particularly in the private
and erotic part of his life.[1]

The second volume of *Main Currents* is called *The Romantic Revolution in America* and it is natural to expect
that the word romantic should appear in it frequently.
So it does, more frequently than one can count, and
seldom with the same meaning, seldom with the sense
that the word, although scandalously vague as it has
been used by the literary historians, is still full of com-

---

[1] See, for example, how Parrington accounts for the "idealizing mind"—Melville's—by the discrepancy between "a wife
in her morning kimono" and "the Helen of his dreams."
Vol. II, p. 259.

plicated but not wholly pointless ideas, that it involves many contrary but definable things; all too often Parrington uses the word romantic with the word romance close at hand, meaning *a* romance, in the sense that *Graustark* or *Treasure Island* is a romance, as though it signified chiefly a gay disregard of the limitations of everyday fact. Romance is refusing to heed the counsels of experience (p. iii); it is ebullience (p. iv); it is utopianism (p. iv); it is individualism (p. vi); it is self-deception (p. 59)—"romantic faith . . . in the beneficent processes of trade and industry" (as held, we inevitably ask, by the romantic Adam Smith?); it is the love of the picturesque (p. 49); it is the dislike of innovation (p. 50) but also the love of change (p. iv); it is the sentimental (p. 192); it is patriotism, and then it is cheap (p. 235). It may be used to denote what is not classical, but chiefly it means that which ignores reality (pp. ix, 136, 143, 147, and *passim*); it is not critical (pp. 225, 235), although in speaking of Cooper and Melville, Parrington admits that criticism can sometimes spring from romanticism.

Whenever a man with whose ideas he disagrees wins from Parrington a reluctant measure of respect, the word romantic is likely to appear. He does not admire Henry Clay, yet something in Clay is not to be despised—his romanticism, although Clay's romanticism is made equivalent with his inability to "come to grips with reality." Romanticism is thus, in most of its significations, the venial sin of *Main Currents;* like carnal passion in the *Inferno,* it evokes not blame but tender sorrow. But it can also be the great and saving virtue which Parrington recognizes. It is ascribed to the transcendental reformers he so much admires; it is said to mark two of his most cherished heroes, Jefferson and Emerson: "they were both romantics and their idealism was only a different expression of a common spirit." Parrington held, we may say, at least two different views of romanticism which suggest two different views of reality. Sometimes he speaks of reality in an honorific way, meaning the substantial stuff of life, the ineluctable facts with which the mind must cope, but sometimes he speaks of it pejoratively and means the world of established social forms; and he speaks of realism in two ways: sometimes as the power of dealing intelligently with fact, sometimes as a cold and conservative resistance to idealism.

Just as for Parrington there is a saving grace and a venial sin, there is also a deadly sin, and this is turning away from reality, not in the excess of generous feeling, but in what he believes to be a deficiency of feeling, as with Hawthorne, or out of what amounts to sinful pride, as with Henry James. He tells us that there was too much realism in Hawthorne to allow him to give his faith to the transcendental reformers: "he was too much of a realist to change fashions in creeds"; "he remained cold to the revolutionary criticism that was eager to pull down the old temples to make room for nobler." It is this cold realism, keeping Hawthorne apart from his enthusiastic contemporaries, that alienates Parrington's sympathy— "Eager souls, mystics and revolutionaries, may propose to refashion the world in accordance with their dreams; but evil remains, and so long as it lurks in the secret places of the heart, utopia is only the shadow of a dream. And so while the Concord thinkers were proclaiming man to be the indubitable child of God, Hawthorne was critically examining the question of evil as it appeared in the light of his own experience. It was the central fascinating problem of his intellectual life, and in pursuit of a solution he probed curiously into the hidden, furtive recesses of the soul." Parrington's disapproval of the enterprise is unmistakable.

Now we might wonder whether Hawthorne's questioning of the naïve and often eccentric faiths of the transcendental reformers was not, on the face of it, a public service. But Parrington implies that it contributes nothing to democracy, and even that it stands in the way of the realization of democracy. If democracy depends wholly on a fighting faith, I suppose he is right. Yet society is after all something that exists at the moment as well as in the future, and if one man wants to probe curiously into the hidden furtive recesses of the contem-

porary soul, a broad democracy and especially one devoted to reality should allow him to do so without
despising him. If what Hawthorne did was certainly
nothing to build a party on, we ought perhaps to forgive
him when we remember that he was only one man and
that the future of mankind did not depend upon him
alone. But this very fact serves only to irritate Parrington; he is put out by Hawthorne's loneliness and believes that part of Hawthorne's insufficiency as a writer
comes from his failure to get around and meet people.
Hawthorne could not, he tells us, establish contact with
the "Yankee reality," and was scarcely aware of the "substantial world of Puritan reality that Samuel Sewall
knew."

To turn from reality might mean to turn to romance,
but Parrington tells us that Hawthorne was romantic
"only in a narrow and very special sense." He was not
interested in the world of, as it were, practical romance,
in the Salem of the clipper ships; from this he turned
away to create "a romance of ethics." This is not an
illuminating phrase but it is a catching one, and it might
be taken to mean that Hawthorne was in the tradition of,
say, Shakespeare; but we quickly learn that, no, Hawthorne had entered a barren field, for although he himself lived in the present and had all the future to mold,
he preferred to find many of his subjects in the past.
We learn too that his romance of ethics is not admirable
because it requires the hard, fine pressing of ideas, and
we are told that "a romantic uninterested in adventure
and afraid of sex is likely to become somewhat graveled
for matter." In short, Hawthorne's mind was a thin one,
and Parrington puts in evidence his use of allegory and
symbol and the very severity and precision of his art to
prove that he suffered from a sadly limited intellect, for
so much fancy and so much art could scarcely be needed
unless the writer were trying to exploit to the utmost the
few poor ideas that he had.

Hawthorne, then, was "forever dealing with shadows,
and he knew that he was dealing with shadows." Perhaps so, but shadows are also part of reality and one

would not want a world without shadows, it would not even be a "real" world. But we must get beyond Parrington's metaphor. The fact is that Hawthorne was dealing beautifully with realities, with substantial things. The man who could raise those brilliant and serious doubts about the nature and possibility of moral perfection, the man who could keep himself aloof from the "Yankee reality" and who could dissent from the orthodoxies of dissent and tell us so much about the nature of moral zeal, is of course dealing exactly with reality.

Parrington's characteristic weakness as a historian is suggested by his title, for the culture of a nation is not truly figured in the image of the current. A culture is not a flow, nor even a confluence; the form of its existence is struggle, or at least debate—it is nothing if not a dialectic. And in any culture there are likely to be certain artists who contain a large part of the dialectic within themselves, their meaning and power lying in their contradictions; they contain within themselves, it may be said, the very essence of the culture, and the sign of this is that they do not submit to serve the ends of any one ideological group or tendency. It is a significant circumstance of American culture, and one which is susceptible of explanation, that an unusually large proportion of its notable writers of the nineteenth century were such repositories of the dialectic of their times—they contained both the yes and the no of their culture, and by that token they were prophetic of the future. Parrington said that he had not set up shop as a literary critic; but if a literary critic is simply a reader who has the ability to understand literature and to convey to others what he understands, it is not exactly a matter of free choice whether or not a cultural historian shall be a literary critic, nor is it open to him to let his virtuous political and social opinions do duty for percipience. To throw out Poe because he cannot be conveniently fitted into a theory of American culture, to speak of him as a biological sport and as a mind apart from the main current, to find his gloom to be merely personal and eccentric, "only the atrabilious wretchedness of a dipsoma-

niac," as Hawthorne's was "no more than the skeptical
questioning of life by a nature that knew no fierce
storms," to judge Melville's response to American life to
be less noble than that of Bryant or of Greeley, to speak
of Henry James as an escapist, as an artist similar to
Whistler, a man characteristically afraid of stress—this is
not merely to be mistaken in aesthetic judgment; rather
it is to examine without attention and from the point of
view of a limited and essentially arrogant conception of
reality the documents which are in some respects the
most suggestive testimony to what America was and is,
and of course to get no answer from them.

Parrington lies twenty years behind us, and in the in-
tervening time there has developed a body of opinion
which is aware of his inadequacies and of the inadequacies of his coadjutors and disciples, who make up what
might be called the literary academicism of liberalism.
Yet Parrington still stands at the center of American
thought about American culture because, as I say, he
expresses the chronic American belief that there exists an
opposition between reality and mind and that one must
enlist oneself in the party of reality.

II

This belief in the incompatibility of mind and reality
is exemplified by the doctrinaire indulgence which liberal intellectuals have always displayed toward Theodore Dreiser, an indulgence which becomes the worthier
of remark when it is contrasted with the liberal severity
toward Henry James. Dreiser and James: with that juxtaposition we are immediately at the dark and bloody
crossroads where literature and politics meet. One does
not go there gladly, but nowadays it is not exactly a
matter of free choice whether one does or does not go.
As for the particular juxtaposition itself, it is inevitable
and it has at the present moment far more significance
than the juxtaposition which once used to be made between James and Whitman. It is not hard to contrive
factitious oppositions between James and Whitman, but

the real difference between them is the difference between the moral mind, with its awareness of tragedy, irony, and multitudinous distinctions, and the transcendental mind, with its passionate sense of the oneness of multiplicity. James and Whitman are unlike not in quality but in kind, and in their very opposition they serve to complement each other. But the difference between James and Dreiser is not of kind, for both men addressed themselves to virtually the same social and moral fact. The difference here is one of quality, and perhaps nothing is more typical of American liberalism than the way it has responded to the respective qualities of the two men.

Few critics, I suppose, no matter what their political disposition, have ever been wholly blind to James's great gifts, or even to the grandiose moral intention of these gifts. And few critics have ever been wholly blind to Dreiser's great faults. But by liberal critics James is traditionally put to the ultimate question: of what use, of what actual political use, are his gifts and their intention? Granted that James was devoted to an extraordinary moral perceptiveness, granted too that moral perceptiveness has something to do with politics and the social life, of what possible practical value in our world of impending disaster can James's work be? And James's style, his characters, his subjects, and even his own social origin and the manner of his personal life are adduced to show that his work cannot endure the question. To James no quarter is given by American criticism in its political and liberal aspect. But in the same degree that liberal criticism is moved by political considerations to treat James with severity, it treats Dreiser with the most sympathetic indulgence. Dreiser's literary faults, it gives us to understand, are essentially social and political virtues. It was Parrington who established the formula for the liberal criticism of Dreiser by calling him a "peasant": when Dreiser thinks stupidly, it is because he has the slow stubbornness of a peasant; when he writes badly, it is because he is impatient of the sterile literary gentility of the bourgeoisie. It is as if wit, and flexibility

of mind, and perception, and knowledge were to be
equated with aristocracy and political reaction, while
dullness and stupidity must naturally suggest a virtuous
democracy, as in the old plays.

The liberal judgment of Dreiser and James goes back
of politics, goes back to the cultural assumptions that
make politics. We are still haunted by a kind of political
fear of the intellect which Tocqueville observed in us
more than a century ago. American intellectuals, when
they are being consciously American or political, are remarkably quick to suggest that an art which is marked
by perception and knowledge, although all very well in
its way, can never get us through gross dangers and difficulties. And their misgivings become the more intense
when intellect works in art as it ideally should, when its
processes are vivacious and interesting and brilliant. It
is then that we like to confront it with the gross dangers
and difficulties and to challenge it to save us at once
from disaster. When intellect in art is awkward or dull
we do not put it to the test of ultimate or immediate
practicality. No liberal critic asks the question of Dreiser
whether *his* moral preoccupations are going to be useful
in confronting the disasters that threaten us. And it is a
judgment on the proper nature of mind, rather than any
actual political meaning that might be drawn from the
works of the two men, which accounts for the unequal
justice they have received from the progressive critics.
If it could be conclusively demonstrated—by, say, documents in James's handwriting—that James explicitly
intended his books to be understood as pleas for co-op-
eratives, labor unions, better housing, and more equita-
ble taxation, the American critic in his liberal and
progressive character would still be worried by James
because his work shows so many of the electric qualities
of mind. And if something like the opposite were proved
of Dreiser, it would be brushed aside—as his doctrinaire
anti-Semitism has in fact been brushed aside—because
his books have the awkwardness, the chaos, the heavi-
ness which we associate with "reality." In the American
metaphysic, reality is always material reality, hard, re-

sistant, unformed, impenetrable, and unpleasant. And that mind is alone felt to be trustworthy which most resembles this reality by most nearly reproducing the sensations it affords.

In *The Rise of American Civilization*, Professor Beard uses a significant phrase when, in the course of an ironic account of James's career, he implies that we have the clue to the irrelevance of that career when we know that James was "a whole generation removed from the odors of the shop." Of a piece with this, and in itself even more significant, is the comment which Granville Hicks makes in *The Great Tradition* when he deals with James's stories about artists and remarks that such artists as James portrays, so concerned for their art and their integrity in art, do not really exist: "After all, who has ever known such artists? Where are the Hugh Verekers, the Mark Ambients, the Neil Paradays, the Overts, Limberts, Dencombes, Delavoys?" This question, as Mr. Hicks admits, had occurred to James himself, but what answer had James given to it? "If the life about us for the last thirty years refused warrant for these examples," he said in the preface to volume XII of the New York Edition, "then so much the worse for that life. . . . There are decencies that in the name of the general self-respect we must take for granted, there's a rudimentary intellectual honor to which we must, in the interest of civilization, at least pretend." And to this Mr. Hicks, shocked beyond argument, makes this reply, which would be astonishing had we not heard it before: "But this is the purest romanticism, this writing about what ought to be rather than what is!"

The "odors of the shop" are real, and to those who breathe them they guarantee a sense of vitality from which James is debarred. The idea of intellectual honor is not real, and to that chimera James was devoted. He betrayed the reality of what is in the interests of what ought to be. Dare we trust him? The question, we remember, is asked by men who themselves have elaborate transactions with what ought to be. Professor Beard spoke in the name of a growing, developing, and improving America. Mr. Hicks, when he wrote *The Great Tradition*, was in general sympathy with a nominally radical movement. But James's own transaction with what ought to be is suspect because it is carried on through what I have called the electrical qualities of mind, through a complex and rapid imagination and with a kind of authoritative immediacy. Mr. Hicks knows that Dreiser is "clumsy" and "stupid" and "bewildered" and "crude in his statement of materialistic monism"; he knows that Dreiser in his personal life—which is in point because James's personal life is always supposed to be so much in point—was not quite emancipated from "his boyhood longing for crass material success," showing "again and again a desire for the ostentatious luxury of the successful business man." But Dreiser is to be accepted and forgiven because his faults are the sad, lovable, honorable faults of reality itself, or of America itself—huge, inchoate, struggling toward expression, caught between the dream of raw power and the dream of morality.

"The liability in what Santayana called the genteel tradition was due to its being the product of mind apart from experience. Dreiser gave us the stuff of our common experience, not as it was hoped to be by any idealizing theorist, but as it actually was in its crudity." The author of this statement certainly cannot be accused of any lack of feeling for mind as Henry James represents it; nor can Mr. Matthiessen be thought of as a follower of Parrington—indeed, in the preface to *American Renaissance* he has framed one of the sharpest and most cogent criticisms of Parrington's method. Yet Mr. Matthiessen, writing in the *New York Times Book Review* about Dreiser's posthumous novel, *The Bulwark*, accepts the liberal cliché which opposes crude experience to mind and establishes Dreiser's value by implying that the mind which Dreiser's crude experience is presumed to confront and refute is the mind of gentility.

This implied amalgamation of mind with gentility is the rationale of the long indulgence of Dreiser, which is extended even to the style of his prose. Everyone is

aware that Dreiser's prose style is full of roughness and
ungainliness, and the critics who admire Dreiser tell us
it does not matter. Of course it does not matter. No
reader with a right sense of style would suppose that it
does matter, and he might even find it a virtue. But it
has been taken for granted that the ungainliness of
Dreiser's style is the only possible objection to be made
to it, and that whoever finds in it any fault at all wants
a prettified genteel style (and is objecting to the ungainliness of reality itself). For instance, Edwin Berry Burgum, in a leaflet on Dreiser put out by the Book Find
Club, tells us that Dreiser was one of those who used—
or, as Mr. Burgum says, utilized—"the diction of the
Middle West, pretty much as it was spoken, rich in colloquialism and frank in the simplicity and directness of
the pioneer tradition," and that this diction took the
place of "the literary English, formal and bookish, of
New England provincialism that was closer to the aristocratic spirit of the mother country than to the tang of
everyday life in the new West." This is mere fantasy.
Hawthorne, Thoreau, and Emerson were for the most
part remarkably colloquial—they wrote, that is, much as
they spoke; their prose was specifically American in
quality, and, except for occasional lapses, quite direct
and simple. It is Dreiser who lacks the sense of colloquial
diction—that of the Middle West or any other. If we are
to talk of bookishness, it is Dreiser who is bookish; he is
precisely literary in the bad sense; he is full of flowers of
rhetoric and shines with paste gems; at hundreds of
points his diction is not only genteel but fancy. It is he
who speaks of "a scene more distingué than this," or of
a woman "artistic in form and feature," or of a man who,
although "strong, reserved, aggressive, with an air of
wealth and experience, was *soi-disant* and not particularly eager to stay at home." Colloquialism held no real
charm for him and his natural tendency is always toward
the "fine:"

. . . . Moralists come and go; religionists fulminate
and declare the pronouncements of God as to this;

but Aphrodite still reigns. Embowered in the festal depths of the spring, set above her altars of porphyry, chalcedony, ivory and gold, see her smile the smile that is at once the texture and essence of delight, the glory and despair of the world! Dream on, oh Buddha, asleep on your lotus leaf, of an undisturbed Nirvana! Sweat, oh Jesus, your last agonizing drops over an unregenerate world! In the forests of Pan still ring the cries of the worshippers of Aphrodite! From her altars the incense of adoration ever rises! And see, the new red grapes dripping where votive hands new-press them!

Charles Jackson, the novelist, telling us in the same leaflet that Dreiser's style does not matter, remarks on how much still comes to us when we have lost by translation the stylistic brilliance of Thomas Mann or the Russians or Balzac. He is in part right. And he is right too when he says that a certain kind of conscious, supervised artistry is not appropriate to the novel of large dimensions. Yet the fact is that the great novelists have usually written very good prose, and what comes through even a bad translation is exactly the power of mind that made the well-hung sentence of the original text. In literature style is so little the mere clothing of thought—need it be insisted on at this late date?—that we may say that from the earth of the novelist's prose spring his characters, his ideas, and even his story itself.[2]

[2] The latest defense of Dreiser's style, that in the chapter on Dreiser in the *Literary History of the United States*, is worth noting: "Forgetful of the integrity and power of Dreiser's whole work, many critics have been distracted into a condemnation of his style. He was, like Twain and Whitman, an organic artist; he wrote what he knew—what he was. His many colloquialisms were part of the coinage of his time, and his sentimental and romantic passages were written in the language of the educational system and the popular literature of his formative years. In his style, as in his material, he was a child of his time, of his class. Self-educated, a type of model of the artist of plebeian origin in America, his language, like his subject matter, is not marked by internal inconsistencies." No doubt Dreiser was an organic artist in the sense that he wrote

To the extent that Dreiser's style is defensible, his thought is also defensible. That is, when he thinks like a novelist, he is worth following—when by means of his rough and ungainly but no doubt cumulatively effective style he creates rough, ungainly, but effective characters and events. But when he thinks like, as we say, a philosopher, he is likely to be not only foolish but vulgar. He thinks as the modern crowd thinks when it decides to think: religion and morality are nonsense, "religionists" and moralists are fakes, tradition is a fraud, what is man but matter and impulses, mysterious "chemisms," what value has life anyway? "What, cooking, eating, coition, job holding, growing, aging, losing, winning, in so changeful and passing a scene as this, important? Bunk! It is some form of titillating illusion with about as much import to the superior forces that bring it all about as the functions and gyrations of a fly. No more. And maybe less." Thus Dreiser at sixty. And yet there is for him always the vulgarly saving suspicion that maybe, when all is said and done, there is Something Behind It All. It is much to the point of his intellectual vulgarity that Dreiser's anti-Semitism was not merely a social prejudice but an idea, a way of dealing with difficulties.

No one, I suppose, has ever represented Dreiser as a masterly intellect. It is even commonplace to say that his ideas are inconsistent or inadequate. But once that admission has been made, his ideas are hustled out of sight while his "reality" and great brooding pity are spoken of. (His pity is to be questioned: pity is to be judged by kind, not amount, and Dreiser's pity—*Jennie*

---

what he knew and what he was, but so, I suppose, is every artist; the question for criticism comes down to *what* he knew and *what* he was. That he was a child of his time and class is also true, but this can be said of everyone without exception; the question for criticism is how he transcended the imposed limitations of his time and class. As for the defense made on the ground of his particular class, it can only be said that liberal thought has come to a strange pass when it assumes that a plebeian origin is accountable for a writer's faults through all his intellectual life.

Gerhardt provides the only exception—is either destructive of its object or it is self-pity.) Why has no liberal critic ever brought Dreiser's ideas to the bar of political practicality, asking what use is to be made of Dreiser's dim, awkward speculation, of his self-justification, of his lust for "beauty" and "sex" and "living" and "life itself," and of the showy nihilism which always seems to him so grand a gesture in the direction of profundity? We live, understandably enough, with the sense of urgency; our clock, like Baudelaire's, has had the hands removed and bears the legend, "It is later than you think." But with us it is always a little too late for mind, yet never too late for honest stupidity; always a little too late for understanding, never too late for righteous, bewildered wrath; always too late for thought, never too late for naïve moralizing. We seem to like to condemn our finest but not our worst qualities by pitting them against the exigency of time.

But sometimes time is not quite so exigent as to justify all our own exigency, and in the case of Dreiser time has allowed his deficiencies to reach their logical, and fatal, conclusion. In *The Bulwark* Dreiser's characteristic ideas come full circle, and the simple, didactic life history of Solon Barnes, a Quaker business man, affirms a simple Christian faith, and a kind of practical mysticism, and the virtues of self-abnegation and self-restraint, and the belief in and submission to the hidden purposes of higher powers, those "superior forces that bring it all about"—once, in Dreiser's opinion, so brutally indifferent, now somehow benign. This is not the first occasion on which Dreiser has shown a tenderness toward religion and a responsiveness to mysticism. *Jennie Gerhardt* and the figure of the Reverend Duncan McMillan in *An American Tragedy* are forecasts of the avowals of *The Bulwark*, and Dreiser's lively interest in power of any sort led him to take account of the power implicit in the cruder forms of mystical performance. Yet these rifts in his nearly monolithic materialism cannot quite prepare us for the blank pietism of *The Bulwark*, not after we have remembered how salient in Dreiser's work has been

the long surly rage against the "religionists" and the
"moralists," the men who have presumed to believe that
life can be given any law at all and who have dared to
suppose that will or mind or faith can shape the savage
and beautiful entity that Dreiser liked to call "life itself."
Now for Dreiser the law may indeed be given, and it is
wholly simple—the safe conduct of the personal life requires only that we follow the Inner Light according to
the regimen of the Society of Friends, or according to
some other godly rule. And now the smiling Aphrodite
set above her altars of porphyry, chalcedony, ivory, and
gold is quite forgotten, and we are told that the sad joy
of cosmic acceptance goes hand in hand with sexual ab-
stinence.

Dreiser's mood of "acceptance" in the last years of his
life is not, as a personal experience, to be submitted to
the tests of intellectual validity. It consists of a sensation
of cosmic understanding, of an overarching sense of
unity with the world in its apparent evil as well as in its
obvious good. It is no more to be quarreled with, or
reasoned with, than love itself—indeed, it is a kind of
love, not so much of the world as of oneself in the world.
Perhaps it is either the cessation of desire or the perfect
balance of desires. It is what used often to be meant by
"peace," and up through the nineteenth century a good
many people understood its meaning. If it was Dreiser's
own emotion at the end of his life, who would not be
happy that he had achieved it? I am not even sure that
our civilization would not be the better for more of us
knowing and desiring this emotion of grave felicity. Yet
granting the personal validity of the emotion, Dreiser's
exposition of it fails, and is, moreover, offensive. Mr.
Matthiessen has warned us of the attack that will be
made on the doctrine of The Bulwark by "those who
believe that any renewal of Christianity marks a new
'failure of nerve.'" But Dreiser's religious avowal is not a
failure of nerve—it is a failure of mind and heart. We
have only to set his book beside any work in which mind
and heart are made to serve religion to know this at once.
Ivan Karamazov's giving back his ticket of admission to

the "harmony" of the universe suggests that *The Bulwark* is not morally adequate, for we dare not, as its hero does, blandly "accept" the suffering of others; and the Book of Job tells us that it does not include enough in its exploration of the problem of evil, and is not stern enough. I have said that Dreiser's religious affirmation was offensive; the offense lies in the vulgar ease of its formulation, as well as in the comfortable untroubled way in which Dreiser moved from nihilism to pietism.[3]

The Bulwark is the fruit of Dreiser's old age, but if we speak of it as a failure of thought and feeling, we cannot suppose that with age Dreiser weakened in mind and heart. The weakness was always there. And in a sense it is not Dreiser who failed but a whole way of dealing with ideas, a way in which we have all been in some degree involved. Our liberal, progressive culture tolerated Dreiser's vulgar materialism with its huge negation, its simple cry of "Bunk!," feeling that perhaps it was not quite intellectually adequate but certainly very *strong*, certainly very *real*. And now, almost as a natural consequence, it has been given, and is not unwilling to take, Dreiser's pietistic religion in all its inadequacy.

Dreiser, of course, was firmer than the intellectual culture that accepted him. He *meant* his ideas, at least so far as a man can mean ideas who is incapable of following them to their consequences. But we, when it came to his ideas, talked about his great brooding pity and shrugged the ideas off. We are still doing it. Robert Elias, the biographer of Dreiser, tells us that "it is part of the logic of [Dreiser's] life that he should have completed *The Bulwark* at the same time that he joined the

---

[3] This ease and comfortableness seem to mark contemporary religious conversions. Religion nowadays has the appearance of what the ideal modern house has been called, "a machine for living," and seemingly one makes up one's mind to acquire and use it not with spiritual struggle but only with a growing sense of its practicability and convenience. Compare *The Seven Storey Mountain*, which Monsignor Sheen calls "a twentieth-century form of the *Confessions* of St. Augustine," with the old, the as it were original, *Confessions* of St. Augustine.

Communists." Just what kind of logic this is we learn from Mr. Elias's further statement. "When he supported left-wing movements and finally, last year, joined the Communist Party, he did so not because he had examined the details of the party line and found them satisfactory, but because he agreed with a general program that represented a means for establishing his cherished goal of greater equality among men." Whether or not Dreiser was following the logic of his own life, he was certainly following the logic of the liberal criticism that accepted him so undiscriminatingly as one of the great, significant expressions of its spirit. This is the liberal criticism, in the direct line of Parrington, which establishes the social responsibility of the writer and then goes on to say that, apart from his duty of resembling reality as much as possible, he is not really responsible for anything, not even for his ideas. The scope of reality being what it is, ideas are held to be mere "details," and, what is more, to be details which, if attended to, have the effect of diminishing reality. But ideals are different from ideas; in the liberal criticism which descends from Parrington ideals consort happily with reality and they urge us to deal impatiently with ideas—a "cherished goal" forbids that we stop to consider how we reach it, or if we may not destroy it in trying to reach it the wrong way.

Sherwood Anderson

I find it hard, and I think it would be false, to write about Sherwood Anderson without speaking of him personally and even emotionally. I did not know him; I was in his company only twice and on neither occasion did I talk with him. The first time I saw him was when he was at the height of his fame; I had, I recall, just been reading *A Story-Teller's Story* and *Tar*, and these autobiographical works had made me fully aware of the change that had taken place in my feelings since a few years before when almost anything that Anderson wrote had seemed a sort of revelation. The second time was about two years before his death; he had by then not figured in my own thought about literature for many years, and I believe that most people were no longer aware of him as an immediate force in their lives. His last two novels (*Beyond Desire* in 1932 and *Kit Brandon* in 1936) had not been good; they were all too clearly an attempt to catch up with the world, but the world had moved too fast; it was not that Anderson was not aware of the state of things but rather that he had suffered the fate of the writer who at one short past moment has had a success with a simple idea which he allowed to remain simple and to become fixed. On both occasions—the first being a gathering, after one of Anderson's lectures, of eager Wisconsin graduate students and of young instructors who were a little worried that they would be thought stuffy and academic by this Odysseus, the first famous man of letters most of us had ever seen; the second being a crowded New York party

—I was much taken by Anderson's human quality, by a certain serious interest he would have in the person he was shaking hands with or talking to for a brief, formal moment, by a certain graciousness or gracefulness which seemed to arise from an innocence of heart.

I mention this very tenuous personal impression because it must really have arisen not at all from my observation of the moment but rather have been projected from some unconscious residue of admiration I had for Anderson's books even after I had made all my adverse judgments upon them. It existed when I undertook this notice of Anderson on the occasion of his death, or else I should not have undertaken it. And now that I have gone back to his books again and have found that I like them even less than I remembered, I find too that the residue of admiration still remains; it is quite vague, yet it requires to be articulated with the clearer feelings of dissatisfaction; and it needs to be spoken of, as it has been, first.

There is a special poignancy in the failure of Anderson's later career. According to the artistic morality to which he and his friends subscribed—Robert Browning seems to have played a large if anonymous part in shaping it—Anderson should have been forever protected against artistic failure by the facts of his biography. At the age of forty-five, as everyone knows, he found himself the manager of a small paint factory in Elyria, Ohio; one day, in the very middle of a sentence he was dictating, he walked out of the factory and gave himself to literature and truth. From the wonder of that escape he seems never to have recovered, and his continued pleasure in it did him harm, for it seems to have made him feel that the problem of the artist was defined wholly by the struggle between sincerity on the one hand and commercialism and gentility on the other. He did indeed say that the artist needed not only courage but craft, yet it was surely the courage by which he set the most store. And we must sometimes feel that he had dared too much for his art and therefore expected too much merely from his boldness, believing that right opinion

must necessarily result from it. Anderson was deeply
concerned with the idea of justification; there was an
odd, quirky, undisciplined religious strain in him that
took this form; and he expected that although Philistia
might condemn him, he would have an eventual justification in the way of art and truth. He was justified in
some personal way, as I have tried to say, and no doubt
his great escape had something to do with this, but it
also had the effect of fatally fixing the character of his
artistic life.

Anderson's greatest influence was probably upon
those who read him in adolescence, the age when we
find the books we give up but do not get over. And it
now needs a little fortitude to pick up again, as many
must have done upon the news of his death, the one
book of his we are all sure to have read, for *Winesburg,
Ohio* is not just a book, it is a personal souvenir. It is
commonly owned in the Modern Library edition, very
likely in the most primitive format of that series, even
before it was tricked out with its vulgar little ballet-
Prometheus; and the brown oilcloth binding, the coarse
paper, the bold type crooked on the page, are dreadfully evocative. Even the introduction by Ernest Boyd is
rank with the odor of the past, of the day when criticism
existed in heroic practical simplicity, when it was all
truth against hypocrisy, idealism against philistinism,
and the opposite of "romanticism" was not "classicism"
but "realism," which—it now seems odd—negated both.
As for the Winesburg stories themselves, they are as
dangerous to read again, as paining and as puzzling, as
if they were old letters we had written or received.

It is not surprising that Anderson should have made
his strongest appeal, although by no means his only one,
to adolescents. For one thing, he wrote of young people
with a special tenderness; one of his best-known stories
is called "I Want To Know Why": it is the great adoles-
cent question, and the world Anderson saw is essentially,
and even when it is inhabited by adults, the world of
the sensitive young person. It is a world that does not
"understand," a world of solitude, of running away from

home, of present dullness and far-off joy and eventual fulfillment; it is a world seen as suffused by one's own personality and yet—and therefore—felt as indifferent to one's own personality. And Anderson used what seems to a young person the very language to penetrate to the heart of the world's mystery, what with its rural or primeval willingness to say things thrice over, its reiterated "Well . . ." which suggests the groping of boyhood, its "Eh?" which implies the inward-turning wisdom of old age.

Most of us will feel now that this world of Anderson's is a pretty inadequate representation of reality and probably always was. But we cannot be sure that it was not a necessary event in our history, like adolescence itself; and no one has the adolescence he would have liked to have had. But an adolescence must not continue beyond its natural term, and as we read through Anderson's canon what exasperates us is his stubborn, satisfied continuance in his earliest attitudes. There is something undeniably impressive about the period of Anderson's work in which he was formulating his characteristic notions. We can take, especially if we have a modifying consciousness of its historical moment, *Windy MacPherson's Son*, despite its last part which is so curiously like a commercial magazine story of the time; *Marching Men* has power even though its political mysticism is repellent; *Winesburg, Ohio* has its touch of greatness; *Poor White* is heavy-handed but not without its force; and some of the stories in *The Triumph of the Egg* have the kind of grim quaintness which is, I think, Anderson's most successful mood, the mood that he occasionally achieves now and then in his later short pieces, such as "Death in the Woods." But after 1921, in *Dark Laughter* and *Many Marriages*, the books that made the greatest critical stir, there emerges in Anderson's work the compulsive, obsessive, repetitive quality which finally impresses itself on us as his characteristic quality.

Anderson is connected with the tradition of the men who maintain a standing quarrel with respectable society and have a perpetual bone to pick with the rational intellect. It is a very old tradition, for the Essenes, the early Franciscans, as well as the early Hasidim, may be said to belong to it. In modern times it has been continued by Blake and Whitman and D. H. Lawrence. Those who belong to the tradition usually do something more about the wrong way the world goes than merely to denounce it—they *act out* their denunciations and assume a role and a way of life. Typically they take up their packs and leave the doomed respectable city, just as Anderson did. But Anderson lacked what his spiritual colleagues have always notably had. We may call it *mind,* but *energy* and *spiritedness,* in their relation to mind, will serve just as well. Anderson never understood that the moment of enlightenment and conversion—the walking out—cannot be merely celebrated but must be developed, so that what begins as an act of will grows to be an act of intelligence. The men of the anti-rationalist tradition mock the mind's pretensions and denounce its restrictiveness; but they are themselves the agents of the most powerful thought. They do not of course really reject mind at all, but only mind as it is conceived by respectable society. "I learned the Torah from all the limbs of my teacher," said one of the Hasidim. They think with their sensations, their emotions, and, some of them, with their sex. While denouncing intellect, they shine forth in a mental blaze of energy which manifests itself in syntax, epigram, and true discovery.

Anderson is not like them in this regard. He did not become a "wise" man. He did not have the gift of being able to throw out a sentence or a metaphor which suddenly illuminates some dark corner of life—his role implied that he should be full of "sayings" and specific insights, yet he never was. But in the preface to *Winesburg, Ohio* he utters one of the few really "wise" things in his work, and, by a kind of irony, it explains something of his own inadequacy. The preface consists of a little story about an old man who is writing what he calls "The Book of the Grotesque." This is the old man's ruling idea:

That in the beginning when the world was young there were a great many thoughts but no such thing as a truth. Man made the truths himself and each truth was a composite of a great many vague thoughts. All about in the world were truths and they were all beautiful.

The old man listed hundreds of the truths in his book. I will not try to tell you all of them. There was the truth of virginity and the truth of passion, the truth of wealth and of poverty, of thrift and of profligacy, of carelessness and abandon. Hundreds and hundreds were the truths and they were all beautiful.

And then the people came along. Each as he appeared snatched up one of the truths and some who were quite strong snatched up a dozen of them.

It was the truths that made the people grotesques. The old man had quite an elaborate theory concerning the matter. It was his notion that the moment one of the people took one of the truths to himself, called it his truth, and tried to live his life by it, he became a grotesque and the truth he embraced became a falsehood.

Anderson snatched but a single one of the truths and it made him, in his own gentle and affectionate meaning of the word, a "grotesque"; eventually the truth itself became a kind of falsehood. It was the truth—or perhaps we must call it a simple complex of truths—of love-passion-freedom, and it was made up of these "vague thoughts": that each individual is a precious secret essence, often discordant with all other essences; that society, and more particularly the industrial society, threatens these essences; that the old good values of life have been destroyed by the industrial dispensation; that people have been cut off from each other and even from themselves. That these thoughts make a truth is certain; and its importance is equally certain. In what way could it have become a falsehood and its possessor a "grotesque"?

The nature of the falsehood seems to lie in this—that Anderson's affirmation of life by love, passion, and free-

dom had, paradoxically enough, the effect of quite
negating life, making it gray, empty, and devoid of
meaning. We are quite used to hearing that this is what
excessive intellection can do; we are not so often warned
that emotion, if it is of a certain kind, can be similarly
destructive. Yet when feeling is understood as an answer,
a therapeutic, when it becomes a sort of critical tool
and is conceived of as excluding other activities of life,
it can indeed make the world abstract and empty. Love
and passion, when considered as they are by Anderson
as a means of attack upon the order of the respectable
world, can contrive a world which is actually without
love and passion and not worth being "free" in.[1]

In Anderson's world there are many emotions, or
rather many instances of a few emotions, but there are
very few sights, sounds, and smells, very little of the stuff
of actuality. The very things to which he gives moral
value because they are living and real and opposed in
their organic nature to the insensate abstractness of an
industrial culture become, as he writes about them,
themselves abstract and without life. His praise of the
racehorses he said he loved gives us no sense of a horse;
his Mississippi does not flow; his tall corn grows out of

[1] In the preface of *The Sherwood Anderson Reader*, Paul
Rosenfeld, Anderson's friend and admirer, has summarized
in a remarkable way the vision of life which Anderson's
work suggests: "Almost, it seems, we touch an absolute existence, a curious semi-animal, semi-divine life. Its chronic
state is banality, prostration, dismemberment, unconsciousness; tensity with indefinite yearning and infinitely stretch-
ing desire. Its manifestation: the non-community of cranky
or otherwise asocial solitaries, dispersed, impotent and imprisoned. . . . Its wonders—the wonders of its chaos—are
fugitive heroes and heroines, mutilated like the dismembered Osiris, the dismembered Dionysius. . . . Painfully
the absolute comes to itself in consciousness of universal
feeling and helplessness. . . . It realizes itself as feeling,
sincerity, understanding, as connection and unity; sometimes at the cost of the death of its creatures. It triumphs
in anyone aware of its existence even in its sullen state.
The moment of realization is tragically brief. Feeling, understanding, unity pass. The divine life sinks back again,
dismembered and unconscious."

the soil of his dominating subjectivity. The beautiful organic things of the world are made to be admirable not for themselves but only for their moral superiority to men and machines. There are many similarities of theme between Anderson and D. H. Lawrence, but Lawrence's far stronger and more sensitive mind kept his faculty of vision fresh and true; Lawrence had eyes for the substantial and even at his most doctrinaire he knew the world of appearance.

And just as there is no real sensory experience in Anderson's writing, there is also no real social experience. His people do not really go to church or vote or work for money, although it is often said of them that they do these things. In his desire for better social relationships Anderson could never quite see the social relationships that do in fact exist, however inadequate they may be. He often spoke, for example, of unhappy, desperate marriages and seemed to suggest that they ought to be quickly dissolved, but he never understood that marriages are often unsatisfactory for the very reasons that make it impossible to dissolve them.

His people have passion without body, and sexuality without gaiety and joy, although it is often through sex that they are supposed to find their salvation. John Jay Chapman said of Emerson that, great as he was, a visitor from Mars would learn less about life on earth from him than from Italian opera, for the opera at least suggested that there were two sexes. When Anderson was at the height of his reputation, it seemed that his report on the existence of two sexes was the great thing about him, the thing that made his work an advance over the literature of New England. But although the visitor from Mars might be instructed by Anderson in the mere fact of bisexuality, he would still be advised to go to the Italian opera if he seeks fuller information. For from the opera, as never from Anderson, he will acquire some of the knowledge which is normally in the possession of natives of the planet, such as that sex has certain manifestations which are socially quite complex, that it is involved with religion, politics, and the fate of nations, above all that it is frequently marked by the liveliest sort of energy.

In their speech his people have not only no wit, but no idiom. To say that they are not "real" would be to introduce all sorts of useless quibbles about the art of character creation; they are simply not *there*. This is not a failure of art; rather, it would seem to have been part of Anderson's intention that they should be not there. His narrative prose is contrived to that end; it is not really a colloquial idiom, although it has certain colloquial tricks; it approaches in effect the inadequate use of a foreign language; old slang persists in it and elegant archaisms are consciously used, so that people are constantly having the "fantods," girls are frequently referred to as "maidens," and things are "like unto" other things. These mannerisms, although they remind us of some of Dreiser's, are not the result, as Dreiser's are, of an effort to be literary and impressive. Anderson's prose has a purpose to which these mannerisms are essential—it has the intention of making us doubt our familiarity with our own world, and not, we must note, in order to make things fresher for us but only in order to make them seem puzzling to us and remote from us. When a man whose name we know is frequently referred to as "the plowmaker," when we hear again and again of "a kind of candy called Milky Way" long after we have learned, if we did not already know, that Milky Way is a candy, when we are told of someone that "He became a radical. He had radical thoughts," it becomes clear that we are being asked by this false naïveté to give up our usual and on the whole useful conceptual grasp of the world we get around in.

Anderson liked to catch people with their single human secret, their essence, but the more he looks for their essence the more his characters vanish into the vast limbo of meaningless life, the less they are human beings. His great American heroes were Mark Twain and Lincoln, but when he writes of these two shrewd, enduring men, he robs them of all their savor and masculinity, of all their bitter resisting mind; they become little more than a pair of sensitive, suffering happy-go-luckies. The more Anderson says about people, the less alive they become— and the less lovable. Is it strange that, with all Anderson's expressed affection for them, we ourselves can never love the people he writes about? But of course we do not love people for their essence or their souls, but for their having a certain body, or wit, or idiom, certain specific relationships with things and other people, and for a dependable continuity of existence: we love them for being there.

We can even for a moment entertain the thought that Anderson himself did not love his characters, else he would not have so thoroughly robbed them of substance and hustled them so quickly off the stage after their small essential moments of crisis. Anderson's love, however, was real enough; it is only that he loves under the aspect of his "truth"; it is love indeed but love become wholly abstract. Another way of putting it is that Anderson sees with the eyes of a religiosity of a very limited sort. No one, I think, has commented on the amount and quality of the mysticism that entered the thought of the writers of the twenties. We may leave Willa Cather aside, for her notion of Catholic order differentiates her; but in addition to Anderson himself, Dreiser, Waldo Frank, and Eugene O'Neill come to mind as men who had recourse to a strong but undeveloped sense of supernal powers.

It is easy enough to understand this crude mysticism as a protest against philosophical and moral materialism; easy enough, too, to forgive it, even when, as in Anderson, the second births and the large revelations seem often to point only to the bosom of a solemn bohemia, and almost always to a lowering rather than a heightening of energy. We forgive it because some part of the blame for its crudity must be borne by the culture of the time. In Europe a century before, Stendhal could execrate a bourgeois materialism and yet remain untempted by the dim religiosity which in America in the twenties seemed one of the likeliest of the few ways by which one might affirm the value of spirit; but then Stendhal could utter his denunciation of philistinism in the name of Mozart's music, the pictures of Cimabue, Masaccio, Giotto, Leonardo, and Michelangelo, the plays of Corneille, Racine, and Shakespeare. Of what is implied by these things Anderson seems never to have had a real intimation. His awareness of the past was limited, perhaps by his fighting faith in the "modern," and this, in a modern, is always a danger. His heroes in art and morality were few: Joyce, Lawrence, Dreiser, and Gertrude Stein, as fellow moderns; Cellini, Turgeniev; there is a long piece in praise of George Borrow; he spoke of Hawthorne with contempt, for he could not understand Hawthorne except as genteel, and he said of Henry James that he was "the novelist of those who hate," for mind seemed to him always a sort of malice. And he saw but faintly even those colleagues in art whom he did admire. His real heroes were the simple and unassuming, a few anonymous Negroes, a few craftsmen, for he gave to the idea of craftsmanship a value beyond the value which it actually does have—it is this as much as anything else that reminds us of Hemingway's relation to Anderson—and a few racing drivers of whom Pop Geers was chief. It is a charming hero worship, but it does not make an adequate antagonism to the culture which Anderson opposed, and in order to make it compelling and effective Anderson reinforced it with what is in effect the high language of religion, speaking of salvation, of the voice that will not be denied, of dropping the heavy burden of this world.

The salvation that Anderson was talking about was no doubt a real salvation, but it was small, and he used for it the language of the most strenuous religious experience. He spoke in visions and mysteries and raptures, but what he was speaking about after all was only the salvation of a small legitimate existence, of a quiet place in the sun and moments of leisurely peace, of not being nagged and shrew-ridden, nor deprived of one's due share of affection. What he wanted for himself and others was perhaps no more than what he got in his last years: a home, neighbors, a small daily work to do, and the right to say his say carelessly and loosely and without the sense of being strictly judged. But between this small, good life and the language which he used about it there is a discrepancy which may be thought of as a willful failure of taste, an intended lapse of the sense of how things fit. Wyndham Lewis, in his attack in *Paleface* on the early triumphant Anderson, speaks of Anderson's work as an assault on responsibility and thoughtful maturity, on the pleasures and uses of the mind, on decent human pride, on Socratic clarity and precision; and certainly when we think of the "marching men" of Anderson's second novel, their minds lost in their marching and singing, leaving to their leader the definitions of their aims, we have what might indeed be the political consequences of Anderson's attitudes if these were carried out to their ultimate implications. Certainly the precious essence of personality to which Anderson was so much committed could not be preserved by any of the people or any of the deeds his own books delight in.

But what hostile critics forget about Anderson is that the cultural situation from which his writing sprang was actually much as he described it. Anderson's truth may have become a falsehood in his hands by reason of limitations in himself or in the tradition of easy populism he chose as his own, but one has only to take it out of his hands to see again that it is indeed a truth. The small legitimate existence, so necessary for the majority of men to achieve, is in our age so very hard, so nearly impossible, for them to achieve. The language Anderson used was certainly not commensurate with the traditional value which literature gives to the things he wanted, but it is not incommensurate with the modern difficulty of attaining these things. And it is his unending consciousness of this difficulty that constitutes for me the residue of admiration for him that I find I still have.

Freud and Literature

I

The Freudian psychology is the only systematic account of the human mind which, in point of subtlety and complexity, of interest and tragic power, deserves to stand beside the chaotic mass of psychological insights which literature has accumulated through the centuries. To pass from the reading of a great literary work to a treatise of academic psychology is to pass from one order of perception to another, but the human nature of the Freudian psychology is exactly the stuff upon which the poet has always exercised his art. It is therefore not surprising that the psychoanalytical theory has had a great effect upon literature. Yet the relationship is reciprocal, and the effect of Freud upon literature has been no greater than the effect of literature upon Freud. When, on the occasion of the celebration of his seventieth birthday, Freud was greeted as the "discoverer of the unconscious," he corrected the speaker and disclaimed the title. "The poets and philosophers before me discovered the unconscious," he said. "What I discovered was the scientific method by which the unconscious can be studied."

A lack of specific evidence prevents us from considering the particular literary "influences" upon the founder of psychoanalysis; and, besides, when we think of the men who so clearly anticipated many of Freud's own ideas—Schopenhauer and Nietzsche, for example—and then learn that he did not read their works until after he had formulated his own theories, we must see that particular influences cannot be in question here but that what we must deal with is nothing less than a whole *Zeitgeist*, a direction of thought. For psychoanalysis is one of the culminations of the Romanticist literature of the nineteenth century. If there is perhaps a contradiction in the idea of a science standing upon the shoulders of a literature which avows itself inimical to science in so many ways, the contradiction will be resolved if we remember that this literature, despite its avowals, was itself scientific in at least the sense of being passionately devoted to a research into the self.

In showing the connection between Freud and this Romanticist tradition, it is difficult to know where to begin, but there might be a certain aptness in starting even back of the tradition, as far back as 1762 with Diderot's *Rameau's Nephew*. At any rate, certain men at the heart of nineteenth-century thought were agreed in finding a peculiar importance in this brilliant little work: Goethe translated it, Marx admired it, Hegel—as Marx reminded Engels in the letter which announced that he was sending the book as a gift—praised and expounded it at length, Shaw was impressed by it, and Freud himself, as we know from a quotation in his *Introductory Lectures*, read it with the pleasure of agreement.

The dialogue takes place between Diderot himself and a nephew of the famous composer. The protagonist, the younger Rameau, is a despised, outcast, shameless fellow; Hegel calls him the "disintegrated consciousness" and credits him with great wit, for it is he who breaks down all the normal social values and makes new combinations with the pieces. As for Diderot, the deuteragonist, he is what Hegel calls the "honest consciousness," and Hegel considers him reasonable, decent, and dull. It is quite clear that the author does not despise his Rameau and does not mean us to. Rameau is lustful and greedy, arrogant yet self-abasing, perceptive yet "wrong," like a child. Still, Diderot seems actually to be giving the fellow a kind of superiority over himself, as though Rameau represents the elements which, dangerous but wholly necessary, lie beneath the reasonable decorum of social life. It would perhaps be pressing too far to find in Rameau Freud's id and in Diderot Freud's ego; yet the connection does suggest itself; and at least we have here the perception which is to be the common characteristic of both Freud and Romanticism, the perception of the hidden element of human nature and of the opposition between the hidden and the visible. We have too the bold perception of just what lies hidden: "If the little savage [i.e., the child] were left to himself, if he preserved all his foolishness and combined the violent passions of a man of thirty with the lack of reason of a child in the cradle, he'd wring his father's neck and go to bed with his mother."

From the self-exposure of Rameau to Rousseau's account of his own childhood is no great step; society might ignore or reject the idea of the "immorality" which lies concealed in the beginning of the career of the "good" man, just as it might turn away from Blake struggling to expound a psychology which would include the forces beneath the propriety of social man in general, but the idea of the hidden thing went forward to become one of the dominant notions of the age. The hidden element takes many forms and it is not necessarily "dark" and "bad"; for Blake the "bad" was the good, while for Wordsworth and Burke what was hidden and unconscious was wisdom and power, which work in despite of the conscious intellect.

The mind has become far less simple; the devotion to the various forms of autobiography—itself an important fact in the tradition—provides abundant examples of the change that has taken place. Poets, making poetry by what seems to them almost a freshly discovered faculty, find that this new power may be conspired against by other agencies of the mind and even deprived of its freedom; the names of Wordsworth, Coleridge, and Arnold at once occur to us again, and Freud quotes Schiller on the danger to the poet that lies in the merely analytical reason. And it is not only the poets who are threatened; educated and sensitive people throughout Europe become aware of the depredations that reason might make upon the affective life, as in the classic instance of John Stuart Mill.

We must also take into account the preoccupation—it began in the eighteenth century, or even in the seventeenth—with children, women, peasants, and savages, whose mental life, it is felt, is less overlaid than that of the educated adult male by the proprieties of social habit. With this preoccupation goes a concern with education and personal development, so consonant with the historical and evolutionary bias of the time. And we must certainly note the revolution in morals which took place at the instance (we might almost say) of the *Bildungsroman,* for in the novels fathered by *Wilhelm Meister* we get the almost complete identification of author and hero and of the reader with both, and this identification almost inevitably suggests a leniency of moral judgment. The autobiographical novel has a further influence upon the moral sensibility by its exploitation of all the modulations of motive and by its hinting that we may not judge a man by any single moment in his life without taking into account the determining past and the expiating and fulfilling future.

It is difficult to know how to go on, for the further we look the more literary affinities to Freud we find, and even if we limit ourselves to bibliography we can at best be incomplete. Yet we must mention the sexual revolution that was being demanded—by Shelley, for example, by the Schlegel of *Lucinde,* by George Sand, and later and more critically by Ibsen; the belief in the sexual origin of art, baldly stated by Tieck, more subtly by Schopenhauer; the investigation of sexual maladjustment by Stendhal, whose observations on erotic feeling seem to us distinctly Freudian. Again and again we see the effective, utilitarian ego being relegated to an inferior position and a plea being made on behalf of the anarchic and self-indulgent id. We find the energetic exploitation of the idea of the mind as a divisible thing, one part of which can contemplate and mock the other. It is not a far remove from this to Dostoevski's brilliant instances of ambivalent feeling. Novalis brings in the preoccupation with the death wish, and this is linked on the one hand with sleep and on the other hand with the perception of the perverse, self-destroying impulses, which in turn leads us to that fascination by the horrible which we find in Shelley, Poe, and Baudelaire. And always there is the profound interest in the dream—"Our dreams," said Gerard de Nerval, "are a second life"—and in the nature of metaphor, which reaches its climax in Rimbaud and the later Symbolists, metaphor becoming less and less communicative as it approaches the relative autonomy of the dream life.

But perhaps we must stop to ask, since these are the components of the *Zeitgeist* from which Freud himself developed, whether it can be said that Freud did indeed produce a wide literary effect. What is it that Freud added that the tendency of literature itself would not have developed without him? If we were looking for a writer who showed the Freudian influence, Proust would perhaps come to mind as readily as anyone else; the very title of his novel, in French more than in English, suggests an enterprise of psychoanalysis and scarcely less so does his method—the investigation of sleep, of sexual deviation, of the way of association, the almost obsessive interest in metaphor; at these and at many other points the "influence" might be shown. Yet I believe it is true that Proust did not read Freud. Or again, exegesis of *The Waste Land* often reads remarkably like the psychoanalytic interpretation of a dream, yet we know that Eliot's methods were prepared for him not by Freud but by other poets.

Nevertheless, it is of course true that Freud's influence on literature has been very great. Much of it is so pervasive that its extent is scarcely to be determined; in one form or another, frequently in perversions or absurd simplifications, it had been infused into our life and become a component of our culture of which it is now hard to be specifically aware. In biography its first effect was sensational but not fortunate. The early Freudian biographers were for the most part Guildensterns who seemed to know the pipes but could not pluck out the heart of the mystery, and the same condemnation applies to the early Freudian critics. But in recent years, with the acclimatization of psychoanalysis and the increased sense of its refinements and complexity, criticism has derived from the Freudian system much that is of great value, most notably the license and the injunction to read the work of literature with a lively sense of its latent and ambiguous meanings, as if it were, as indeed it is, a being no less alive and contradictory than the man who created it. And this new response to the literary work has had a corrective effect upon our conception of literary biography. The literary critic or biographer who makes use of the Freudian theory is no less threatened by the dangers of theoretical systematization than he was in the early days, but he is likely to be more aware of these dangers; and I think it is true to say that now the motive of his interpretation is not that of exposing the secret shame of the writer and limiting the meaning of his work, but, on the contrary, that of finding grounds for sympathy with the writer and for increasing the possible significances of the work.

The names of the creative writers who have been more or less Freudian in tone or assumption would of course be legion. Only a relatively small number, however, have made serious use of the Freudian ideas. Freud himself seems to have thought this was as it should be: he is said to have expected very little of the works that were sent to him by writers with inscriptions of gratitude for all they had learned from him. The Surrealists have, with a certain inconsistency, depended upon Freud for the "scientific" sanction of their program. Kafka, with an apparent awareness of what he was doing, has explored the Freudian conceptions of guilt and punishment, of the dream, and of the fear of the father. Thomas Mann, whose tendency, as he himself says, was always in the direction of Freud's interests, has been most susceptible to the Freudian anthropology, finding a special charm in the theories of myths and magical practices. James Joyce, with his interest in the numerous states of receding consciousness, with his use of words as things and of words which point to more than one thing, with his pervading sense of the interrelation and interpenetration of all things, and, not least important, his treatment of familial themes, has perhaps most thoroughly and consciously exploited Freud's ideas.

II

It will be clear enough how much of Freud's thought has significant affinity with the anti-rationalist element of the Romanticist tradition. But we must see with no less distinctness how much of his system is militantly rationalistic. Thomas Mann is at fault when, in his first essay on Freud, he makes it seem that the "Apollonian," the rationalistic, side of psychoanalysis is, while certainly important and wholly admirable, somehow secondary and even accidental. He gives us a Freud who is committed to the "night side" of life. Not at all: the rationalistic element of Freud is foremost; before everything else he is positivistic. If the interpreter of dreams came to medical science through Goethe, as he tells us he did, he entered not by way of the *Walpurgisnacht* but by the essay which played so important a part in the lives of so many scientists of the nineteenth century, the famous disquisition on Nature.

This correction is needed not only for accuracy but also for any understanding of Freud's attitude to art. And for that understanding we must see how intense is the passion with which Freud believes that positivistic rationalism, in its golden-age pre-Revolutionary purity, is the very form and pattern of intellectual virtue. The aim of psychoanalysis, he says, is the control of the night side of life. It is "to strengthen the ego, to make it more independent of the super-ego, to widen its field of vision, and so to extend the organization of the id." "Where id was," —that is, where all the irrational, non-logical, pleasure-seeking dark forces were—"there shall ego be,"—that is, intelligence and control. "It is," he concludes, with a reminiscence of Faust, "reclamation work, like the draining of the Zuyder Zee." This passage is quoted by Mann

when, in taking up the subject of Freud a second time,
he does indeed speak of Freud's positivistic program; but
even here the bias induced by Mann's artistic interest in
the "night side" prevents him from giving the other aspect of Freud its due emphasis. Freud would never have
accepted the role which Mann seems to give him as the
legitimizer of the myth and the dark irrational ways of
the mind. If Freud discovered the darkness for science
he never endorsed it. On the contrary, his rationalism
supports all the ideas of the Enlightenment that deny
validity to myth or religion; he holds to a simple materialism, to a simple determinism, to a rather limited sort of
epistemology. No great scientist of our day has thun-
dered so articulately and so fiercely against all those who
would sophisticate with metaphysics the scientific principles that were good enough for the nineteenth century. Conceptualism or pragmatism is anathema to him
through the greater part of his intellectual career, and
this, when we consider the nature of his own brilliant
scientific methods, has surely an element of paradox in
it.

From his rationalistic positivism comes much of
Freud's strength and what weakness he has. The strength
is the fine, clear tenacity of his postive aims, the goal of
therapy, the desire to bring to men a decent measure of
earthly happiness. But upon the rationalism must also be
placed the blame for the often naïve scientific principles
which characterize his early thought—they are later
much modified—and which consist largely of claiming for
his theories a perfect correspondence with an external
reality, a position which, for those who admire Freud
and especially for those who take seriously his views on
art, is troublesome in the extreme.

Now Freud has, I believe, much to tell us about art,
but whatever is suggestive in him is not likely to be found
in those of his works in which he deals expressly with art
itself. Freud is not insensitive to art—on the contrary—nor
does he ever intend to speak of it with contempt. Indeed,
he speaks of it with a real tenderness and counts it one of
the true charms of the good life. Of artists, especially of

writers, he speaks with admiration and even a kind of
awe, though perhaps what he most appreciates in literature are specific emotional insights and observations; as
we have noted, he speaks of literary men, because they
have understood the part played in life by the hidden
motives, as the precursors and coadjutors of his own science.

And yet eventually Freud speaks of art with what we
must indeed call contempt. Art, he tells us, is a "substitute gratification," and as such is "an illusion in contrast
to reality." Unlike most illusions, however, art is "almost
always harmless and beneficent" for the reason that "it
does not seek to be anything but an illusion. Save in the
case of a few people who are, one might say, obsessed by
Art, it never dares make any attack on the realm of reality." One of its chief functions is to serve as a "narcotic."
It shares the characteristics of the dream, whose element
of distortion Freud calls a "sort of inner dishonesty." As
for the artist, he is virtually in the same category with
the neurotic. "By such separation of imagination and intellectual capacity," Freud says of the hero of a novel,
"he is destined to be a poet or a neurotic, and he belongs
to that race of beings whose realm is not of this world."

Now there is nothing in the logic of psychoanalytical
thought which requires Freud to have these opinions.
But there is a great deal in the practice of the psychoanalytical therapy which makes it understandable that
Freud, unprotected by an adequate philosophy, should
be tempted to take the line he does. The analytical therapy deals with illusion. The patient comes to the physician to be cured, let us say, of a fear of walking in the
street. The fear is real enough, there is no illusion on that
score, and it produces all the physical symptoms of a
more rational fear, the sweating palms, pounding heart,
and shortened breath. But the patient knows that there
is no cause for the fear, or rather that there is, as he says,
no "real cause": there are no machine guns, man traps,
or tigers in the street. The physician knows, however,
that there is indeed a "real" cause for the fear, though it
has nothing at all to do with what is or is not in the

street; the cause is within the patient, and the process of the therapy will be to discover, by gradual steps, what this real cause is and so free the patient from its effects.

Now the patient in coming to the physician, and the physician in accepting the patient, make a tacit compact about reality; for their purpose they agree to the limited reality by which we get our living, win our loves, catch our trains and our colds. The therapy will undertake to train the patient in proper ways of coping with this reality. The patient, of course, has been dealing with this reality all along, but in the wrong way. For Freud there are two ways of dealing with external reality. One is practical, effective, positive; this is the way of the conscious self, of the ego which must be made independent of the super-ego and extend its organization over the id, and it is the right way. The antithetical way may be called, for our purpose now, the "fictional" way. Instead of doing something about, or to, external reality, the individual who uses this way does something to, or about, his affective states. The most common and "normal" example of this is daydreaming, in which we give ourselves a certain pleasure by imagining our difficulties solved or our desires gratified. Then, too, as Freud discovered, sleeping dreams are, in much more complicated ways, and even though quite unpleasant, at the service of this same "fictional" activity. And in ways yet more complicated and yet more unpleasant, the actual neurosis from which our patient suffers deals with an external reality which the mind considers still more unpleasant than the painful neurosis itself.

For Freud as psychoanalytic practitioner there are, we may say, the polar extremes of reality and illusion. Reality is an honorific word, and it means what is *there;* illusion is a pejorative word, and it means a response to what is *not there.* The didactic nature of a course of psychoanalysis no doubt requires a certain firm crudeness in making the distinction; it is after all aimed not at theoretical refinement but at practical effectiveness. The polar extremes are practical reality and neurotic illusion, the latter judged by the former. This, no doubt, is as it should be; the patient is not being trained in metaphysics and epistemology.

This practical assumption is not Freud's only view of the mind in its relation to reality. Indeed what may be called the essentially Freudian view assumes that the mind, for good as well as bad, helps create its reality by selection and evaluation. In this view, reality is malleable and subject to creation; it is not static but is rather a series of situations which are dealt with in their own terms. But beside this conception of the mind stands the conception which arises from Freud's therapeutic-practical assumptions; in this view, the mind deals with a reality which is quite fixed and static, a reality that is wholly "given" and not (to use a phrase of Dewey's) "taken." In his epistemological utterances, Freud insists on this second view, although it is not easy to see why he should do so. For the reality to which he wishes to reconcile the neurotic patient is, after all, a "taken" and not a "given" reality. It is the reality of social life and of value, conceived and maintained by the human mind and will. Love, morality, honor, esteem—these are the components of a created reality. If we are to call art an illusion then we must call most of the activities and satisfactions of the ego illusions; Freud, of course, has no desire to call them that.

What, then, is the difference between, on the one hand, the dream and the neurosis, and, on the other hand, art? That they have certain common elements is of course clear; that unconscious processes are at work in both would be denied by no poet or critic; they share too, though in different degrees, the element of fantasy. But there is a vital difference between them which Charles Lamb saw so clearly in his defense of the sanity of true genius: "The . . . poet dreams being awake. He is not possessed by his subject but he has dominion over it."

That is the whole difference: the poet is in command of his fantasy, while it is exactly the mark of the neurotic that he is possessed by his fantasy. And there is a further difference which Lamb states; speaking of the poet's relation to reality (he calls it Nature), he says, "He is beautifully loyal to that sovereign directress, even when he appears most to betray her"; the illusions of art are made to serve the purpose of a closer and truer relation with reality. Jacques Barzun, in an acute and sympathetic discussion of Freud, puts the matter well: "A good analogy between art and *dreaming* has led him to a false one between art and *sleeping*. But the difference between a work of art and a dream is precisely this, that the work of art *leads us back to the outer reality by taking account of it*." Freud's assumption of the almost exclusively hedonistic nature and purpose of art bar him from the perception of this.

Of the distinction that must be made between the artist and the neurotic Freud is of course aware; he tells us that the artist is not like the neurotic in that he knows how to find a way back from the world of imagination and "once more get a firm foothold in reality." This however seems to mean no more than that reality is to be dealt with when the artist suspends the practice of his art; and at least once when Freud speaks of art dealing with reality he actually means the rewards that a successful artist can win. He does not deny to art its function and its usefulness; it has a therapeutic effect in releasing mental tension; it serves the cultural purpose of acting as a "substitute gratification" to reconcile men to the sacrifices they have made for culture's sake; it promotes the social sharing of highly valued emotional experiences; and it recalls men to their cultural ideals. This is not everything that some of us would find that art does, yet even this is a good deal for a "narcotic" to do.

III

I started by saying that Freud's ideas could tell us something about art, but so far I have done little more than try to show that Freud's very conception of art is inadequate. Perhaps, then, the suggestiveness lies in the application of the analytic method to specific works of art or to the artist himself? I do not think so, and it is only fair to say that Freud himself was aware both of the limits and the limitations of psychoanalysis in art, even though he does not always in practice submit to the former or admit the latter.

Freud has, for example, no desire to encroach upon the artist's autonomy; he does not wish us to read his monograph on Leonardo and then say of the "Madonna of the Rocks" that it is a fine example of homosexual, autoerotic painting. If he asserts that in investigation the "psychiatrist cannot yield to the author," he immediately insists that the "author cannot yield to the psychiatrist," and he warns the latter not to "coarsen everything" by using for all human manifestations the "substantially useless and awkward terms" of clinical procedure. He admits, even while asserting that the sense of beauty probably derives from sexual feeling, that psychoanalysis "has less to say about beauty than about most other things." He confesses to a theoretical indifference to the form of art and restricts himself to its content. Tone, feeling, style, and the modification that part makes upon part he does not consider. "The layman," he says, "may expect perhaps too much from analysis . . . for it must be admitted that it throws no light upon the two problems which probably interest him the most. It can do nothing toward elucidating the nature of the artistic gift, nor can it explain the means by which the artist works— artistic technique."

What, then, does Freud believe that the analytical method can do? Two things: explain the "inner meanings" of the work of art and explain the temperament of the artist as man.

A famous example of the method is the attempt to solve the "problem" of *Hamlet* as suggested by Freud and as carried out by Dr. Ernest Jones, his early and distinguished follower. Dr. Jones's monograph is a work of painstaking scholarship and of really masterly ingenuity. The research undertakes not only the clearing up of the mystery of Hamlet's character, but also the discovery of "the clue to much of the deeper workings of Shakespeare's mind." Part of the mystery in question is of course why Hamlet, after he had so definitely resolved to do so, did not avenge upon his hated uncle his father's death. But there is another mystery to the play—what Freud calls "the mystery of its effect," its magical appeal that draws so much interest toward it. Recalling the many failures to solve the riddle of the play's charm, he wonders if we are to be driven to the conclusion "that its magical appeal rests solely upon the impressive thoughts in it and the splendor of its language." Freud believes that we can find a source of power beyond this.

We remember that Freud has told us that the meaning of a dream is its intention, and we may assume that the meaning of a drama is its intention, too. The Jones research undertakes to discover what it was that Shakespeare intended to say about Hamlet. It finds that the intention was wrapped by the author in a dreamlike obscurity because it touched so deeply both his personal life and the moral life of the world; what Shakespeare intended to say is that Hamlet cannot act because he is incapacitated by the guilt he feels at his unconscious attachment to his mother. There is, I think, nothing to be quarreled with in the statement that there is an Oedipus situation in *Hamlet;* and if psychoanalysis has indeed added a new point of interest to the play, that is to its credit.[1] And, just so, there is no reason to quarrel with Freud's conclusion when he undertakes to give us the meaning of *King Lear* by a tortuous tracing of the mythological implications of the theme of the three caskets, of the relation of the caskets to the Norns, the Fates, and the Graces, of the connection of these triadic females

---

[1] However, A. C. Bradley, in his discussion of Hamlet (*Shakespearean Tragedy*), states clearly the intense sexual disgust which Hamlet feels and which, for Bradley, helps account for his uncertain purpose; and Bradley was anticipated in this view by Löning. It is well known, and Dover Wilson has lately emphasized the point, that to an Elizabethan audience Hamlet's mother was not merely tasteless, as to a modern audience she seems, in hurrying to marry Claudius, but actually adulterous in marrying him at all because he was, as her brother-in-law, within the forbidden degrees.

with Lear's daughters, of the transmogrification of the
death goddess into the love goddess and the identification of Cordelia with both, all to the conclusion that the
meaning of *King Lear* is to be found in the tragic refusal
of an old man to "renounce love, choose death, and make
friends with the necessity of dying." There is something
both beautiful and suggestive in this, but it is not *the*
meaning of *King Lear* any more than the Oedipus motive is *the* meaning of *Hamlet*.

It is not here a question of the validity of the evidence,
though that is of course important. We must rather object to the conclusions of Freud and Dr. Jones on the
ground that their proponents do not have an adequate
conception of what an artistic meaning is. There is no
single meaning to any work of art; this is true not merely
because it is better that it should be true, that is, because
it makes art a richer thing, but because historical and
personal experience show it to be true. Changes in historical context and in personal mood change the meaning of a work and indicate to us that artistic understanding is not a question of fact but of value. Even if the
author's intention were, as it cannot be, precisely deter-
minable, the meaning of a work cannot lie in the author's
intention alone. It must also lie in its effect. We can say
of a volcanic eruption on an inhabited island that it
"means terrible suffering," but if the island is uninhab-
ited or easily evacuated it means something else. In
short, the audience partly determines the meaning of the
work. But although Freud sees something of this when
he says that in addition to the author's intention we must
take into account the mystery of *Hamlet's* effect, he nevertheless goes on to speak as if, historically, *Hamlet's* effect had been single and brought about solely by the
"magical" power of the Oedipus motive to which, unconsciously, we so violently respond. Yet there was, we
know, a period when *Hamlet* was relatively in eclipse,
and it has always been scandalously true of the French,
a people not without filial feeling, that they have been
somewhat indifferent to the "magical appeal" of *Hamlet*.

I do not think that anything I have said about the in-

adequacies of the Freudian method of interpretation
limits the number of ways we can deal with a work of
art. Bacon remarked that experiment may twist nature
on the rack to wring out its secrets, and criticism may
use any instruments upon a work of art to find its meanings. The elements of art are not limited to the world of
art. They reach into life, and whatever extraneous knowledge of them we gain—for example, by research into the
historical context of the work—may quicken our feelings
for the work itself and even enter legitimately into those
feelings. Then, too, anything we may learn about the artist himself may be enriching and legitimate. But one research into the mind of the artist is simply not practica-
ble, however legitimate it may theoretically be. That is,
the investigation of his unconscious intention as it exists
apart from the work itself. Criticism understands that
the artist's statement of his conscious intention, though it
is sometimes useful, cannot finally determine meaning.
How much less can we know from his unconscious intention considered as something apart from the whole work?
Surely very little that can be called conclusive or scientific. For, as Freud himself points out, we are not in a
position to question the artist; we must apply the technique of dream analysis to his symbols, but, as Freud
says with some heat, those people do not understand his
theory who think that a dream may be interpreted without the dreamer's free association with the multitudinous
details of his dream.

We have so far ignored the aspect of the method
which finds the solution to the "mystery" of such a play
as *Hamlet* in the temperament of Shakespeare himself
and then illuminates the mystery of Shakespeare's temperament by means of the solved mystery of the play.
Here it will be amusing to remember that by 1935 Freud
had become converted to the theory that it was not
Shakespeare of Stratford but the Earl of Oxford who
wrote the plays, thus invalidating the important bit of
evidence that Shakespeare's father died shortly before
the composition of *Hamlet*. This is destructive enough to
Dr. Jones's argument, but the evidence from which Dr.

Jones draws conclusions about literature fails on grounds more relevant to literature itself. For when Dr. Jones, by means of his analysis of *Hamlet*, takes us into "the deeper workings of Shakespeare's mind," he does so with a perfect confidence that he knows what *Hamlet* is and what its relation to Shakespeare is. It is, he tells us, Shakespeare's "chief masterpiece," so far superior to all his other works that it may be placed on "an entirely separate level." And then, having established his ground on an entirely subjective literary judgment, Dr. Jones goes on to tell us that *Hamlet* "probably expresses the core of Shakespeare's philosophy and outlook as no other work of his does." That is, all the contradictory or complicating or modifying testimony of the other plays is dismissed on the basis of Dr. Jones's acceptance of the peculiar position which, he believes, *Hamlet* occupies in the Shakespeare canon. And it is upon this quite inadmissible judgment that Dr. Jones bases his argument: "It may be expected *therefore* that anything which will give us the key to the inner meaning of the play will *necessarily* give us the clue to much of the deeper workings of Shakespeare's mind." (The italics are mine.)

I should be sorry if it appeared that I am trying to say that psychoanalysis can have nothing to do with literature. I am sure that the opposite is so. For example, the whole notion of rich ambiguity in literature, of the interplay between the apparent meaning and the latent—not "hidden"—meaning, has been reinforced by the Freudian concepts, perhaps even received its first impetus from them. Of late years, the more perceptive psychoanalysts have surrendered the early pretensions of their teachers to deal "scientifically" with literature. That is all to the good, and when a study as modest and precise as Dr. Franz Alexander's essay on *Henry IV* comes along, an essay which pretends not to "solve" but only to illuminate the subject, we have something worth having. Dr. Alexander undertakes nothing more than to say that in the development of Prince Hal we see the classic struggle of the ego to come to normal adjustment, beginning with the rebellion against the father, going on to the conquest of the super-ego (Hotspur, with his rigid notions of honor and glory), then to the conquests of the *id* (Falstaff, with his anarchic self-indulgence), then to the identification with the father (the crown scene) and the assumption of mature responsibility. An analysis of this sort is not momentous and not exclusive of other meanings; perhaps it does no more than point up and formulate what we all have already seen. It has the tact to *accept* the play and does not, like Dr. Jones's study of *Hamlet*, search for a "hidden motive" and a "deeper working," which implies that there is a reality to which the play stands in the relation that a dream stands to the wish that generates it and from which it is separable; it is this reality, this "deeper working," which, according to Dr. Jones, produced the play. But *Hamlet* is not merely the product of Shakespeare's thought, it is the very instrument of his thought, and if meaning is intention, Shakespeare did not intend the Oedipus motive or anything less than *Hamlet*; if meaning is effect then it is *Hamlet* which affects us, not the Oedipus motive. *Coriolanus* also deals, and very terribly, with the Oedipus motive, but the effect of the one drama is very different from the effect of the other.

IV

If, then, we can accept neither Freud's conception of the place of art in life nor his application of the analytical method, what is it that he contributes to our understanding of art or to its practice? In my opinion, what he contributes outweighs his errors; it is of the greatest importance, and it lies in no specific statement that he makes about art but is, rather, implicit in his whole conception of the mind.

For, of all mental systems, the Freudian psychology is the one which makes poetry indigenous to the very constitution of the mind. Indeed, the mind, as Freud sees it, is in the greater part of its tendency exactly a poetry-making organ. This puts the case too strongly, no doubt, for it seems to make the working of the unconscious mind

equivalent to poetry itself, forgetting that between the
unconscious mind and the finished poem there super-
vene the social intention and the formal control of the
conscious mind. Yet the statement has at least the virtue
of counterbalancing the belief, so commonly expressed
or implied, that the very opposite is true, and that
poetry is a kind of beneficent aberration of the mind's
right course.

Freud has not merely naturalized poetry; he has discovered its status as a pioneer settler, and he sees it as a
method of thought. Often enough he tries to show how,
as a method of thought, it is unreliable and ineffective
for conquering reality; yet he himself is forced to use it
in the very shaping of his own science, as when he speaks
of the topography of the mind and tells us what a kind
of defiant apology that the metaphors of space relationship which he is using are really most inexact since the
mind is not a thing of space at all, but that there is no
other way of conceiving the difficult idea except by
metaphor. In the eighteenth century Vico spoke of the
metaphorical, imagistic language of the early stages of
culture; it was left to Freud to discover how, in a scientific age, we still feel and think in figurative formations,
and to create, what psychoanalysis is, a science of tropes,
of metaphor and its variants, synecdoche and meton-
ymy.

Freud showed, too, how the mind, in one of its parts,
could work without logic, yet not without that directing
purpose, that control of intent from which, perhaps it
might be said, logic springs. For the unconscious mind
works without the syntactical conjunctions which are
logic's essence. It recognizes no *because,* no *therefore,*
no *but;* such ideas as similarity, agreement, and community are expressed in dreams imagistically by com-
pressing the elements into a unity. The unconscious mind
in its struggle with the conscious always turns from the
general to the concrete and finds the tangible trifle more
congenial than the large abstraction. Freud discovered
in the very organization of the mind those mechanisms
by which art makes its effects, such devices as the con-

densations of meanings and the displacement of accent.

All this is perhaps obvious enough and, though I should like to develop it in proportion both to its importance and to the space I have given to disagreement with Freud, I will not press it further. For there are two other elements in Freud's thought which, in conclusion, I should like to introduce as of great weight in their bearing on art.

Of these, one is a specific idea which, in the middle of his career (1920), Freud put forward in his essay *Beyond the Pleasure Principle*. The essay itself is a speculative attempt to solve a perplexing problem in clinical analysis, but its relevance to literature is inescapable, as Freud sees well enough, even though his perception of its critical importance is not sufficiently strong to make him revise his earlier views of the nature and function of art. The idea is one which stands besides Aristotle's notion of the catharsis, in part to supplement, in part to modify it.

Freud has come upon certain facts which are not to be reconciled with his earlier theory of the dream. According to this theory, all dreams, even the unpleasant ones, could be understood upon analysis to have the intention of fulfilling the dreamer's wishes. They are in the service of what Freud calls the pleasure principle, which is opposed to the reality principle. It is, of course, this explanation of the dream which had so largely conditioned Freud's theory of art. But now there is thrust upon him the necessity for reconsidering the theory of the dream, for it was found that in cases of war neurosis —what we once called shellshock—the patient, with the utmost anguish, recurred in his dreams to the very situation, distressing as it was, which had precipitated his neurosis. It seemed impossible to interpret these dreams by any assumption of a hedonistic intent. Nor did there seem to be the usual amount of distortion in them: the patient recurred to the terrible initiatory situation with great literalness. And the same pattern of psychic behavior could be observed in the play of children; there were some games which, far from fulfilling wishes, seemed to concentrate upon the representation of those aspects of the child's life which were most unpleasant and threatening to his happiness.

To explain such mental activities Freud evolved a theory for which he at first refused to claim much but to which, with the years, he attached an increasing importance. He first makes the assumption that there is indeed in the psychic life a repetition-compulsion which goes beyond the pleasure principle. Such a compulsion cannot be meaningless, it must have an intent. And that intent, Freud comes to believe, is exactly and literally the developing of fear. "These dreams," he says, "are attempts at restoring control of the stimuli by developing apprehension, the pretermission of which caused the traumatic neurosis." The dream, that is, is the effort to reconstruct the bad situation in order that the failure to meet it may be recouped; in these dreams there is no obscured intent to evade but only an attempt to meet the situation, to make a new effort of control. And in the play of children it seems to be that "the child repeats even the unpleasant experiences because through his own activity he gains a far more thorough mastery of the strong impression than was possible by mere passive experience."

Freud, at this point, can scarcely help being put in mind of tragic drama; nevertheless, he does not wish to believe that this effort to come to mental grips with a situation is involved in the attraction of tragedy. He is, we might say, under the influence of the Aristotelian tragic theory which emphasizes a qualified hedonism through suffering. But the pleasure involved in tragedy is perhaps an ambiguous one; and sometimes we must feel that the famous sense of cathartic resolution is perhaps the result of glossing over terror with beautiful language rather than an evacuation of it. And sometimes the terror even bursts through the language to stand stark and isolated from the play, as does Oedipus's sightless and bleeding face. At any rate, the Aristotelian theory does not deny another function for tragedy (and for comedy, too) which is suggested by Freud's theory of the traumatic neurosis—what might be called the mithridatic function, by which tragedy is used as the homeopathic administration of pain to inure ourselves to the greater pain which life will force upon us. There is in the cathartic theory of tragedy, as it is usually understood, a conception of tragedy's function which is too negative and which inadequately suggests the sense of active mastery which tragedy can give.

In the same essay in which he sets forth the conception of the mind embracing its own pain for some vital purpose, Freud also expresses a provisional assent to the idea (earlier stated, as he reminds us, by Schopenhauer) that there is perhaps a human drive which makes of death the final and desired goal. The death instinct is a conception that is rejected by many of even the most thoroughgoing Freudian theorists (as, in his last book, Freud mildly noted); the late Otto Fenichel in his authoritative work on the neurosis argues cogently against it. Yet even if we reject the theory as not fitting the facts in any operatively useful way, we still cannot miss its grandeur, its ultimate tragic courage in acquiescence to fate. The idea of the reality principle and the idea of the death instinct form the crown of Freud's broader speculation on the life of man. Their quality of grim poetry is characteristic of Freud's system and the ideas it generates for him.

And as much as anything else that Freud gives to literature, this quality of his thought is important. Although the artist is never finally determined in his work by the intellectual systems about him, he cannot avoid their influence; and it can be said of various competing systems that some hold more promise for the artist than others. When, for example, we think of the simple humanitarian optimism which, for two decades, has been so pervasive, we must see that not only has it been politically and philosophically inadequate, but also that it implies, by the smallness of its view of the varieties of human possibility, a kind of check on the creative faculties. In Freud's view of life no such limitation is implied. To be sure, certain elements of his system seem hostile to the usual notions of man's dignity. Like every great critic of human nature—and Freud is that—he finds in human pride the ultimate cause of human wretchedness, and he takes pleasure in knowing that his ideas stand with those of Copernicus and Darwin in making pride more difficult to maintain. Yet the Freudian man is, I venture to think, a creature of far more dignity and far more interest than the man which any other modern system has been able to conceive. Despite popular belief to the contrary, man, as Freud conceives him, is not to be understood by any simple formula (such as sex) but is rather an inextricable tangle of culture and biology. And not being simple, he is not simply good; he has, as Freud says somewhere, a kind of hell within him from which rise everlastingly the impulses which threaten his civilization. He has the faculty of imagining for himself more in the way of pleasure and satisfaction than he can possibly achieve. Everything that he gains he pays for in more than equal coin; compromise and the compounding with defeat constitute his best way of getting through the world. His best qualities are the result of a struggle whose outcome is tragic. Yet he is a creature of love; it is Freud's sharpest criticism of the Adlerian psychology that to aggression it gives everything and to love nothing at all.

One is always aware in reading Freud how little cynicism there is in his thought. His desire for man is only that he should be human, and to this end his science is devoted. No view of life to which the artist responds can insure the quality of his work, but the poetic qualities of Freud's own principles, which are so clearly in the line of the classic tragic realism, suggest that this is a view which does not narrow and simplify the human world for the artist but on the contrary opens and complicates it.

The Princess Casamassima

I

In 1888, on the second of January, which in any year is likely to be a sad day, Henry James wrote to his friend William Dean Howells that his reputation had been dreadfully injured by his last two novels. The desire for his productions, he said, had been reduced to zero, editors no longer asked for his work, they even seemed ashamed to publish the stories they had already bought. But James was never without courage. "However, I don't despair," he wrote, "for I think I am now really in better form than I ever have been in my life and I propose yet to do many things." And then, no doubt with the irony all writers use when they dare to speak of future recognition, but also, surely, with the necessary faith, he concludes the matter: "Very likely too, some day, all my buried prose will kick off its various tombstones at once."

And so it happened. The "some day" has arrived and we have been hearing the clatter of marble as James's buried prose kicks off its monuments in a general resurrection. On all sides James is being given the serious and joyous interest he longed for in his lifetime.

One element of our interest must be the question of how some of James's prose ever came to be buried at all. It is not hard to understand why certain of James's books did not catch the contemporary fancy. But the two books on which James placed the blame for his diminishing popularity were *The Bostonians* and *The Princess Casamassima*, and of all James's novels these are the two which are most likely to make an immediate appeal to the reader of today. That they should not have delighted their contemporary public, but on the contrary should have turned it against James, makes a lively problem in the history of taste.[1]

In the masterpieces of his late years James became a difficult writer. This is the fact and nothing is gained for James by denying it. He himself knew that these late works were difficult; he wished them to be dealt with as if they were difficult. When a young man from Texas —it was Mr. Stark Young—inquired indirectly of James how he should go about reading his novels, James did not feel that this diffidence was provincial but happily drew up lists which would lead the admirable young man from the easy to the hard. But the hostility with which *The Bostonians* and *The Princess Casamassima* were received cannot be explained by any difficulty either of manner or intention, for in these books there is none. The prose, although personally characteristic, is perfectly in the tradition of the nineteenth-century novel. It is warm, fluent, and on the whole rather less elaborate and virtuose than Dickens' prose. The motives of the characters are clear and direct—certainly they are far from the elaborate punctilio of the late masterpieces. And the charge that is sometimes made against the later work, that it exists in a social vacuum, clearly does not pertain here. In these novels James is at the point in his career at which society, in the largest and even the grossest sense, is offering itself to his mind with great

[1] Whoever wishes to know what the courage of the artist must sometimes be could do no better than to read the British reviews of *The Bostonians* and *The Princess Casamassima*. In a single year James brought out two major works; he thought they were his best to date and expected great things of them; he was told by the reviewers that they were not really novels at all; he was scorned and sneered at and condescended to and dismissed. In adjacent columns the ephemeral novels of the day were treated with gentle respect. The American press rivaled the British in the vehemence with which it condemned *The Bostonians*, but it was more tolerant of *The Princess Casamassima*.

force. He understands society as crowds and police, as a field of justice and injustice, reform and revolution. The social texture of his work is grainy and knotted with practicality and detail. And more: his social observation is of a kind that we must find startlingly prescient when we consider that it was made some sixty years ago.

It is just this prescience, of course, that explains the resistance of James's contemporaries. What James saw he saw truly, but it was not what the readers of his time were themselves equipped to see. That we now are able to share his vision required the passage of six decades and the events which brought them to climax. Henry James in the eighties understood what we have painfully learned from our grim glossary of wars and concentration camps, after having seen the state and human nature laid open to our horrified inspection. "But I have the imagination of disaster—and see life as ferocious and sinister": James wrote this to A. C. Benson in 1896, and what so bland a young man as Benson made of the statement, what anyone then was likely to make of it, is hard to guess. But nowadays we know that such an imagination is one of the keys to truth.

It was, then, "the imagination of disaster" that cut James off from his contemporaries and it is what recommends him to us now. We know something about the profound disturbance of the sexual life which seems to go along with hypertrophy of the will and how this excess of will seems to be a response to certain maladjustments in society and to direct itself back upon them; D. H. Lawrence taught us much about this, but Lawrence himself never attempted a more daring conjunction of the sexual and the political life than Henry James succeeds with in *The Bostonians*. We know much about misery and downtroddenness and of what happens when strong and gifted personalities are put at a hopeless disadvantage, and about the possibilities of extreme violence, and about the sense of guilt and unreality which may come to members of the upper classes and the strange complex efforts they make to find innocence and reality, and about the conflict between the claims of art and of social duty—these are among the themes which make the pattern of *The Princess Casamassima*. It is a novel which has at its very center the assumption that Europe has reached the full of its ripeness and is passing over into rottenness, that the peculiarly beautiful light it gives forth is in part the reflection of a glorious past and in part the phosphorescence of a present decay, that it may meet its end by violence and that this is not wholly unjust, although never before has the old sinful continent made so proud and pathetic an assault upon our affections.

II

The Princess Casamassima belongs to a great line of novels which runs through the nineteenth century as, one might say, the very backbone of its fiction. These novels, which are defined as a group by the character and circumstance of their heroes, include Stendhal's *The Red and the Black*, Balzac's *Père Goriot* and *Lost Illusions*, Dickens' *Great Expectations*, Flaubert's *Sentimental Education;* only a very slight extension of the definition is needed to allow the inclusion of Tolstoi's *War and Peace* and Dostoevski's *The Idiot*.

The defining hero may be known as the Young Man from the Provinces. He need not come from the provinces in literal fact, his social class may constitute his province. But a provincial birth and rearing suggest the simplicity and the high hopes he begins with—he starts with a great demand upon life and a great wonder about its complexity and promise. He may be of good family but he must be poor. He is intelligent, or at least aware, but not at all shrewd in worldly matters. He must have acquired a certain amount of education, should have learned something about life from books, although not the truth.

The hero of *The Princess Casamassima* conforms very exactly to type. The province from which Hyacinth Robinson comes is a city slum. "He sprang up at me out of the London pavement," says James in the preface to the novel in the New York Edition. In 1883, the first year of his long residence in England, James was in the habit of prowling the streets, and they yielded him the image "of some individual sensitive nature or fine mind, some small obscure creature whose education should have been almost wholly derived from them, capable of profiting by all the civilization, all the accumulation to which they testify, yet condemned to see things only from outside—in mere quickened consideration, mere wistfulness and envy and despair."

Thus equipped with poverty, pride, and intelligence, the Young Man from the Provinces stands outside life and seeks to enter. This modern hero is connected with the tales of the folk. Usually his motive is the legendary one of setting out to seek his fortune, which is what the folktale says when it means that the hero is seeking himself. He is really the third and youngest son of the woodcutter, the one to whom all our sympathies go, the gentle and misunderstood one, the bravest of all. He is likely to be in some doubt about his parentage; his father the woodcutter is not really his father. Our hero has, whether he says so or not, the common belief of children that there is some mystery about his birth; his real parents, if the truth were known, are of great and even royal estate. Julien Sorel of *The Red and the Black* is the third and youngest son of an actual woodcutter, but he is the spiritual son of Napoleon. In our day the hero of *The Great Gatsby* is not really the son of Mr. Gatz; he is said to have sprung "from his Platonic conception of himself," to be, indeed, "the son of God." And James's Hyacinth Robinson, although fostered by a poor dressmaker and a shabby fiddler, has an English lord for his real father.

It is the fate of the Young Man to move from an obscure position into one of considerable eminence in Paris or London or St. Petersburg, to touch the life of the rulers of the earth. His situation is as chancy as that of any questing knight of medieval romance. He is confronted by situations whose meanings are dark to him, in which his choice seems always decisive. He understands everything to be a "test." Parsifal at the castle of the Fisher King is not more uncertain about the right thing to do than the Young Man from the Provinces picking his perilous way through the irrationalities of the society into which he has been transported. That the Young Man be introduced into great houses and involved with large affairs is essential to his story, which must not be confused with the cognate story of the Sensitive Young Man. The provincial hero must indeed be sensitive, and in proportion to the brassiness of the world; he may even be an artist; but it is not his part merely to be puzzled and hurt; he is not the hero of *The Way of All Flesh* or *Of Human Bondage* or *Mooncalf*. Unlike the merely sensitive hero, he is concerned to know how the political and social world are run and enjoyed; he wants a share of power and pleasure and in consequence he takes real risks, often of his life. The "swarming facts" that James tells us Hyacinth is to confront are "freedom and ease, knowledge and power, money, opportunity, and satiety."

The story of the Young Man from the Provinces is thus a strange one, for it has its roots both in legend and in the very heart of the modern actuality. From it we have learned most of what we know about modern society, about class and its strange rituals, about power and influence and about money, the hard fluent fact in which modern society has its being. Yet through the massed social fact there runs the thread of legendary romance, even of downright magic. We note, for example, that it seems necessary for the novelist to deal in transformation. Some great and powerful hand must reach down into the world of seemingly chanceless routine and pick up the hero and set him down in his complex and dangerous fate. Pip meets Magwitch on the marsh, a felon-godfather; Pierre Bezuhov unexpectedly inherits the fortune that permits this uncouth young man to make his tour of Russian society; powerful unseen forces play around the proud head of Julien Sorel to make possible his astonishing upward career; Rastignac, simply by being one of the boarders at the Maison Vauquer

which also shelters the great Vautrin, moves to the very
center of Parisian intrigue; James Gatz rows out to a
millionaire's yacht, a boy in dungarees, and becomes Jay
Gatsby, an Oxford man, a military hero.

Such transformations represent, with only slight exag-
geration, the literal fact that was to be observed every
day. From the late years of the eighteenth century
through the early years of the twentieth, the social structure of the West was peculiarly fitted—one might say
designed—for changes in fortune that were magical and
romantic. The upper-class ethos was strong enough to
make it remarkable that a young man should cross the
borders, yet weak enough to permit the crossing in exceptional cases. A shiftless boy from Geneva, a starve-
ling and a lackey, becomes the admiration of the French
aristocracy and is permitted by Europe to manipulate
its assumptions in every department of life: Jean Jacques
Rousseau is the father of all the Young Men from the
Provinces, including the one from Corsica.

The Young Man's story represents an actuality, yet
we may be sure that James took special delight in its
ineluctable legendary element. James was certainly the
least primitive of artists, yet he was always aware of his
connection with the primitive. He set great store by the
illusion of probability and verisimilitude, but he knew
that he dealt always with illusion; he was proud of the
devices of his magic. Like any primitive storyteller, he
wished to hold the reader against his will, to *enchant*,
as we say. He loved what he called "the story as story";
he delighted to work, by means of the unusual, the extravagant, the melodramatic, and the supernatural, upon
what he called "the blessed faculty of wonder"; and he
understood primitive story to be the root of the modern
novelist's art. F. O. Matthiessen speaks of the fairytale
quality of *The Wings of the Dove;* so sophisticated a
work as *The Ambassadors* can be read as one of those
tales in which the hero finds that nothing is what it
seems and that the only guide through the world must
be the goodness of his heart.

Like any great artist of story, like Shakespeare or

Balzac or Dickens or Dostoevski, James crowds probability rather closer than we nowadays like. It is not that he gives us unlikely events but that he sometimes thickens the number of interesting events beyond our ordinary expectation. If this, in James or in any storyteller, leads to a straining of our sense of verisimilitude, there is always the defense to be made that the special job of literature is, as Marianne Moore puts it, the creation of "imaginary gardens with real toads in them." The reader who detects that the garden is imaginary should not be led by his discovery to a wrong view of the reality of the toads. In settling questions of reality and truth in fiction, it must be remembered that, although the novel in certain of its forms resembles the accumulative and classificatory sciences, which are the sciences most people are most at home with, in certain other of its forms the novel approximates the sciences of experiment. And an experiment is very like an imaginary garden which is laid out for the express purpose of supporting a real toad of fact. The apparatus of the researcher's bench is not nature itself but an artificial and extravagant contrivance, much like a novelist's plot, which is devised to force or foster a fact into being. This seems to have been James's own view of the part that is played in his novels by what he calls "romance." He seems to have had an analogy with experiment very clearly in mind when he tells us that romance is "experience liberated, so to speak; experience disengaged, disembroiled, disencumbered, exempt from the conditions that usually attach to it." Again and again he speaks of the contrivance of a novel in ways which will make it seem like illegitimate flummery to the reader who is committed only to the premises of the naturalistic novel, but which the intelligent scientist will understand perfectly.

Certainly *The Princess Casamassima* would seem to need some such defense as this, for it takes us, we are likely to feel, very far along the road to romance, some will think to the very point of impossibility. It asks us to accept a poor young man whose birth is darkly secret, his father being a dissipated but authentic English lord, his mother a French courtesan-seamstress who murders the father; a beautiful American-Italian princess who descends in the social scale to help "the people"; a general mingling of the very poor with persons of exalted birth; and then a dim mysterious leader of revolution, never seen by the reader, the machinations of an underground group of conspirators, an oath taken to carry out an assassination at some unspecified future day, the day arriving, the hour of the killing set, the instructions and the pistol given.

Confronted by paraphernalia like this, even those who admire the book are likely to agree with Rebecca West when, in her exuberant little study of James, she tells us that it is "able" and "meticulous" but at the same time "distraught" and "wild," that the "loveliness" in it comes from a transmutation of its "perversities"; she speaks of it as a "mad dream" and teases its vast unlikelihood, finding it one of the big jokes in literature that it was James, who so prided himself on his lack of naïveté, who should have brought back to fiction the high implausibility of the old novels which relied for their effects on dark and stormy nights, Hindu servants, mysterious strangers, and bloody swords wiped on richly embroidered handkerchiefs.

Miss West was writing in 1916, when the English naturalistic novel, with its low view of possibility, was in full pride. Our notion of political possibility was still to be changed by a small group of quarrelsome conspiratorial intellectuals taking over the control of Russia. Even a loyal Fabian at that time could consider it one of the perversities of *The Princess Casamassima* that two of its lower-class characters should say of a third that he had the potentiality of becoming Prime Minister of England; today Paul Muniment sits in the Cabinet and is on the way to Downing Street. In the thirties the book was much admired by those who read it in the light of knowledge of our own radical movements; it then used to be said that although James had dreamed up an impossible revolutionary group he had nonetheless managed to derive from it some notable insights into the temper of radicalism; these admirers grasped the toad of fact and felt that it was all the more remarkably there because the garden is so patently imaginary.

Yet an understanding of James's use of "romance"—and there is "romance" in Hyacinth's story—must not preclude our understanding of the striking literal accuracy of *The Princess Casamassima*. James himself helped to throw us off the scent when in his preface to the novel he told us that he made no research into Hyacinth's subterranean politics. He justified this by saying that "the value I wished most to render and the effect I wished most to produce were precisely those of our not knowing, of society's not knowing, but only guessing and suspecting and trying to ignore, what 'goes on' irreconcilably, subversively, beneath the vast smug surface." And he concludes the preface with the most beautifully arrogant and truest thing a novelist ever said about his craft: "What it all came back to was, no doubt, something like *this* wisdom—that if you haven't, for fiction the root of the matter in you, haven't the sense of life and the penetrating imagination, you are a fool in the very presence of the revealed and assured; but that if you *are* so armed, you are not really helpless, not without your resource, even before mysteries abysmal." If, to learn about the radical movement of his time, James really did no more than consult his penetrating imagination—which no doubt was nourished like any other on conversation and the daily newspaper—then we must say that in no other novelist did the root of the matter go so deep and so wide. For the truth is that there is not a political event of *The Princess Casamassima*, not a detail of oath or mystery or danger, which is not confirmed by multitudinous records.

III

We are inclined to flatter our own troubles with the belief that the late nineteenth century was a peaceful time. But James knew its actual violence. England was, to be sure, rather less violent than the Continent, but the history of England in the eighties was one of profound social unrest often intensified to disorder. In March of 1886, the year in which *The Princess Casamassima* appeared in book form, James wrote to his brother William of a riot in his street, of ladies' carriages being stopped and the "occupants hustled, rifled, slapped, and kissed." He does not think that the rioters were unemployed workingmen, more likely that they were "the great army of roughs and thieves." But he says that there is "immense destitution" and that "everyone is getting poorer —from causes which, I fear, will continue." In the same year he wrote to Charles Eliot Norton that the state of the British upper class seems to be "in many ways very much the same rotten and *collapsible* one of the French aristocracy before the revolution."

James envisaged revolution, and not merely as a convenience for his fiction. But he imagined a kind of revolution with which we are no longer familiar. It was not a Marxian revolution. There is no upsurge of an angry proletariat led by a disciplined party which plans to head a new strong state. Such a revolution has its conservative aspect—it seeks to save certain elements of bourgeois culture for its own use, for example, science and the means of production and even some social agencies. The revolutionary theory of *The Princess Casamassima* has little in common with this. There is no organized mass movement; there is no discipline party but only a strong conspiratorial center. There are no plans for taking over the state and almost no ideas about the society of the future. The conspiratorial center plans only for destruction, chiefly personal terrorism. But James is not naïvely representing a radical Graustark; he is giving a very accurate account of anarchism.

In 1872, at its meeting in The Hague, the First International voted the expulsion of the anarchists. Karl Marx had at last won his long battle with Bakunin. From that point on, "scientific socialism" was to dominate revolutionary thought. Anarchism ceased to be a main current of political theory. But anarchism continued as a force to be reckoned with, especially in the Latin countries, and it produced a revolutionary type of great courage and sometimes of appealing interest. Even in decline the theory and action of anarchism dominated the imagination of Europe.

It is not possible here to give a discriminating account of anarchism in all its aspects; to distinguish between the mutation which verges on nihilism and that which is called communist-anarchism, or between its representatives, Sergei Nechayev, who had the character of a police spy, and Kropotkin or the late Carlo Tresca, who were known for their personal sweetness; or to resolve the contradiction between the violence of its theory and action and the gentle world toward which these are directed. It will have to be enough to say that anarchism holds that the natural goodness of man is absolute and that society corrupts it, and that the guide to anarchist action is the desire to destroy society in general and not merely a particular social form.

When, therefore, Hyacinth Robinson is torn between his desire for social justice and his fear lest the civilization of Europe be destroyed, he is dealing reasonably with anarchist belief. "The unchaining of what is today called the evil passions and the destruction of what is called public order" was the consummation of Bakunin's aim which he defended by saying that "the desire for destruction is at the same time a creative desire." It was not only the state but all social forms that were to be demolished according to the doctrine of *amorphism;* any social form held the seeds of the state's rebirth and must therefore be extirpated. Intellectual disciplines were social forms like any other. At least in its early days anarchism expressed hostility toward science. Toward the arts the hostility was less, for the early leaders were often trained in the humanities and their inspiration was largely literary; in the nineties there was a strong alliance between the French artists and the anarchist groups. But in the logic of the situation art was bound to come under the anarchist fire. Art is inevitably associated with civil peace and social order and indeed with the ruling classes. Then too any large intense movement of moral-political action is likely to be jealous of art and to feel that it is in competition with the full awareness of human suffering. Bakunin on several occasions spoke of it as of no account when the cause of human happiness was considered. Lenin expressed something of the same sort when, after having listened with delight to a sonata by Beethoven, he said that he could not listen to music too often. "It affects your nerves, makes you want to say stupid, nice things, and stroke the heads of people who could create such beauty while living in this vile hell. And you mustn't stroke anyone's head—you might get your hand bitten off." And similarly the Princess of James's novel feels that her taste is but the evidence of her immoral aristocratic existence and that art is a frivolous distraction from revolution.

The nature of the radicals in *The Princess Casamassima* may, to the modern reader, seem a distortion of fact. The people who meet at the Sun and Moon to mutter their wrongs over their beer are not revolutionists and scarcely radicals; most of them are nothing more than dull malcontents. Yet they represent with complete accuracy the political development of a large part of the working class of England at the beginning of the eighties. The first great movement of English trade unionism had created an aristocracy of labor largely cut off from the mass of the workers, and the next great movement had not yet begun; the political expression of men such as met at the Sun and Moon was likely to be as fumbling as James represents it.

James has chosen the occupations of these men with great discrimination. There are no factory workers among them; at that time anarchism did not attract factory workers so much as the members of the skilled and relatively sedentary trades: tailors, shoemakers, weavers, cabinetmakers, and ornamental-metal workers. Hyacinth's craft of bookbinding was no doubt chosen because James knew something about it and because, being at once a fine and a mechanic art, it perfectly suited

Hyacinth's fate, but it is to the point that bookbinders were largely drawn to anarchism.

When Paul Muniment tells Hyacinth that the club of the Sun and Moon is a "place you have always over-estimated," he speaks with the authority of one who has connections more momentous. The anarchists, although of course they wished to influence the masses and could on occasion move them to concerted action, did not greatly value democratic or quasi-democratic mass organizations. Bakunin believed that "for the international organization of all Europe one hundred revolutionists, strongly and seriously bound together, are sufficient." The typical anarchist organization was hierarchical and secret. When in 1867 Bakunin drew up plans of organization, he instituted three "orders": a public group to be known as the International Alliance of Social Democracy; then above this and not known to it the Order of National Brothers; above this and not known to it the Order of International Brothers, very few in number. James's Muniment, we may suppose, is a National Brother.

For the indoctrination of his compact body of revolutionists, Bakunin, in collaboration with the amazing Sergei Nechayev, compiled *The Revolutionary Catechism*. This vade mecum might be taken as a guidebook to *The Princess Casamassima*. It instructs the revolutionist that he may be called to live in the great world and to penetrate into any class of society: the aristocracy, the church, the army, the diplomatic corps. It tells how one goes about compromising the wealthy in order to command their wealth, just as the Princess is compromised. There are instructions on how to deal with people who, like James's Captain Sholto, are drawn to the movement by questionable motives; on how little one is to trust the women of the upper classes who may be seeking sensation or salvation—the Princess calls it reality—through revolutionary action. It is a ruthless little book: eventually Bakunin himself complains that nothing—no private letter, no wife, no daughter—is safe from the conspiratorial zeal of his co-author Nechayev.

The situation in which Hyacinth involves himself, his pledge to commit an assassination upon demand of the secret leadership, is not the extreme fancy of a cloistered novelist, but a classic anarchist situation. Anarchism could arouse mass action, as in the riots at Lyon in 1882, but typically it showed its power by acts of terror committed by courageous individuals glad to make personal war against society. Bakunin canonized for anarchism the Russian bandit Stenka Razin; Balzac's Vautrin and Stendhal's Valbayre (of *Lamiel*) are prototypes of anarchist heroes. Always ethical as well as instrumental in its theory, anarchism conceived assassination not only as a way of advertising its doctrine and weakening the enemy's morale, but also as punishment or revenge or warning. Of the many assassinations or attempts at assassination that fill the annals of the late years of the century, not all were anarchist, but those that were not were influenced by anarchist example. In 1878 there were two attempts on the life of the Kaiser, one on the King of Spain, one on the King of Italy; in 1880 another attempt on the King of Spain; in 1881 Alexander II of Russia was killed after many attempts; in 1882 the Phoenix Park murders were committed, Lord Frederick Cavendish, Secretary for Ireland, and Undersecretary Thomas Burke being killed by extreme Irish nationalists; in 1883 there were several dynamite conspiracies in Great Britain and in 1885 there was an explosion in the House of Commons; in 1883 there was an anarchist plot to blow up, all at once, the Emperor Wilhelm, the Crown Prince, Bismarck, and Moltke. These are but a few of the terroristic events of which James would have been aware in the years just before he began *The Princess Casamassima*, and later years brought many more.

Anarchism never established itself very firmly in England as it did in Russia, France, and Italy. In these countries it penetrated to the upper classes. The actions of the Princess are not unique for an aristocrat of her time, nor is she fabricating when she speaks of her acquaintance with revolutionists of a kind more advanced than Hyacinth is likely to know. In Italy she would have met on terms of social equality such notable anarchists as Count Carlo Cafiero and the physician Enrico Malatesta, who was the son of a wealthy family. Kropotkin was a descendant of the Ruriks and, as the novels of James's friend Turgenev testify, extreme radicalism was not uncommon among the Russian aristocracy. In France in the eighties and still more markedly in the nineties there were artistic, intellectual, and even aristocratic groups which were closely involved with the anarchists.

The great revolutionary of *The Princess Casamassima* is Hoffendahl, whom we never see although we feel his real existence. Hoffendahl is, in the effect he has upon others, not unlike what is told of Bakunin himself in his greatest days, when he could enthrall with his passion even those who could not understand the language he spoke in. But it is possible that James also had the famous Johann Most in mind. Most figured in the London press in 1881 when he was tried because his newspaper, *Freiheit,* exulted in the assassination of the Czar. He was found guilty of libel and inciting to murder and sentenced to sixteen months at hard labor. The jury that convicted him recommended mercy on the ground that he was a foreigner and "might be suffering violent wrong." The jury was right—Most had suffered in the prisons of Germany after a bitter youth. It is not clear whether he, like James's Hoffendahl, had had occasion to stand firm under police torture, but there can be no doubt of his capacity to do so. After having served his jail sentence, he emigrated to America, and it has been said of him that terrorist activities in this country centered about him. He was implicated in the Haymarket Affair and imprisoned for having incited the assassin of President McKinley; Emma Goldman and Alexander Berkman were his disciples, and they speak of him in language such as Hyacinth uses of Hoffendahl. It is worth noting that Most was a bookbinder by trade.

In short, when we consider the solid accuracy of James's political detail at every point, we find that we must give up the notion that James could move only in the thin air of moral abstraction. A writer has said of *The Princess Casamassima* that it is "a capital example of James's impotence in matters sociological." The very opposite is so. Quite apart from its moral and aesthetic authority, *The Princess Casamassima* is a brilliantly precise representation of social actuality.

IV

In his preface to *The Princess* in the New York Edition, James tells us of a certain autobiographical element that went into the creation of Hyacinth Robinson. "To find his possible adventures interesting," James says, "I had only to conceive his watching the same public show, the same innumerable appearances I had myself watched and of watching very much as I had watched."

This, at first glance, does not suggest a very intense connection between author and hero. But at least it assures us that at some point the novel is touched by the author's fantasy about himself. It is one of the necessities of successful modern story that the author shall have somewhere entrusted his personal fantasy to the tale; but it may be taken as very nearly a rule that the more the author disguises the personal nature of his fantasy, the greater its force will be. Perhaps he is best off if he is not wholly aware that he is writing about himself at all: his fantasy, like an actual dream, is powerful in the degree that its "meaning" is hidden.

If Hyacinth does indeed express James's personal fantasy, we are led to believe that the fantasy has reference to a familial situation. James puts an insistent emphasis upon his hero's small stature. Hyacinth's mere size is decisive in the story. It exempts him from certain adult situations; for example, where Paul Muniment overcomes the class barrier to treat the Princess as a woman, taking so full an account of her sexual existence and his own that we expect him to make a demand upon her, Hyacinth is detached from the sexual possibility and disclaims it. The intention is not to show him as unmanly but as too young to make the claims of maturity; he is the child of the book, always the very youngest person. And this child-man lives in a novel full of parental figures. Hyacinth has no less than three sets of parents: Lord Frederick and Florentine, Miss Pynsent and Mr. Vetch, Eustache Poupin and Madame Poupin, and this is not to mention the French-revolutionary grandfather and the arch-conspirator Hoffendahl; and even Millicent Henning appears, for one memorable Sunday, in a maternal role. The decisive parental pair are, of course, the actual parents, Lord Frederick and Florentine, who represent—some will feel too schematically—the forces which are in conflict in Hyacinth. Undertaking to kill the Duke as a step in the destruction of the ruling class, Hyacinth is in effect plotting the murder of his own father; and one reason that he comes to loathe the pledged deed is his belief that, by repeating poor Florentine's action, he will be bringing his mother to life in all her pitiful shame.

It is as a child that Hyacinth dies; that is, he dies of the withdrawal of love. James contrives with consummate skill the lonely circumstance of Hyacinth's death. Nothing can equal for delicacy of ironic pathos the incidents of the last part of the book, in which Hyacinth, who has his own death warrant in his pocket, the letter ordering the assassination, looks to his adult friends for a reason of love which will explain why he does not have to serve it on himself, or how, if he must serve it, he can believe in the value of his deed. But the grown-up people have occupations from which he is excluded and they cannot believe in his seriousness. Paul Muniment and the Princess push him aside, not unkindly, only condescendingly, only as one tells a nice boy that there are certain things he cannot understand, such things as power and love and justification.

The adult world last represents itself to Hyacinth in the great scene of lust in the department store. To make its point the crueler, James has previously contrived for Hyacinth a wonderful Sunday of church and park with

Millicent Henning[2]; Millicent enfolds Hyacinth in an undemanding, protective love that is not fine or delicate but for that reason so much the more useful; but when in his last hunt for connection Hyacinth seeks out Millicent in her shop, he sees her standing "still as a layfigure" under Captain Sholto's gaze, exhibiting "the long grand lines" of her body under pretense of "modeling" a dress. And as Hyacinth sees the Captain's eyes "travel up and down the front of Millicent's person," he knows that he has been betrayed.

So much manipulation of the theme of parent and child, so much interest in lost protective love, suggests that the connection of Hyacinth and his author may be more intense than at first appears. And there is one consideration that reinforces the guess that this fantasy of a child and his family has a particular and very personal relation to James in his own family situation. The matter which is at issue in *The Princess Casamassima*, the dispute between art and moral action, the controversy between the glorious unregenerate past and the regenerate future, was not of merely general interest to Henry James, nor, indeed, to any of the notable members of the James family. Ralph Barton Perry in his *Thought and Character of William James* finds the question so real and troubling in William's life that he devotes a chapter to it. William, to whom the antithesis often represented itself as between Europe-art and America-

---

[2] The reviewer for *The Athenaeum* remarked it as "an odd feature of the book that nearly all the action, or nearly all of which the date is indicated, takes place on Sundays." The observation was worth making, for it suggests how certain elements of the book's atmosphere are achieved: what better setting for loneliness and doubt than Sunday in a great city? And since the action of the book must depend on the working schedule of the working-class characters, who, moreover, live at considerable distance from one another, what more natural than that they should meet on Sundays? But the reviewer thinks that "possibly a London week-day suggests a life too strenuous to be lived by the aimless beings whom Mr. James depicts." The "aimless beings" note was one that was struck by most of the more-or-less liberal reviewers.

action, settled in favor of America and action. Henry settled, it would seem, the other way—certainly in favor of art. But whether Henry's option necessarily involved, as William believed, a decision in favor of the past, a love of the past for, as people like to say, the past's sake, may be thought of as the essential matter of dispute between William and Henry.

The dispute was at the very heart of their relationship. They had the matter out over the years. But in the having-out William was the aggressor, and it is impossible to suppose that his statement of the case did not cause Henry pain. William came to suspect that the preoccupation with art was very close to immorality. He was perhaps not so wrong as the clichés in defense of art would make him out to be; his real error lay in his not knowing what art, as a thing to contemplate or as a thing to make, implied for his brother. His suspicion extended to Henry's work. He was by no means without sympathy for it, but he thought that Henry's great gifts were being put at the service of the finicking and refined; he was impatient of what was not robust in the same way he was. Henry, we may be sure, would never have wanted a diminution of the brotherly frankness that could tell him that *The Bostonians* might have been very fine if it had been only a hundred pages long; but the remark and others of similar sort could only have left his heart a little sore.

When, then, we find Henry James creating for his Hyacinth a situation in which he must choose between political action and the fruits of the creative spirit of Europe, we cannot but see that he has placed at the center of his novel a matter whose interest is of the most personal kind. Its personal, its familial, nature is emphasized by Alice James's share in the dispute, for she and William were at one against their brother in aggressively holding a low view of England, and William's activism finds a loud and even shrill echo in Alice, whose passionate radicalism was, as Henry said of her, "her most distinguishing feature." But far more important is the father's relation to the family difference. The authority of the elder Henry James could be fairly claimed by both his sons, for he was brilliantly contradictory on the moral status of art. If William could come to think of art as constituting a principle which was antagonistic to the principle of life, his father had said so before him. And Henry could find abundant support for his own position in his father's frequent use of the artist as one who, because he seeks to create and not to possess, most closely approximates in mankind the attributes of divinity.

The Princess Casamassima may, then, be thought of as an intensely autobiographical book, not in the sense of being the author's personal record but in the sense of being his personal act. For we may imagine that James, beautifully in control of his novel, dominant in it as almost no decent person can be in a family situation, is continuing the old dispute on his own terms and even taking a revenge. Our imagination of the "revenge" does not require that we attribute a debasing malice to James —quite to the contrary, indeed, for the revenge is gentle and innocent and noble. It consists, this revenge, only in arranging things in such a way that Paul Muniment and the Princess shall stand for James's brother and sister and then so to contrive events as to show that, at the very moment when this brilliant pair think they are closest to the conspiratorial arcanum, the real thing, the true center, they are in actual fact furthest from it.[3] Paul

[3] When I say that Paul and the Princess "stand for" William and Alice, I do not mean that they are portraits of William and Alice. It is true that, in the conditioning context of the novel, Paul suggests certain equivalences with William James: in his brisk masculinity, his intelligence, his downright common sense and practicality, most of all in his relation to Hyacinth. What we may most legitimately guess to be a representation is the *ratio* of the characters—Paul: Hyacinth : : William:Henry. The Princess has Alice's radical ideas; she is called "the most remarkable woman in Europe," which in effect is what Henry James said Alice would have been if the full exercise of her will and intellect had not been checked by her illness. But such equivalence is not portraiture and the novel is not a family *roman à clef*. And yet the matter of portraiture cannot be so easily settled, for it has been noticed by those who are acquainted with the life and character of Alice James that there are

and the Princess believe themselves to be in the confidence of *Them,* the People Higher Up, the International Brothers, or whatever, when really they are held in suspicion in these very quarters. They condescend to Hyacinth for his frivolous concern with art, but Hyacinth, unknown to them, has received his letter of fatal commission; he has the death warrant in his pocket, another's and his own; despite his having given clear signs of lukewarmness to the cause, he is trusted by the secret powers where his friends are not. In his last days Hyacinth has become aware of his desire no longer to bind books but to write them: the novel can be thought of as Henry James's demonstrative message, to the world in general, to his brother and sister in particular, that the artist quite as much as any man of action carries his ultimate commitment and his death warrant in his pocket. "Life's nothing," Henry James wrote to a young friend, "—unless heroic and sacrificial."

James even goes so far as to imply that the man of art may be close to the secret center of things when the man of action is quite apart from it. Yet Hyacinth cannot carry out the orders of the people who trust him. Nor of course can he betray them—the pistol which, in the book's last dry words, "would certainly have served much better for the Duke," Hyacinth turns upon himself. A vulgar and facile progressivism can find this to be a proof of James's "impotence in matters sociological"—"the problem remains unsolved." Yet it would seem that a

---

many points of similarity between her and Rosy Muniment. Their opinions are, to be sure, at opposite poles, for Rosy is a staunch Tory and a dreadful snob, but the very patness of the opposition may reasonably be thought significant. In mind and pride of mind, in outspokenness, in will and the license given to will by illness, there is similarity between the sister of Paul and the sister of William and Henry. There is no reason why anyone interested in Henry James should not be aware of this, provided that it not be taken as the negation of Henry's expressed love for Alice and William—provided, too, that it be taken as an aspect of his particular moral imagination, a matter which is discussed later.

true knowledge of society comprehends the reality of the social forces it presumes to study and is aware of contradictions and consequences; it knows that sometimes society offers an opposition of motives in which the antagonists are in such a balance of authority and appeal that a man who so wholly perceives them as to embody them in his very being cannot choose between them and is therefore destroyed. This is known as tragedy.

V

We must not misunderstand the nature of Hyacinth's tragic fate. Hyacinth dies sacrificially, but not as a sacrificial lamb, wholly innocent; he dies as a human hero who has incurred a certain amount of guilt.

The possibility of misunderstanding Hyacinth's situation arises from our modern belief that the artist is one of the types of social innocence. Our competitive, acquisitive society ritualistically condemns what it practices—with us money gives status, yet we consider a high regard for money a debasing thing and we set a large value on disinterested activity. Hence our cult of the scientist and the physician, who are presumed to be free of the acquisitive impulses. The middle class, so far as it is liberal, admires from varying distances the motives and even the aims of revolutionists: it cannot imagine that revolutionists have anything to "gain" as the middle class itself understands gain. And although sometimes our culture says that the artist is a subversive idler, it is nowadays just as likely to say that he is to be admired for his innocence, for his activity is conceived as having no end beyond itself except possibly some benign social purpose, such as "teaching people to understand each other."

But James did not see art as, in this sense, innocent. We touch again on autobiography, for on this point there is a significant connection between James's own life and Hyacinth's.

In Chapter xxv of *A Small Boy and Others*, his first autobiographic volume, James tells how he was initiated into a knowledge of style in the Galerie d'Apollon of the

Louvre. As James represents the event, the varieties of style in that gallery assailed him so intensely that their impact quite transcended aesthetic experience. For they seemed to speak to him not visually at all but in some "complicated sound" and as a "deafening chorus"; they gave him what he calls "a general sense of glory." About this sense of glory he is quite explicit. "The glory meant ever so many things at once, not only beauty and art and supreme design, but history and fame and power, the world in fine raised to the richest and noblest expression."

Hazlitt said that "the language of poetry naturally falls in with the language of power," and goes on to develop an elaborate comparison between the processes of the imagination and the processes of autocratic rule. He is not merely indulging in a flight of fancy or a fashion of speaking; no stancher radical democrat ever lived than Hazlitt and no greater lover of imaginative literature, yet he believed that poetry has an affinity with political power in its autocratic and aristocratic form and that it is not a friend of the democratic virtues. We are likely not to want to agree with Hazlitt; we prefer to speak of art as if it lived in a white bungalow with a garden, had a wife and two children, and were harmless and quiet and cooperative. But James is of Hazlitt's opinion; his first great revelation of art came as an analogy with the triumphs of the world; art spoke to him of the imperious will, with the music of an army with banners. Perhaps it is to the point that James's final act of imagination, as he lay dying, was to call his secretary and give her as his last dictation what purported to be an autobiographical memoir by Napoleon Bonaparte.

But so great an aggression must carry some retribution with it, and as James goes on with the episode of the Galerie d'Apollon, he speaks of the experience as having the effect not only of a "love-philtre" but also of a "fear-philtre." Aggression brings guilt and then fear. And James concludes the episode with the account of a nightmare in which the Galerie figures; he calls it "the most appalling and yet most admirable" nightmare of his life. He dreamed that he was defending himself from an intruder, trying to keep the door shut against a terrible invading form; then suddenly there came "the great thought that I, in my appalled state, was more appalling than the awful agent, creature or presence"; whereupon he opened the door and, surpassing the invader for "straight aggression and dire intention," pursued him down a long corridor in a great storm of lightning and thunder; the corridor was seen to be the Galerie d'Apollon. We do not have to presume very far to find the meaning in the dream, for James gives us all that we might want; he tells us that the dream was important to him, that, having experienced art as "history and fame and power," his arrogation seemed a guilty one and represented itself as great fear which he overcame by an inspiration of straight aggression and dire intention and triumphed in the very place where he had had his imperious fantasy. An admirable nightmare indeed. One needs to be a genius to counterattack nightmare; perhaps this is the definition of genius.

When James came to compose Hyacinth's momentous letter from Venice, the implications of the analogue of art with power had developed and become clearer and more objective. Hyacinth has had his experience of the glories of Europe, and when he writes to the Princess his view of human misery is matched by a view of the world "raised to the richest and noblest expression." He understands no less clearly than before "the despotisms, the cruelties, the exclusions, the monopolies and the rapacities of the past." But now he recognizes that "the fabric of civilization as we know it" is inextricably bound up with this injustice; the monuments of art and learning and taste have been reared upon coercive power. Yet never before has he had the full vision of what the human spirit can accomplish to make the world "less impracticable and life more tolerable." He finds that he is ready to fight for art—and what art suggests of glorious life—against the low and even hostile estimate which his revolutionary friends have made of it, and this involves of course some reconciliation with established coercive power.

It is easy enough, by certain assumptions, to condemn Hyacinth and even to call him names. But first we must see what his position really means and what heroism there is in it. Hyacinth recognizes what very few people wish to admit, that civilization has a price, and a high one. Civilizations differ from one another as much in what they give up as in what they acquire; but all civilizations are alike in that they renounce something for something else. We do right to protest this in any given case that comes under our notice and we do right to get as much as possible for as little as possible; but we can never get everything for nothing. Nor, indeed, do we really imagine that we can. Thus, to stay within the present context, every known theory of popular revolution gives up division of the world "raised to the richest and noblest expression." To achieve the ideal of widespread security, popular revolutionary theory condemns the ideal of adventurous experience. It tries to avoid doing this explicitly and it even, although seldom convincingly, denies that it does it at all. But all the instincts or necessities of radical democracy are against the superbness and arbitrariness which often mark great spirits. It it sometimes said in the interests of an ideal or abstract completeness that the choice need not be made, that security can be imagined to go with richness and nobility of expression. But we have not seen it in the past and nobody really strives to imagine it in the future. Hyacinth's choice is made under the pressure of the counterchoice made by Paul and the Princess; their "general rectification" implies a civilization from which the idea of life raised to the richest and noblest expression will quite vanish.

There have been critics who said that Hyacinth is a snob and the surrogate of James's snobbery. But if Hyacinth is a snob, he is of the company of Rabelais, Shakespeare, Scott, Dickens, Balzac, and Lawrence, men who saw the lordliness and establishment of the aristocrat and the gentleman as the proper condition for the spirit of man, and who, most of them, demanded it for themselves, as poor Hyacinth never does, for "it was not so much that he wished to enjoy as that he wished to know; his desire was not to be pampered but to be initiated." His snobbery is no other than that of John Stuart Mill when he discovered that a grand and spacious room could have so enlarging an effect upon his mind; when Hyacinth at Medley had his first experience of a great old house, he admired nothing so much as the ability of a thing to grow old without loss but rather with gain of dignity and interest; "the spectacle of long duration unassociated with some sordid infirmity or poverty was new to him; for he had lived with people among whom old age meant, for the most part, a grudged and degraded survival." Hyacinth has Yeats's awareness of the dream that a great house embodies, that here the fountain of life "overflows without ambitious pains,"

> And mounts more dizzy high the more it rains
> As though to choose whatever shape it wills
> And never stoop to a mechanical
> Or servile shape, at others' beck and call.

But no less than Yeats he has the knowledge that the rich man who builds the house and the architect and artists who plan and decorate it are "bitter and violent men" and that the great houses "but take our greatness with our violence" and our "greatness with our bitterness."[4]

By the time Hyacinth's story draws to its end, his mind is in a perfect equilibrium, not of irresolution but of awareness. His sense of the social horror of the world is not diminished by his newer sense of the glory of the world. On the contrary, just as his pledge of his life to the revolutionary cause had in effect freed him to understand human glory, so the sense of the glory quickens his response to human misery—never, indeed, is he so sensitive to the sordid life of the mass of mankind as after he has had the revelation of art. And just as he is in an equilibrium of awareness, he is also in an equilib-

[4] "Ancestral Houses" in *Collected Poems*. The whole poem may be read as a most illuminating companion-piece to *The Princess Casamassima*.

rium of guilt. He has learned something of what may lie behind abstract ideals, the envy, the impulse to revenge and to dominance. He is the less inclined to forgive what he sees because, as we must remember, the triumph of the revolution presents itself to him as a certainty and the act of revolution as an ecstasy. There is for him as little doubt of the revolution's success as there is of the fact that his mother had murdered his father. And when he thinks of revolution, it is as a tremendous tide, a colossal force; he is tempted to surrender to it as an escape from his isolation—one would be lifted by it "higher on the sun-touched billows than one could ever be by a lonely effort of one's own." But if the revolutionary passion thus has its guilt, Hyacinth's passion for life at its richest and noblest is no less guilty. It leads him to consent to the established coercive power of the world, and this can never be innocent. One cannot "accept" the suffering of others, no matter for what ideal, no matter if one's own suffering be also accepted, without incurring guilt. It is the guilt in which every civilization is implicated.

Hyacinth's death, then, is not his way of escaping from irresolution. It is truly a sacrifice, an act of heroism. He is a hero of civilization because he dares do more than civilization does: embodying two ideals at once, he takes upon himself, in full consciousness, the guilt of each. He acknowledges both his parents. By his death he instructs us in the nature of civilized life and by his consciousness he transcends it.

VI

Suppose that truth be the expression, not of intellect, nor even, as we sometimes now think, of will, but of love. It is an outmoded idea, and yet if it has still any force at all it will carry us toward an understanding of the truth of *The Princess Casamassima*. To be sure, the legend of James does not associate him with love; indeed, it is a fact symptomatic of the condition of American letters that Sherwood Anderson, a writer who himself spoke much of love, was able to say of James that he was the novelist of "those who hate." Yet as we read *The Princess Casamassima* it is possible to ask whether any novel was ever written which, dealing with decisive moral action and ultimate issues, makes its perceptions and its judgments with so much loving-kindness.

Since James wrote, we have had an increasing number of novels which ask us to take cognizance of those whom we call the underprivileged. These novels are of course addressed to those of us who have the money and the leisure to buy books and read them and the security to assail our minds with accounts of the miseries of our fellow men; on the whole, the poor do not read about the poor. And in so far as the middle class has been satisfied and gratified by the moral implications of most of these books, it is not likely to admire Henry James's treatment of the poor. For James represents the poor as if they had dignity and intelligence in the same degree as people of the reading class. More, he assumes this and feels no need to insist that it is so. This is a grace of spirit that we are so little likely to understand that we may resent it. Few of our novelists are able to write about the poor so as to make them something more than the pitied objects of our facile sociological minds. The literature of our liberal democracy pets and dandles its underprivileged characters, and, quite as if it had the right to do so, forgives them what faults they may have. But James is sure that in such people, who are numerous, there are the usual human gradations of understanding, interest, and goodness. Even if my conjecture about the family connection of the novel be wholly mistaken, it will at least suggest what is unmistakably true, that James could write about a workingman quite as if he were as large, willful, and complex as the author of *The Principles of Psychology*. At the same time that everything in the story of *The Princess Casamassima* is based on social difference, everything is also based on the equality of the members of the human family. People at the furthest extremes of class are easily brought into relation because they are all contained in the novelist's affection. In that context it is natural for the Princess and Lady Aurora Langrish to make each other's acquaintance by the side of Rosy Muniment's bed and to contend for the notice of Paul. That James should create poor people so proud and intelligent as to make it impossible for anyone, even the reader who has paid for the privilege, to condescend to them, so proud and intelligent indeed that it is not wholly easy for them to be "good," is, one ventures to guess, an unexpressed, a never-to-be-expressed reason for finding him "impotent in matters sociological." We who are liberal and progressive know that the poor are our equals in every sense except that of being equal to us.

But James's special moral quality, his power of love, is not wholly comprised by his impulse to make an equal distribution of dignity among his characters. It goes beyond this to create his unique moral realism, his particular gift of human understanding. If in his later novels James, as many say he did, carried awareness of human complication to the point of virtuosity, he surely does not do so here, and yet his knowledge of complication is here very considerable. But this knowledge is not an analytical one, or not in the usual sense in which that word is taken, which implies a cool dissection. If we imagine a father of many children who truly loves them all, we may suppose that he will see very vividly their differences from one another, for he has no wish to impose upon them a similarity which would be himself; and he will be quite willing to see their faults, for his affection leaves him free to love them, not because they are faultless but because they are they; yet while he sees their faults he will be able, from long connection and because there is no reason to avoid the truth, to perceive the many reasons for their actions. The discriminations and modifications of such a man would be enormous, yet the moral realism they would constitute would not arise from an analytical intelligence as we usually conceive it but from love.

The nature of James's moral realism may most easily be exemplified by his dealings with the character of Rosy

Muniment. Rosy is in many ways similar to Jennie Wren, the dolls' dressmaker of *Our Mutual Friend;* both are crippled, courageous, quaint, sharp-tongued, and dominating, and both are admired by the characters among whom they have their existence. Dickens unconsciously recognizes the cruelty that lies hidden in Jennie, but consciously he makes nothing more than a brusque joke of her habit of threatening people's eyes with her needle. He allows himself to be deceived and is willing to deceive us. But James manipulates our feelings about Rosy into a perfect ambivalence. He forces us to admire her courage, pride, and intellect and seems to forbid us to take account of her cruelty because she directs it against able-bodied or aristocratic people. Only at the end does he permit us the release of our ambivalence—the revelation that Hyacinth doesn't like Rosy and that we don't have to is an emotional relief and a moral enlightenment. But although we by the author's express permission are free to dislike Rosy, the author does not avail himself of the same privilege. In the family of the novel Rosy's status has not changed.

Moral realism is the informing spirit of *The Princess Casamassima* and it yields a kind of social and political knowledge which is hard to come by. It is at work in the creation of the character of Millicent Henning, whose strength, affectionateness, and warm sensuality move James to the series of remarkable prose arias in her praise which punctuate the book; yet while he admires her, he knows the particular corruptions which our civilization is working upon her, for he is aware not only of her desire to pull down what is above her but also of her desire to imitate and conform to it and to despise what she herself is. Millicent is proud of doing nothing with her hands; she despises Hyacinth because he is so poor in spirit as to consent to *make* things and get dirty in the process, and she values herself because she does nothing less genteel than exhibit what others have made; and in one of the most pregnant scenes of the book James involves her in the peculiarly corrupt and feeble sexuality which is associated in our culture with exhibiting and looking at luxurious objects.

But it is in the creation of Paul Muniment and the Princess that James's moral realism shows itself in fullest power. If we seek an explanation of why *The Princess Casamassima* was not understood in its own day, we find it in the fact that the significance of this remarkable pair could scarcely have emerged for the reader of 1886. But we of today can say that they and their relationship constitute one of the most masterly comments on modern life that has ever been made.

In Paul Muniment a genuine idealism coexists with a secret desire for personal power. It is one of the brilliances of the novel that his ambition is never made explicit. Rosy's remark about her brother, "What my brother really cares for—well, one of these days, when you know you'll tell me," is perhaps as close as his secret ever comes to statement. It is conveyed to us by his tone, as a decisive element of his charm, for Paul radiates what the sociologists, borrowing the name from theology, call *charisma,* the charm of power, the gift of leadership. His natural passion for power must never become explicit, for it is one of the beliefs of our culture that power invalidates moral purpose. The ambiguity of Paul Muniment has been called into being by the nature of modern politics in so far as they are moral and idealistic. For idealism has not changed the nature of leadership, but it has forced the leader to change his nature, requiring him to present himself as a harmless and self-abnegating man. It is easy enough to speak of this ambiguity as a form of hypocrisy, yet the opposition between morality and power from which it springs is perfectly well conceived. But even if well conceived, it is endlessly difficult to execute and it produces its own particular confusions, falsefications, and even lies. The moral realist sees it as the source of characteristically modern ironies, such as the liberal exhausting the scrupulosity which made him deprecate all power and becoming extravagantly tolerant of what he had once denounced, or the idealist who takes license from his ideals for the unrestrained exercise of power.

The Princess, as some will remember, is the Christina Light of James's earlier novel, *Roderick Hudson*, and she considers, as Madame Grandoni says of her, "that in the darkest hour of her life, she sold herself for a title and a fortune. She regards her doing so as such a terrible piece of frivolity that she can never for the rest of her days be serious enough to make up for it." Seriousness has become her ruling passion, and in the great sad comedy of the story it is her fatal sin, for seriousness is not exempt from the tendency of ruling passions to lead to error. And yet it has an aspect of heroism, this hunt of hers for reality, for a strong and final basis of life. "Then it's real, it's solid!" she exclaims when Hyacinth tells her that he has seen Hoffendahl and has penetrated to the revolutionary holy of holies. It is her quest for reality that leads her to the poor, to the very poorest poor she can find, and that brings a light of joy to her eye at any news of suffering or deprivation, which must surely be, if anything is, an irrefrangible reality. As death and danger are—her interest in Hyacinth is made the more intense by his pledged death, and she herself eventually wants to undertake the mortal mission. A perfect drunkard of reality, she is ever drawn to look for stronger and stronger drams.

Inevitably, of course, the great irony of her fate is that the more passionately she seeks reality and the happier she becomes in her belief that she is close to it, the further removed she is. Inevitably she must turn away from Hyacinth because she reads his moral seriousness as frivolousness; and inevitably she is led to Paul who, as she thinks, affirms her in a morality which is as real and serious as anything can be, an absolute morality which gives her permission to devaluate and even destroy all that she has known of human good because it has been connected with her own frivolous, self-betraying past. She cannot but mistake the nature of reality, for she believes it is a thing, a position, a finality, a bedrock. She is, in short, the very embodiment of the modern will which masks itself in virtue, making itself appear harmless, the will that hates itself and finds its manifestations guilty and is able to exist only if it operates in the name of virtue, that despises the variety and modulations of the human story and longs for an absolute humanity, which is but another way of saying a nothingness. In her alliance with Paul she constitutes a striking symbol of that powerful part of modern culture that exists by means of its claim to political innocence and by its false seriousness—the political awareness that is not aware, the social consciousness which hates full consciousness, the moral earnestness which is moral luxury.

The fatal ambiguity of the Princess and Paul is a prime condition of Hyacinth Robinson's tragedy. If we comprehend the complex totality that James has thus conceived, we understand that the novel is an incomparable representation of the spiritual circumstances of our civilization. I venture to call it incomparable because, although other writers have provided abundant substantiation of James's insight, no one has, like him, told us the truth in a single luminous act of creation. If we ask by what magic James was able to do what he did, the answer is to be found in what I have identified as the source of James's moral realism. For the novelist can tell the truth about Paul and the Princess only if, while he represents them in their ambiguity and error, he also allows them to exist in their pride and beauty: the moral realism that shows the ambiguity and error cannot refrain from showing the pride and beauty. Its power to tell the truth arises from its power of love. James had the imagination of disaster and that is why he is immediately relevant to us; but together with the imagination of disaster he had what the imagination of disaster often destroys and in our time is daily destroying, the imagination of love.

The Function of the
Little Magazine

The Partisan Reader[1] may be thought of as an ambiguous monument. It commemorates a victory—*Partisan Review* has survived for a decade, and has survived with a vitality of which the evidence may be found in the book which marks the anniversary. Yet to celebrate the victory is to be at once aware of the larger circumstance of defeat in which it was gained. For what we speak of as if it were a notable achievement is no more than this: that a magazine which has devoted itself to the publication of good writing of various kinds has been able to continue in existence for ten years and has so far established itself that its audience now numbers some six thousand readers.[2]

Here is an epitome of our cultural situation. Briefly put, it is that there exists a great gulf between our educated class and the best of our literature.

I use the word *educated* in its commonest sense to indicate those people who value their ability to live some part of their lives with serious ideas. I limit the case to these people and do not refer to the great mass of people because that would involve us in an ultimate social question and I have in mind only the present cultural question. And I do not mean to assert that *Partisan Review* in itself contains the best of our literature, but

[1] This essay was first published as the introduction to *The Partisan Reader: Ten Years of Partisan Review, 1933-1944: An Anthology*, edited by William Phillips and Philip Rahv (New York: The Dial Press, 1946).
[2] Four years later the number has risen to ten thousand.

only that it is representative of some of the tendencies that are producing the best.

The great gulf to which I refer did not open suddenly. Some fifty years ago, William Dean Howells observed that the readers of the "cultivated" American magazines were markedly losing interest in literary contributions. Howells is here a useful witness, not only because he had his finger in so many important literary pies and was admirably aware of the economics and sociology of literature, but also because he himself was an interesting example of the literary culture whose decline he was noting. The Ohio of Howells' boyhood had only recently emerged from its frontier phase and in its manner of life it was still what we would call primitive. Yet in this Ohio, while still a boy, Howells had devoted himself to the literary life. He was unusual but he was not unique or lonely; he had friends who also felt called to literature or scholarship. His elders did not think the young man strange. Literature had its large accepted place in this culture. The respectable lawyers of the locality subscribed to the great British quarterlies. The printing office of Howells' father was the resort of the village wits, who, as the son tells us, "dropped in, and liked to stand with their backs to the stove and challenge opinion concerning Holmes and Poe, Irving and Macaulay, Pope and Byron, Dickens and Shakespeare." Problems of morality and religious faith were freely and boldly discussed. There was no intellectual isolationism, and the village felt, at least eventually, the reverberations of the European movement of mind. Howells learned an adequate German from the German settlers and became a disciple of Heine. The past was alive, and the boy, rooting in a barrel of books in his father's log cabin, found much to read about old Spain—at the age of fifteen, having conceived a passion for *Don Quixote*, he vowed to write the life of Cervantes. At the outbreak of the Civil War, when Howells was twenty-three, Abraham Lincoln, wishing to reward the young author for a campaign biography, offered him, at the instance of John Hay and the urging of the Ohio politicians, the consulship at Venice. It was then the common practice to place literary men in foreign diplomatic posts.

I am not trying to paint an idyllic picture of the literary life of our nineteenth century. It was a life full of social anomaly and economic hardship. I am only trying to suggest that in the culture of the time literature was assumed. What was true of Howells in Ohio was also true of Mark Twain in Missouri. Nothing could be falser than the view that Mark Twain was a folk writer. Like his own Tom Sawyer, he was literate and literary to the core, even snobbishly so. The local literary culture that he loved to mock, the graveyard poetry, the foolish Byronism, the adoration of Scott, was the literature of the London drawing rooms naturalized as a folk fact in Missouri. We were once a nation that took its cultural stand on the intense literariness of McGuffey's *Eclectic Readers*. When Oscar Wilde and Matthew Arnold came here on tour, they may have figured chiefly as curiosities, but at least these literary men were nothing less than that.

In the nineteenth century, in this country as in Europe, literature underlay every activity of mind. The scientist, the philosopher, the historian, the theologian, the economist, the social theorist, and even the politician, were required to command literary abilities which would now be thought irrelevant to their respective callings. The man of original ideas spoke directly to "the intelligent public," to the lawyer, the doctor, the merchant, and even—and much more than now, as is suggested by the old practice of bringing out very cheap editions of important books—to the working masses. The role of the "popularizer" was relatively little known; the originator of an idea was expected to make his own full meaning clear.

Of two utterances of equal quality, one of the nineteenth and one of the twentieth century, we can say that the one of the nineteenth century had the greater *power*. If the mechanical means of communication were then less efficient than now, the intellectual means were far more efficient. There may even be a significant ratio between the two. Perhaps, as John Dos Passos has suggested, where books and ideas are relatively rare, true literacy may be higher than where they are superabundant.[3] At any rate, it was the natural expectation that a serious idea would be heard and considered. Baudelaire is the poet from whom our modern disowned poets have taken their characteristic attitudes, yet Baudelaire himself was still able to think of "success," to believe in the possibility of being seriously listened to by the very society he flouted, and he even carried his belief to the point of standing for election to the Academy.

This power of the word, this power of the idea, we no longer count on in the same degree. It is now more than twenty years since a literary movement in this country has had what I have called power. The literary movement of social criticism of the 1920's is not finally satisfying, but it had more energy to advance our civilization than anything we can now see, and its effects were large and good. No tendency since has had an equal strength. The falling off from this energy may not be permanent. It could, of course, become permanent. There are circumstances that suggest it might become so. After all, the emotional space of the human mind is large but not infinite, and perhaps it will be pre-empted by the substitutes for literature—the radio, the movies, and certain magazines—which are antagonistic to literature not merely because they are competing genres but also because of the political and cultural assumptions that control them. Further, the politics with which we are now being confronted may be of such kind as to

[3] This seems to be borne out not only by the great example of Lincoln's prose, but also by the assumptions of the humorous writers, by the style of the newspapers of the day, by the letters of people who read very few books—see, for instance, the letter which Mark Twain's father wrote his son to give him the gist of a course he had taken with a traveling professor of grammar and rhetoric. The command of language was believed to be one of the means by which one could become a person of standing and effectiveness. The tradition of American oratory is now only comic, yet perhaps the verbal ritual of the Fourth of July was the tribute paid by simplicity to intellect.

crush the possibility of that interplay between free will and circumstance upon which all literature depends. These conditions can scarcely encourage us. On the other hand, they must not be allowed to obsess us so that we cannot work. They involve ultimate considerations, and, apart from the fact that it is always futile to make predictions about culture, the practical activity of literature requires that a sense of the present moment be kept paramount.

To the general lowering of the status of literature and of the interest in it, the innumerable "little magazines" have been a natural and heroic response. Since the beginning of the century, meeting difficulties of which only their editors can truly conceive, they have tried to keep the roads open. From the elegant and brilliant *Dial* to the latest little scrub from the provinces, they have done their work, they have kept our culture from being cautious and settled, or merely sociological, or merely pious. They are snickered at and snubbed, sometimes deservedly, and no one would venture to say in a precise way just what effect they have—except that they keep the new talents warm until the commercial publisher with his customary air of noble resolution is ready to take his chance, except that they make the official representatives of literature a little uneasy, except that they keep a countercurrent moving which perhaps no one will be fully aware of until it ceases to move.

Among these magazines, these private and precarious ventures, *Partisan Review* does a work that sets it apart. Although it is a magazine of literary experiment, it differs from the other little magazines in the emphasis it puts upon ideas and intellectual attitudes. And to understand its special role in our culture, we must further particularize the cultural situation I have described; we must become aware of the discrepancy that exists between the political beliefs of our educated class and the literature that, by its merit, should properly belong to that class.

In its political feeling our educated class is predominantly liberal. Attempts to define liberalism are not likely to meet with success—I mean only that our educated class has a ready if mild suspiciousness of the profit motive, a belief in progress, science, social legislation, planning, and international cooperation, perhaps especially where Russia is in question. These beliefs do great credit to those who hold them. Yet it is a comment, if not on our beliefs then on our way of holding them, that not a single first-rate writer has emerged to deal with these ideas, and the emotions that are consonant with them, in a great literary way.

Our liberal ideology has produced a large literature of social and political protest, but not, for several decades, a single writer who commands our real literary admiration; we all respond to the flattery of agreement, but perhaps even the simplest reader among us knows in his heart the difference between that emotion and the real emotions of literature. It is a striking fact about this literature of contemporary liberalism that it is commercially very successful—at the behest of the liberal middle class, that old vice of "commercialism," which we all used to scold, is now at a disadvantage before the "integrity" which it once used to corrupt. Our dominant literature is profitable in the degree that it is earnest, sincere, solemn. At its best it has the charm of a literature of piety. It has neither imagination nor mind.

And if on the other hand we name those writers who, by the general consent of the most serious criticism, by consent too of the very class of educated people of which we speak, are to be thought of as the monumental figures of our time, we see that to these writers the liberal ideology has been at best a matter of indifference. Proust, Joyce, Lawrence, Eliot, Yeats, Mann (in his creative work), Kafka, Rilke, Gide—all have their own love of justice and the good life, but in not one of them does it take the form of a love of the ideas and emotions which liberal democracy, as known by our educated class, has declared respectable. So that we can say that no connection exists between our liberal educated class and the best of the literary mind of our time. And this is to say that there is no connection between the political ideas of our educated class and the deep places of the imagination. The same fatal separation is to be seen in the tendency of our educated liberal class to reject the tough, complex psychology of Freud for the easy rationalistic optimism of Horney and Fromm.

The alienation of the educated class from the most impressive literature of our time has of course been noted before. And certain critics have been eager to attribute the lack of connection to the literal difficulty of the writers themselves and to blame this difficulty on the writers' intellectual snobbishness and irresponsibility; as the war approached they even went so far as to regard as subversive to democracy all writers who did not, as one of them put it, "turn away from the preferences of the self-appointed few, and toward the needs and desires of the many." One might be the more willing to accept this diagnosis if the critics who made it were more adept in their understanding of what, after all, a good many people can understand, or if they were not so very quick to give all their sympathy and all their tolerance to works of an obviously inferior sort merely because they are easy to read, and "affirmative," and "life-giving," and written for the needs and desires of the many. If tolerance is in question, I am inclined rather to suppose that it should go to those writers from whom, whatever their difficulty, we hear the unmistakable note of seriousness —a note which, when we hear it, should suggest to us that those who sound it are not devoting their lives to committing literary suicide.

It would be futile to offer a diagnosis which would go counter to the one of literary snobbery and irresponsibility, a diagnosis which would undertake, perhaps, to throw the blame for the cultural situation upon the quality of the education of our educated class, or upon the political intelligence of this class. The situation is too complex and too important for so merely contentious a procedure. Neither blame nor flattery can do anything to close the breach that I have described.

But to organize a new union between our political ideas and our imagination—in all our cultural purview there is no work more necessary. It is to this work that *Partisan Review* has devoted itself for more than a decade.

It is of some importance that *Partisan Review* began its career as an organ which, in the cultural field, was devoted to the interests of the Communist Party. Considering it for the moment quite apart from politics, the cultural program of the Communist Party in this country has, more than any other single intellectual factor, given the license to that divorce between politics and the imagination of which I have spoken. Basing itself on a great act of mind and on a great faith in mind, it has succeeded in rationalizing intellectual limitation and has, in twenty years, produced not a single work of distinction or even of high respectability. After *Partisan Review* had broken with the Communist Party, some large part of its own intellectual vitality came from its years of conflict with Communist culture at a time when our educated class, in its guilt and confusion, was inclined to accept in serious good faith the cultural leadership of the Party. In recent years the political intensity of *Partisan Review* has somewhat diminished, yet its political character remains.

As it should remain, because our fate, for better or worse, is political. It is therefore not a happy fate, even if it has an heroic sound, but there is no escape from it, and the only possibility of enduring it is to force into our definition of politics every human activity and every subtlety of every human activity. There are manifest dangers in doing this, but greater dangers in not doing it. Unless we insist that politics is imagination and mind, we will learn that imagination and mind are politics, and of a kind that we will not like. *Partisan Review* has conceived its particular function to be the making of this necessary insistence, and within its matrix of politics it has wished to accommodate the old and the new, the traditional and the experimental, the religious and the positivistic, the hopeful and the despairing. In its implicit effort to bring about the union of the political idea with the imagination, it has drawn on a wider range of human interests and personality than any other cultural periodical of our time. And yet it has its own clear unity: it is the unity conferred on diversity by intelligence and imagination.

But if we grant the importance of the work, we are bound to ask how effectively it can be carried out by a magazine of this kind and of similar circulation. We are dealing again with power. The question of power has not always preoccupied literature. And ideally it is not the question which should first come to mind in thinking about literature. Quality is the first, and perhaps should be the only, consideration. But in our situation today, when we think of quality, we must ask what chance a particular quality has to survive, and how it can be a force to act in its own defense and in the defense of those social circumstances which will permit it to establish and propagate itself in the world. This is not a desirable state of affairs. "Art is a weapon" and "Ideas are weapons" were phrases that a few years ago had a wide and happy currency; and sometimes, as we look at the necessities of our life, we have the sense that the weapon metaphor all too ruthlessly advances—food is now a weapon, sleep and love will soon be weapons, and our final slogan perhaps will be, "Life is a weapon." And yet the question of power is forced upon us.

At least let us not fall into the temptations it always offers, of grossness and crudeness. The critics to whom I have referred yield to these temptations when they denounce the coterie and the writer who does not write for "the many." The matter is not so simple as these earnest minds would have it. From the democratic point of view, we must say that in a true democracy nothing should be done *for* the people. The writer who defines his audience by its limitations is indulging in the unforgivable arrogance. The writer must define his audience by its abilities, by its perfections, so far as he is gifted to conceive them. He does well, if he cannot see his right audience within immediate reach of his voice, to direct his words to his spiritual ancestors, or to posterity, or even, if need be, to a coterie. The writer serves his daemon and his subject. And the democracy that does not know that the daemon and the subject must be served is not, in any ideal sense of the word, a democracy at all.

The word coterie should not frighten us too much. Neither should it charm us too much; writing for a small group does not insure integrity any more than writing for the many; the coterie can corrupt as surely, and sometimes as quickly, as the big advertising appropriation. But the smallness of the coterie does not limit the "human" quality of the work. Some coterie authors will no doubt always be difficult and special, like Donne and Hopkins; but this says nothing of their humanity. The populist critics seem to deny the possibility of broad humanity to those who do not have a large audience in mind, yet the writers they would cite as exemplifying breadth of humanity did not themselves feel that the effect of their imagination depended on the size of their audience. "Very bookish, this housebred man. His work smells of the literary coterie"—this is T. E. Shaw's opinion of the author of the *Odyssey*. Chaucer wrote for a small court group; Shakespeare, as his sonnets show, had something of the aspect of the coterie poet; Milton was content that his audience be few, although he insisted that it be fit. The Romanticists wrote for a handful while the nation sneered. Dostoevski wrote for a journal that considered that it was doing well when its subscribers numbered four thousand. And our Whitman, now the often unread symbol of the democratic life, was through most of his career the poet of what was even less than a coterie.

This stale argument should not have to be offered at all, and it is a grim portent of our cultural situation that, in the name of democracy, critics should dare attempt to make it the sign of a poet's shame that he is not widely read.

When we try to estimate the power of literature, we must not be misled by the fancy pictures of history. Now and then periods do occur when the best literature overflows its usual narrow bounds and reaches a large mass of the people. Athens had such a period and we honor it for that. The nineteenth century also had this kind of overflowing. It is what we must always hope for and work for. But in actual fact the occasions are rare when the best literature becomes, as it were, the folk literature, and generally speaking literature has always been carried on within small limits and under great difficulties. Most people do not like the loneliness and the physical quiescence of the activity of contemplation, and many do not have the time or the spirit left for it. But whenever it becomes a question of measuring the power of literature, Shelley's old comment recurs, and "it exceeds all imagination to conceive what would have been the moral condition of the world" if literature did not continue in existence with its appeal to limited groups, keeping the road open.

This does not answer the question of a period like ours when a kind of mechanical literacy is spreading more and more, when more and more people insist, as they should, on an equality of cultural status and are in danger of being drawn to what was called by Tocqueville, who saw the situation in detail a century ago, the "hypocrisy of luxury," the satisfaction with the thing that looks like the real thing but is not the real thing. A magazine with six thousand readers cannot seem very powerful here, and yet to rest with this judgment would be to yield far too easily to the temptations of grossness and crudeness which appear whenever the question of power is raised. We must take into account what would be our moral and political condition if the impulse which such a magazine represents did not exist, the impulse to make sure that the daemon and the subject are served, the impulse to insist that the activity of politics be united with the imagination under the aspect of mind.

Huckleberry Finn

In 1876 Mark Twain published *The Adventures of Tom Sawyer* and in the same year began what he called "another boys' book." He set little store by the new venture and said that he had undertaken it "more to be at work than anything else." His heart was not in it—"I like it only tolerably well as far as I have got," he said, "and may possibly pigeonhole or burn the MS when it is done." He pigeonholed it long before it was done and for as much as four years. In 1880 he took it out and carried it forward a little, only to abandon it again. He had a theory of unconscious composition and believed that a book must write itself; the book which he referred to as "Huck Finn's Autobiography" refused to do the job of its own creation and he would not coerce it.

But then in the summer of 1887 Mark Twain was possessed by a charge of literary energy which, as he wrote to Howells, was more intense than any he had experienced for many years. He worked all day and every day, and periodically he so fatigued himself that he had to recruit his strength by a day or two of smoking and reading in bed. It is impossible not to suppose that this great creative drive was connected with—was perhaps the direct result of—the visit to the Mississippi he had made earlier in the year, the trip which forms the matter of the second part of *Life on the Mississippi*. His boyhood and youth on the river he so profoundly loved had been at once the happiest and most significant part of Mark Twain's life; his return to it in middle age stirred memories which revived and refreshed the idea of *Huckleberry Finn*. Now at last the book was not only ready but eager to write itself. But it was not to receive much conscious help from its author. He was always full of second-rate literary schemes and now, in the early weeks of the summer, with *Huckleberry Finn* waiting to complete itself, he turned his hot energy upon several of these sorry projects, the completion of which gave him as much sense of satisfying productivity as did his eventual absorption in *Huckleberry Finn*.

When at last *Huckleberry Finn* was completed and published and widely loved, Mark Twain became somewhat aware of what he had accomplished with the book that had been begun as journeywork and depreciated, postponed, threatened with destruction. It is his masterpiece, and perhaps he learned to know that. But he could scarcely have estimated it for what it is, one of the world's great books and one of the central documents of American culture.

Wherein does its greatness lie? Primarily in its power of telling the truth. An awareness of this quality as it exists in *Tom Sawyer* once led Mark Twain to say of the earlier work that "it is *not* a boys' book at all. It will be read only by adults. It is written only for adults." But this was only a manner of speaking, Mark Twain's way of asserting, with a discernible touch of irritation, the degree of truth he had achieved. It does not represent his usual view either of boys' books or of boys. No one, as he well knew, sets a higher value on truth than a boy. Truth is the whole of a boy's conscious demand upon the world of adults. He is likely to believe that the adult world is in a conspiracy to lie to him, and it is this belief, by no means unfounded, that arouses Tom and Huck and all boys to their moral sensitivity, their everlasting concern with justice, which they call fairness. At the same time it often makes them skillful and profound liars in their own defense, yet they do not tell the ultimate lie of adults: they do not lie to themselves. That is why Mark Twain felt that it was impossible to carry Tom Sawyer beyond boyhood—in maturity "he would lie just like all the other one-horse men of literature and the reader would conceive a hearty contempt for him."

Certainly one element in the greatness of *Huckleberry Finn*, as also in the lesser greatness of *Tom Sawyer*, is that it succeeds first as a boys' book. One can read it at ten and then annually ever after, and each year find that it is as fresh as the year before, that it has changed only in becoming somewhat larger. To read it young is like planting a tree young—each year adds a new growth ring of meaning, and the book is as little likely as the tree to become dull. So, we may imagine, an Athenian boy grew up together with the *Odyssey*. There are few other books which we can know so young and love so long.

The truth of *Huckleberry Finn* is of a different kind from that of *Tom Sawyer*. It is a more intense truth, fiercer and more complex. *Tom Sawyer* has the truth of honesty—what it says about things and feelings is never false and always both adequate and beautiful. *Huckleberry Finn* has this kind of truth, too, but it has also the truth of moral passion; it deals directly with the virtue and depravity of man's heart.

Perhaps the best clue to the greatness of *Huckleberry Finn* has been given to us by a writer who is as different from Mark Twain as it is possible for one Missourian to be from another. T. S. Eliot's poem, "The Dry Salvages," the third of his *Four Quartets*, begins with a meditation on the Mississippi, which Mr. Eliot knew in his St. Louis boyhood:

I do not know much about gods; but I think that the river
Is a strong brown god . . .

And the meditation goes on to speak of the god as

                              almost forgotten
By the dwellers in cities—ever, however, implacable,
Keeping his seasons and rages, destroyer, reminder of
What men choose to forget. Unhonoured, unpropitiated
By worshippers of the machine, but waiting, watching
    and waiting.[1]

[1] Copyright, 1943, by T. S. Eliot, reprinted by permission of Harcourt, Brace and Company.

Huckleberry Finn is a great book because it is about a god—about, that is, a power which seems to have a mind and will of its own, and which to men of moral imagination appears to embody a great moral idea.

Huck himself is the servant of the river-god, and he comes very close to being aware of the divine nature of the being he serves. The world he inhabits is perfectly equipped to accommodate a deity, for it is full of presences and meanings which it conveys by natural signs and also by preternatural omens and taboos: to look at the moon over the left shoulder, to shake the tablecloth after sundown, to handle a snakeskin, are ways of offending the obscure and prevalent spirits. Huck is at odds, on moral and aesthetic grounds, with the only form of established religion he knows, and his very intense moral life may be said to derive almost wholly from his love of the river. He lives in a perpetual adoration of the Mississippi's power and charm. Huck, of course, always expresses himself better than he can know, but nothing draws upon his gift of speech like his response to his deity. After every sally into the social life of the shore, he returns to the river with relief and thanksgiving; and at each return, regular and explicit as a chorus in a Greek tragedy, there is a hymn of praise to the god's beauty, mystery, and strength, and to his noble grandeur in contrast with the pettiness of men.

Generally the god is benign, a being of long sunny days and spacious nights. But, like any god, he is also dangerous and deceptive. He generates fogs which bewilder, and contrives echoes and false distances which confuse. His sand bars can ground and his hidden snags can mortally wound a great steamboat. He can cut away the solid earth from under a man's feet and take his house with it. The sense of the danger of the river is what saves the book from any touch of the sentimentality and moral ineptitude of most works which contrast the life of nature with the life of society.

The river itself is only divine; it is not ethical and good. But its nature seems to foster the goodness of those who love it and try to fit themselves to its ways. And we must observe that we cannot make—that Mark Twain does not make—an absolute opposition between the river and human society. To Huck much of the charm of the river life is human: it is the raft and the wigwam and Jim. He has not run away from Miss Watson and the Widow Douglas and his brutal father to a completely individualistic liberty, for in Jim he finds his true father, very much as Stephen Dedalus in James Joyce's *Ulysses* finds his true father in Leopold Bloom.[2] The boy and the Negro slave form a family, a primitive community—and it is a community of saints.

Huck's intense and even complex moral quality may possibly not appear on a first reading, for one may be caught and convinced by his own estimate of himself, by his brags about his lazy hedonism, his avowed preference for being alone, his dislike of civilization. The fact is, of course, that he is involved in civilization up to his ears. His escape from society is but his way of reaching what society ideally dreams of for itself. Responsibility is the very essence of his character, and it is perhaps to the point that the original of Huck, a boyhood companion of Mark Twain's named Tom Blenkenship, did, like Huck, "light out for the Territory," only to become a justice of the peace in Montana, "a good citizen and greatly respected."

Huck does indeed have all the capacities for simple happiness he says he has, but circumstances and his own moral nature make him the least carefree of boys—he is always "in a sweat" over the predicament of someone else. He has a great sense of the sadness of human life, and although he likes to be alone, the words "lonely" and "loneliness" are frequent with him. The note of his spe-

---

[2] In Joyce's *Finnegans Wake* both Mark Twain and Huckleberry Finn appear frequently. The theme of rivers is, of course, dominant in the book; and Huck's name suits Joyce's purpose, for Finn is one of the many names of his hero. Mark Twain's love of and gift for the spoken language make another reason for Joyce's interest in him.

cial sensibility is struck early in the story: "Well, when Tom and me got to the edge of the hilltop we looked away down into the village and could see three or four lights twinkling where there were sick folks, maybe; and the stars over us was sparkling ever so fine; and down by the village was the river, a whole mile broad, and awful still and grand." The identification of the lights as the lamps of sick-watches defines Huck's character.

His sympathy is quick and immediate. When the circus audience laughs at the supposedly drunken man who tries to ride the horse, Huck is only miserable: "It wasn't funny to me . . . ; I was all of a tremble to see his danger." When he imprisons the intending murderers on the wrecked steamboat, his first thought is of how to get someone to rescue them, for he considers "how dreadful it was, even for murderers, to be in such a fix. I says to myself, there ain't no telling but I might come to be a murderer myself yet, and then how would I like it." But his sympathy is never sentimental. When at last he knows that the murderers are beyond help, he has no inclination to false pathos. "I felt a little bit heavy-hearted about the gang, but not much, for I reckoned that if they could stand it I could." His will is genuinely good and he has no need to torture himself with guilty second thoughts.

Not the least remarkable thing about Huck's feeling for people is that his tenderness goes along with the assumption that his fellow men are likely to be dangerous and wicked. He travels incognito, never telling the truth about himself and never twice telling the same lie, for he trusts no one and the lie comforts him even when it is not necessary. He instinctively knows that the best way to keep a party of men away from Jim on the raft is to beg them to come aboard to help his family stricken with smallpox. And if he had not already had the knowledge of human weakness and stupidity and cowardice, he would soon have acquired it, for all his encounters forcibly teach it to him—the insensate feud of the Graingerfords and Shepherdsons, the invasion of the raft by the Duke and the King, the murder of Boggs, the lynching party, and the speech of Colonel Sherburn. Yet his profound and bitter knowledge of human depravity never prevents him from being a friend to man.

No personal pride interferes with his well-doing. He knows what status is and on the whole he respects it—he is really a very *respectable* person and inclines to like "quality folks"—but he himself is unaffected by it. He himself has never had status, he has always been the lowest of the low, and the considerable fortune he had acquired in *The Adventures of Tom Sawyer* is never real to him. When the Duke suggests that Huck and Jim render him the personal service that accords with his rank, Huck's only comment is, "Well, that was easy so we done it." He is injured in every possible way by the Duke and the King, used and exploited and manipulated, yet when he hears that they are in danger from a mob, his natural impulse is to warn them. And when he fails of his purpose and the two men are tarred and feathered and ridden on a rail, his only thought is, "Well, it made me sick to see it; and I was sorry for them poor pitiful rascals, it seemed like I couldn't ever feel any hardness against them any more in the world."

And if Huck and Jim on the raft do indeed make a community of saints, it is because they do not have an ounce of pride between them. Yet this is not perfectly true, for the one disagreement they ever have is over a matter of pride. It is on the occasion when Jim and Huck have been separated by the fog. Jim has mourned Huck as dead, and then, exhausted, has fallen asleep. When he awakes and finds that Huck has returned, he is overjoyed; but Huck convinces him that he has only dreamed the incident, that there has been no fog, no separation, no chase, no reunion, and then allows him to make an elaborate "interpretation" of the dream he now believes he has had. Then the joke is sprung, and in the growing light of the dawn Huck points to the debris of leaves on the raft and the broken oar.

> Jim looked at the trash, and then looked at me, and back at the trash again. He had got the dream fixed so strong in his head that he couldn't seem

to shake it loose and get the facts back into its place again right away. But when he did get the thing straightened around he looked at me steady without ever smiling, and says:

"What do dey stan' for? I'se gwyne to tell you. When I got all wore out wid work, en wid de callin' for you, en went to sleep, my heart wuz mos' broke bekase you wuz los', en I didn' k'yer no mo' what became er me en de raf'. En when I wake up en fine you back agin, all safe en soun', de tears come, en I could a got down on my knees en kiss yo' foot, I's so thankful. En all you wuz thinkin' 'bout wuz how you could make a fool uv ole Jim wid a lie. Dat truck dah is *trash;* en trash is what people is dat puts dirt on de head er dey fren's en makes 'em ashamed."

Then he got up slow and walked to the wigwam, and went in there without saying anything but that.

The pride of human affection has been touched, one of the few prides that has any true dignity. And at its utterance, Huck's one last dim vestige of pride of status, his sense of his position as a white man, wholly vanishes: "It was fifteen minutes before I could work myself up to go and humble myself to a nigger; but I done it, and I warn't sorry for it afterwards either."

This incident is the beginning of the moral testing and development which a character so morally sensitive as Huck's must inevitably undergo. And it becomes an heroic character when, on the urging of affection, Huck discards the moral code he has always taken for granted and resolves to help Jim in his escape from slavery. The intensity of his struggle over the act suggests how deeply he is involved in the society which he rejects. The satiric brilliance of the episode lies, of course, in Huck's solving his problem not by doing "right" but by doing "wrong." He has only to consult his conscience, the conscience of a Southern boy in the middle of the last century, to know that he ought to return Jim to slavery. And as soon as he makes the decision according to conscience and decides to inform on Jim, he has all the warmly gratifying emotions of conscious virtue. "Why, it was astonishing, the way I felt as light as a feather right straight off, and my troubles all gone. . . . I felt good and all washed clean of sin for the first time I had ever felt so in my life, and I knowed I could pray now." And when at last he finds that he cannot endure his decision but must sacrifice the comforts of the pure heart and help Jim in his escape, it is not because he has acquired any new ideas about slavery—he believes that he detests Abolitionists; he himself answers when he is asked if the explosion of a steamboat boiler had hurt anyone, "No'm, killed a nigger," and of course finds nothing wrong in the responsive comment, "Well, it's lucky because sometimes people do get hurt." Ideas and ideals can be of no help to him in his moral crisis. He no more condemns slavery than Tristram and Lancelot condemn marriage; he is as consciously *wicked* as any illicit lover of romance and he consents to be damned for a personal devotion, never questioning the justice of the punishment he has incurred.

Huckleberry Finn was once barred from certain libraries and schools for its alleged subversion of morality. The authorities had in mind the book's endemic lying, the petty thefts, the denigrations of respectability and religion, the bad language, and the bad grammar. We smiled at that excessive care, yet in point of fact *Huckleberry Finn* is indeed a subversive book—no one who reads thoughtfully the dialectic of Huck's great moral crisis will ever again be wholly able to accept without some question and some irony the assumptions of the respectable morality by which he lives, nor will ever again be certain that what he considers the clear dictates of moral reason are not merely the engrained customary beliefs of his time and place.

We are not likely to miss in *Huckleberry Finn* the subtle, implicit moral meaning of the great river. But we are likely to understand these moral implications as having to do only with personal and individual conduct. And since the sum of individual pettiness is on the whole pretty constant, we are likely to think of the book as applicable to mankind in general and at all times and in all places, and we praise it by calling it "universal." And so it is; but like many books to which that large adjective applies, it is also local and particular. It has a particular moral reference to the United States in the period after the Civil War. It was then when, in Mr. Eliot's phrase, the river was forgotten, and precisely by the "dwellers in cities," by the "worshippers of the machine."

The Civil War and the development of the railroads ended the great days when the river was the central artery of the nation. No contrast could be more moving than that between the hot, turbulent energy of the river life of the first part of *Life on the Mississippi* and the melancholy reminiscence of the second part. And the war that brought the end of the rich Mississippi days also marked a change in the quality of life in America which, to many men, consisted of a deterioration of American moral values. It is of course a human habit to look back on the past and to find it a better and more innocent time than the present. Yet in this instance there seems to be an objective basis for the judgment. We cannot disregard the testimony of men so diverse as Henry Adams, Walt Whitman, William Dean Howells, and Mark Twain himself, to mention but a few of the many who were in agreement on this point. All spoke of something that had gone out of American life after the war, some simplicity, some innocence, some peace. None of them was under any illusion about the amount of ordinary human wickedness that existed in the old days, and Mark Twain certainly was not. The difference was in the public attitude, in the things that were now accepted and made respectable in the national ideal. It was, they all felt, connected with new emotions about money. As Mark Twain said, where formerly "the people had desired money," now they "fall down and worship it." The new gospel was, "Get money. Get it quickly. Get it in abundance. Get it in prodigious abundance. Get it dishonestly if you can, honestly if you must."[3]

---

[3] *Mark Twain in Eruption*, edited by Bernard De Voto, p. 77.

With the end of the Civil War capitalism had established itself. The relaxing influence of the frontier was coming to an end. Americans increasingly became "dwellers in cities" and "worshippers of the machine." Mark Twain himself became a notable part of this new dispensation. No one worshipped the machine more than he did, or thought he did—he ruined himself by his devotion to the Paige typesetting machine, by which he hoped to make a fortune even greater than he had made by his writing, and he sang the praises of the machine age in *A Connecticut Yankee in King Arthur's Court*. He associated intimately with the dominant figures of American business enterprise. Yet at the same time he hated the new way of life and kept bitter memoranda of his scorn, commenting on the low morality or the bad taste of the men who were shaping the ideal and directing the destiny of the nation.

Mark Twain said of *Tom Sawyer* that it "is simply a hymn, put into prose form to give it a worldly air." He might have said the same, and with even more reason, of *Huckleberry Finn*, which is a hymn to an older America forever gone, an America which had its great national faults, which was full of violence and even of cruelty, but which still maintained its sense of reality, for it was not yet enthralled by money, the father of ultimate illusion and lies. Against the money-god stands the river-god, whose comments are silent—sunlight, space, uncrowded time, stillness, and danger. It was quickly forgotten once its practical usefulness had passed, but, as Mr. Eliot's poem says, "The river is within us. . . ."

In form and style *Huckleberry Finn* is an almost perfect work. Only one mistake has ever been charged against it, that it concludes with Tom Sawyer's elaborate, too elaborate, game of Jim's escape. Certainly this episode is too long—in the original draft it was much longer—and certainly it is a falling off, as almost anything would have to be, from the incidents of the river. Yet it has a certain formal aptness—like, say, that of the Turkish initiation which brings Molière's *Le Bourgeois Gentilhomme* to its close. It is a rather mechanical development of an idea, and yet some device is needed to permit Huck to return to his anonymity, to give up the role of hero, to fall into the background which he prefers, for he is modest in all things and could not well endure the attention and glamour which attend a hero at a book's end. For this purpose nothing could serve better than the mind of Tom Sawyer with its literary furnishings, its conscious romantic desire for experience and the hero's part, and its ingenious schematization of life to achieve that aim.

The form of the book is based on the simplest of all novel-forms, the so-called picaresque novel, or novel of the road, which strings its incidents on the line of the hero's travels. But, as Pascal says, "rivers are roads that move," and the movement of the road in its own mysterious life transmutes the primitive simplicity of the form: the road itself is the greatest character in this novel of the road, and the hero's departures from the river and his returns to it compose a subtle and significant pattern. The linear simplicity of the picaresque novel is further modified by the story's having a clear dramatic organization: it has a beginning, a middle, and an end, and a mounting suspense of interest.

As for the style of the book, it is not less than definitive in American literature. The prose of *Huckleberry Finn* established for written prose the virtues of American colloquial speech. This has nothing to do with pronunciation or grammar. It has something to do with ease and freedom in the use of language. Most of all it has to do with the structure of the sentence, which is simple, direct, and fluent, maintaining the rhythm of the word-groups of speech and the intonations of the speaking voice.

In the matter of language, American literature had a special problem. The young nation was inclined to think that the mark of the truly literary product was a grandiosity and elegance not to be found in the common speech. It therefore encouraged a greater breach between its vernacular and its literary language than, say, English literature of the same period ever allowed. This accounts for the hollow ring one now and then hears even in the work of our best writers in the first half of the last century. English writers of equal stature would never have made the lapses into rhetorical excess that are common in Cooper and Poe and that are to be found even in Melville and Hawthorne.

Yet at the same time that the language of ambitious literature was high and thus always in danger of falseness, the American reader was keenly interested in the actualities of daily speech. No literature, indeed, was ever so taken up with matters of speech as ours was. "Dialect," which attracted even our serious writers, was the accepted common ground of our popular humorous writing. Nothing in social life seemed so remarkable as the different forms which speech could take—the brogue of the immigrant Irish or the mispronunciation of the German, the "affectation" of the English, the reputed precision of the Bostonian, the legendary twang of the Yankee farmer, and the drawl of the Pike County man. Mark Twain, of course, was in the tradition of humor that exploited this interest, and no one could play with it nearly so well. Although today the carefully spelled-out dialects of nineteenth-century American humor are likely to seem dull enough, the subtle variations of speech in *Huckleberry Finn,* of which Mark Twain was justly proud, are still part of the liveliness and flavor of the book.

Out of his knowledge of the actual speech of America Mark Twain forged a classic prose. The adjective may seem a strange one, yet it is apt. Forget the misspellings and the faults of grammar, and the prose will be seen to move with the greatest simplicity, directness, lucidity, and grace. These qualities are by no means accidental. Mark Twain, who read widely, was passionately interested in the problems of style; the mark of the strictest literary sensibility is everywhere to be found in the prose of *Huckleberry Finn.*

It is this prose that Ernest Hemingway had chiefly in mind when he said that "all modern American literature comes from one book by Mark Twain called *Huckleberry*

Finn." Hemingway's own prose stems from it directly and consciously; so does the prose of the two modern writers who most influenced Hemingway's early style, Gertrude Stein and Sherwood Anderson (although neither of them could maintain the robust purity of their model); so, too, does the best of William Faulkner's prose, which, like Mark Twain's own, reinforces the colloquial tradition with the literary tradition. Indeed, it may be said that almost every contemporary American writer who deals conscientiously with the problems and possibilities of prose must feel, directly or indirectly, the influence of Mark Twain. He is the master of the style that escapes the fixity of the printed page, that sounds in our ears with the immediacy of the heard voice, the very voice of unpretentious truth.

Kipling

Kipling belongs irrevocably to our past, and although
the renewed critical attention he has lately been given
by Edmund Wilson and T. S. Eliot is friendlier and more
interesting than any he has received for a long time, it
is less likely to make us revise our opinions than to revive
our memories of him. But these memories, when revived,
will be strong, for if Kipling belongs to our past, he belongs there very firmly, fixed deep in childhood feeling.
And especially for liberals of a certain age he must always be an interesting figure, for he had an effect upon
us in that obscure and important part of our minds
where literary feeling and political attitude meet, an effect so much the greater because it was so early experienced; and then for many of us our rejection of him
was our first literary-political decision.

My own relation with Kipling was intense and I believe typical. It began, properly enough, with *The Jungle
Book*. This was my first independently chosen and avidly
read book, my first literary discovery, all the more wonderful because I had come upon it in an adult "set," one
of the ten green volumes of the Century Edition that
used to be found in many homes. (The "set" has become unfashionable and that is a blow to the literary
education of the young, who, once they had been lured
to an author, used to remain loyal to him until they had
read him by the yard.) The satisfactions of *The Jungle
Book* were large and numerous. I suppose a boy's ves-
tigial animal totemism was pleased; there were the mar-
velous but credible abilities of Mowgli; there were the

deadly enmities and grandiose revenges, strangely and tragically real. And it was a world peopled by wonderful parents, not only Mother Wolf and Father Wolf, but also—the fathers were far more numerous than the mothers—Bagheera the panther, Baloo the bear, Hathi the elephant, and the dreadful but decent Kaa the python, a whole council of strength and wisdom which was as benign as it was dangerous, and no doubt much of the delight came from discovering the benignity of this feral world. And then there was the fascination of the Pack and its Law. It is not too much to say that a boy had thus his first introduction to a generalized notion of society. It was a notion charged with feeling—the Law was mysterious, firm, certain, noble, in every way admirable beyond any rule of home or school.

Mixed up with this feeling about the Pack and the Law, and perfectly expressing it, was the effect of Kipling's gnomic language, both in prose and in verse, for you could not entirely skip the verse that turned up in the prose, and so you were led to trust yourself to the *Barrack Room Ballads* at a time when you would trust no other poetry. That gnomic quality of Kipling's, that knowing allusiveness which later came to seem merely vulgar, was, when first experienced, a delightful thing. By understanding Kipling's ellipses and allusions, you partook of what was Kipling's own special delight, the joy of being "in." Max Beerbohm has satirized Kipling's yearning to be admitted to any professional arcanum, his fawning admiration of the man in uniform, the man with the know-how and the technical slang. It is the emotion of a boy—he lusts for the exclusive circle, for the sect with the password, and he profoundly admires the technical, secret-laden adults who run the world, the overalled people, majestic in their occupation, superb in their preoccupation, the dour engineer and the thoughtful plumber. To this emotion, developed not much beyond a boy's, Kipling was addicted all his life, and eventually it made him silly and a bore. But a boy reading Kipling was bound to find all this sense of arcanum very pertinent; as, for example, it expressed itself in *Plain*

Tales from the Hills, it seemed the very essence of adult life. Kipling himself was not much more than a boy when he wrote these remarkable stories—remarkable because, no matter how one judges them, one never forgets the least of them—and he saw the adult world as full of rites of initiation, of closed doors and listeners behind them, councils, boudoir conferences, conspiracies, innuendoes, and special knowledge. It was very baffling, and certainly as an introduction to literature it went counter to all our present educational theory, according to which a child should not be baffled at all but should read only about what he knows of from experience; but one worked it out by a sort of algebra, one discovered the meaning of the unknowns through the knowns, and just as one got without definition an adequate knowledge of what a *sais* was, or a *dâk*-bungalow, and what the significance of *pukka* was, so one penetrated to what went on between the Gadsbys and to why Mrs. Hauksbee was supposed to be charming and Mrs. Reiver not. Kipling's superior cryptic tone was in effect an invitation to understand all this—it suggested first that the secret was being kept not only from oneself but from everyone else and then it suggested that the secret was not so much being kept as revealed, if one but guessed hard enough. And this elaborate manner was an invitation to be "in" not only on life but on literature; to follow its hints with a sense of success was to become an initiate of literature, a Past Master, a snob of the esoteric Mystery of the Word.

"Craft" and "craftily" were words that Kipling loved (no doubt they were connected with his deep Masonic attachment), and when he used them he intended all their several meanings at once—shrewdness, a special technique, a special *secret* technique communicated by some master of it, and the bond that one user of the technique would naturally have with another. This feeling about the Craft, the Mystery, grew on Kipling and colored his politics and even his cosmological ideas quite for the worse, but to a boy it suggested the virtue of disinterested professional commitment. If one ever fell in love with the cult of art, it was not because one had been proselytized by some intelligent Frenchman, but because one had absorbed Kipling's creedal utterances about the virtues of craft and had read *The Light that Failed* literally to pieces.

These things we must be sure to put into the balance when we make up our account with Kipling—these and a few more. To a middle-class boy he gave a literary sanction for the admiration of the illiterate and shiftless parts of humanity. He was the first to suggest what may be called the anthropological view, the perception that another man's idea of virtue and honor may be different from one's own but quite to be respected. We must remember this when we condemn his mindless imperialism. Indians naturally have no patience whatever with Kipling and they condemn even his best book, *Kim,* saying that even here, where his devotion to the Indian life is most fully expressed, he falsely represents the Indians. Perhaps this is so, yet the dominant emotions of *Kim* are love and respect for the aspects of Indian life that the ethos of the West does not usually regard even with leniency. *Kim* established the value of things a boy was not likely to find approved anywhere else—the rank, greasy, over-rich things, the life that was valuable outside the notions of orderliness, success, and gentility. It suggested not only a multitude of different ways of life, but even different modes of thought. Thus, whatever one might come to feel personally about religion, a reading of *Kim* could not fail to establish religion's factual reality, not as a piety, which was the apparent extent of its existence in the West, but as something at the very root of life; in *Kim* one saw the myth in the making before one's very eyes and understood how and why it was made, and this, when later one had the intellectual good luck to remember it, had more to say about history and culture than anything in one's mere experience. *Kim,* like *The Jungle Book,* is full of wonderful fathers, all dedicated men in their different ways, each representing a different possibility of existence; and the charm of each is the greater because the boy need not commit himself to one alone but, like Kim himself, may follow Ali into the shrewdness and sensuality of the bazaars, and be initiated by Colonel Strickland into the cold glamour of the Reason of State, and yet also make himself the son of the Lama, the very priest of contemplation and peace.

And then a boy in a large New York high school could find a blessed release from the school's offensive pieties about "service" and "character" in the scornful individualism of *Stalky & Co.* But it was with *Stalky & Co.* that the spell was broken, and significantly enough by H. G. Wells. In his *Outline of History* Wells connected the doings of Stalky, McTurk, and Beetle with British imperialism, and he characterized both in a way that made one see how much callousness, arrogance, and brutality one had been willing to accept. From then on the disenchantment grew. Exactly because Kipling was so involved with one's boyhood, one was quick to give him up in one's adolescence. The Wellsian liberalism took hold, and Shaw offered a new romance of wit and intellect. The new movements in literature came in to make Kipling seem inconsequential and puerile, to require that he be dismissed as official and, as one used to say, intending something aesthetic and emotional rather than political, "bourgeois." He ceased to be the hero of life and literature and became the villain, although even then a natural gratitude kept green the memory of the pleasure he had given.

But the world has changed a great deal since the days when that antagonism between Kipling and enlightenment was at its early intensity, and many intellectual and political things have shifted from their old assigned places. The liberalism of Wells and Shaw long ago lost its ascendency, and indeed in its later developments it showed what could never in the early days have been foreseen, an actual affinity with certain elements of Kipling's own constellation of ideas. And now when, in the essay which serves as the introduction to his selection of Kipling's verse, Mr. Eliot speaks of "the fascination of exploring a mind so different from my own," we surprise ourselves—as perhaps Mr. Eliot intended that we should

—by seeing that the similarities between the two minds are no less striking than the differences. Time surely has done its usual but always dramatic work of eroding our clear notions of cultural antagonisms when Kipling can be thought of as in any way akin to Eliot. Yet as Mr. Eliot speaks of the public intention and the music-hall tradition of Kipling's verse, anyone who has heard a record of Mr. Eliot reading *The Waste Land* will be struck by how much that poem is publicly intended, shaped less for the study than for the platform or the pulpit, by how much the full dialect rendition of the cockney passages suggests that it was even shaped for the music hall, by how explicit the poet's use of his voice makes the music we are so likely to think of as internal and secretive. Then it is significant that among the dominant themes of both Kipling and Eliot are those of despair and the fear of nameless psychological horror. Politically they share an excessive reliance on administration and authority. They have the same sense of being beset and betrayed by the ignoble mob; Kipling invented and elaborated the image of the Pict, the dark little hating man, "too little to love or to hate," who, if left alone, "can drag down the state"; and this figure plays its well-known part in Mr. Eliot's poetry, being for both poets the stimulus to the pathos of xenophobia.

Mr. Eliot's literary apologia for Kipling consists of asking us to judge him not as a deficient writer of poetry but as an admirable writer of verse. Upon this there follow definitions of a certain ingenuity, but the distinction between poetry and verse does not really advance beyond the old inadequate one—I believe that Mr. Eliot himself has specifically rejected it—which Matthew Arnold put forward in writing about Dryden and Pope. I cannot see the usefulness of the distinction; I can even see critical danger in it; and when Mr. Eliot says that Kipling's verse sometimes becomes poetry, it seems to me that verse, in Mr. Eliot's present sense, is merely a word used to denote poetry of a particular kind, in which certain intensities are rather low. Nowadays, it is true, we are not enough aware of the pleasures of poetry of low intensity, by which, in our modern way, we are likely to mean poetry in which the processes of thought are not, by means of elliptical or tangential metaphor and an indirect syntax, advertised as being under high pressure; Crabbe, Cowper, and Scott are rejected because they are not Donne or Hopkins or Mr. Eliot himself, or even poets of far less consequence than these; and no doubt Chaucer would be depreciated on the same grounds, if we were at all aware of him these days. I should have welcomed Mr. Eliot's speaking out in a general way in support of the admirable, and, as I think, necessary, tradition of poetry of low intensity. But by making it different in kind from poetry of high intensity and by giving it a particular name which can only be of invidious import, he has cut us off still more sharply from its virtues.

Kipling, then, must be taken as a poet. Taken so, he will scarcely rank very high, although much must be said in his praise. In two evenings, or even in a single very long one, you can read through the bulky Inclusive Edition of his verse, on which Mr. Eliot's selection is based, and be neither wearied, in part because you will not have been involved, nor uninterested, because Kipling was a man of great gifts. You will have moments of admiration, sometimes of unwilling admiration, and even wish that Mr. Elliot had included certain poems in his selection that he has left out. You will be frequently irritated by the truculence and sometimes amused by its unconsciousness—who but Kipling would write a brag about English understatement? Carlyle roaring the virtues of Silence is nothing to it—but when you have done you will be less inclined to condemn than to pity: the constant iteration of the bravado will have been illuminated by a few poems that touch on the fear and horror which Mr. Wilson speaks of at length and which Mr. Eliot refers to; you feel that the walls of wrath and the ramparts of empire are being erected against the mind's threat to itself. This is a real thing, whether we call it good or bad, and its force of reality seems to grow rather than diminish in memory, seems to be greater after one's actual reading is behind one; the quality of this reality is that which we assign to primitive and elemental things, and, judge it as we will, we dare not be indifferent or superior to it.

In speaking of Kipling's politics, Mr. Eliot contents himself with denying that Kipling was a fascist; a tory, he says, is a very different thing, a tory considers fascism the last debasement of democracy. But this, I think, is not quite ingenuous of Mr. Eliot. A tory, to be sure, is not a fascist, and Kipling is not properly to be called a fascist, but neither is his political temperament to be adequately described merely by reference to a tradition which is honored by Dr. Johnson, Burke, and Walter Scott. Kipling is not like these men; he is not generous, and, although he makes much to-do about manliness, he is not manly; and he has none of the *mind* of the few great tories. His toryism often had in it a lower-middle-class snarl of defeated gentility, and it is this, rather than his love of authority and force, that might suggest an affinity with fascism. His imperialism is reprehensible not because it *is* imperialism but because it is a puny and mindless imperialism. In short, Kipling is unloved and unlovable not by reason of his beliefs but by reason of the temperament that gave them literary expression.

I have said that the old antagonism between liberalism and Kipling is now abated by time and events, yet it is still worth saying, and it is not extravagant to say, that Kipling was one of liberalism's major intellectual misfortunes. John Stuart Mill, when he urged all liberals to study the conservative Coleridge, said that we should pray to have enemies who make us worthy of ourselves. Kipling was an enemy who had the opposite effect. He tempted liberals to be content with easy victories of right feeling and with moral self-congratulation. For example, the strength of toryism at its best lies in its descent from a solid administrative tradition, while the weakness of liberalism, arising from its history of reliance upon legislation, is likely to be a fogginess about administration (or, when the fog clears away a little, a fancy and absolute notion of administration such as

Wells and Shaw gave way to). Kipling's sympathy was always with the administrator and he is always suspicious of the legislator. This is foolish, but it is not the most reprehensible error in the world, and it is a prejudice which, in the hands of an intelligent man, say a man like Walter Bagehot or like Fitzjames Stephen, might make clear to the man of principled theory, to the liberal, what the difficulties not merely of government but of *governing* really are. And that is what Kipling set out to do, but he so charged his demonstration with hatred and contempt, with rancor and caste feeling, he so emptied the honorable tory tradition of its intellectual content, that he simply could not be listened to or believed, he could only be reacted against. His extravagance sprang from his hatred of the liberal intellectual —he was, we must remember, the aggressor in the quarrel—and the liberal intellectual responded by hating everything that Kipling loved, even when it had its element of virtue and enlightenment.

We must make no mistake about it—Kipling was an honest man and he loved the national virtues. But I suppose no man ever did more harm to the national virtues than Kipling did. He mixed them up with a swagger and swank, with bullying, ruthlessness, and self-righteousness, and he set them up as necessarily antagonistic to intellect. He made them stink in the nostrils of youth. I remember that in my own undergraduate days we used specifically to exclude physical courage from among the virtues; we were exaggerating the point of a joke of Shaw's and reacting from Kipling. And up to the war I had a yearly struggle with undergraduates over Wordsworth's poem, "The Character of the Happy Warrior," which is, I suppose, the respectable father of the profligate "If." [1] It seemed too moral and "manly," the students said, and once when I remarked that John Wordsworth had apparently been just such a man as his brother had described, and told them about his dutiful and courageous death at sea, they said flatly that they

[1] The war over, the struggle is on again.

were not impressed. This was not what most of them really thought, but the idea of courage and duty had been steeped for them in the Kipling vat and they rejected the idea with the color. In England this response seems to have gone even further.[2] And when the war came, the interesting and touching phenomenon of the cult of Richard Hillary, which Arthur Koestler has described, was the effort of the English young men to find the national virtues without the Kipling color, to know and resist their enemies without self-glorification.

In our day the idea of the nation has become doubtful and debilitated all over the world, or at least wherever it is not being enforced by ruthless governments or wherever it is not being nourished by immediate danger or the tyranny of other nations. Men more and more think it best to postulate their loyalty either to their class, or to the idea of a social organization more comprehensive than that of the nation, or to a cultural ideal or a spiritual fatherland. Yet in the attack which has been made on the national idea, there are, one suspects, certain motives that are not expressed, motives that have less to do with reason and order than with the modern impulse to say that politics is not really a proper human activity at all; the reluctance to give loyalty to any social organization which falls short of some ideal organization of the future may imply a disgust not so much with the merely national life as with civic life itself. And on the positive side too something is still to be said for nations, the case against them is not yet closed. Of course in literature nothing ever is said; every avowal of national pride or love or faith rings false and serves but to reinforce the tendency of rejection, as the example of the response to Kipling shows. Yet Kipling himself, on one occasion, dealt successfully with the national theme and in doing so implied the reason for the general failure— the "Recessional" hymn is a remarkable and perhaps a

[2] George Orwell's essay on Kipling in *Dickens, Dali and Others* deals bluntly and fairly with the implications of easy "liberal" and "aesthetic" contempt for *everything* Kipling stood for.

great national poem; its import of humility and fear at the moment of national success suggests that the idea of the nation, although no doubt a limited one, is still profound enough to require that it be treated with a certain measure of seriousness and truth-telling. But the occasion is exceptional with Kipling, who by the utterances that are characteristic of him did more than any writer of our time to bring the national idea into discredit.

The Immortality Ode

I

Criticism, we know, must always be concerned with the poem itself. But a poem does not always exist only in itself: sometimes it has a very lively existence in its false or partial appearances. These simulacra of the actual poem must be taken into account by criticism; and sometimes, in its effort to come at the poem as it really is, criticism does well to allow the simulacra to dictate at least its opening moves. In speaking about Wordsworth's "Ode: Intimations of Immortality from Recollections of Early Childhood," I should like to begin by considering an interpretation of the poem which is commonly made.[1] According to this interpretation—I choose for its brevity Dean Sperry's statement of a view which is held by many other admirable critics—the Ode is "Wordsworth's conscious farewell to his art, a dirge sung over his departing powers."

How did this interpretation—erroneous, as I believe—come into being? The Ode may indeed be quoted to substantiate it, but I do not think it has been drawn directly from the poem itself. To be sure, the Ode is not wholly perspicuous. Wordsworth himself seems to have thought it difficult, for in the Fenwick notes he speaks of the need for competence and attention in the reader. The difficulty does not lie in the diction, which is simple, or even in the syntax, which is sometimes obscure, but rather in certain contradictory statements which the

[1] The text of the poem is given at the end of this essay.

poem makes, and in the ambiguity of some of its crucial words. Yet the erroneous interpretation I am dealing with does not arise from any intrinsic difficulty of the poem itself but rather from certain extraneous and unexpressed assumptions which some of its readers make about the nature of the mind.

Nowadays it is not difficult for us to understand that such tacit assumptions about the mental processes are likely to lie hidden beneath what we say about poetry. Usually, despite our general awareness of their existence, it requires great effort to bring these assumptions explicitly into consciousness. But in speaking of Wordsworth one of the commonest of our unexpressed ideas comes so close to the surface of our thought that it needs only to be grasped and named. I refer to the belief that poetry is made by means of a particular poetic faculty, a faculty which may be isolated and defined.

It is this belief, based wholly upon assumption, which underlies all the speculations of the critics who attempt to provide us with explanations of Wordsworth's poetic decline by attributing it to one or another of the events of his life. In effect any such explanation is a way of *defining* Wordsworth's poetic faculty: what the biographical critics are telling us is that Wordsworth wrote great poetry by means of a faculty which depended upon his relations with Annette Vallon, or by means of a faculty which operated only so long as he admired the French Revolution, or by means of a faculty which flourished by virtue of a particular pitch of youthful sense-perception or by virtue of a certain attitude toward Jeffrey's criticism or by virtue of a certain relation with Coleridge.

Now no one can reasonably object to the idea of mental determination in general, and I certainly do not intend to make out that poetry is an unconditioned activity. Still, this particular notion of mental determination which implies that Wordsworth's genius failed when it was deprived of some single emotional circumstance is so much too simple and so much too mechanical that I think we must inevitably reject it. Certainly what we know of poetry does not allow us to refer the making of it to any single faculty. Nothing less than the whole mind, the whole man, will suffice for its origin. And such was Wordsworth's own view of the matter.

There is another unsubstantiated assumption at work in the common biographical interpretation of the Ode. This is the belief that a natural and inevitable warfare exists between the poetic faculty and the faculty by which we conceive or comprehend general ideas. Wordsworth himself did not believe in this antagonism—indeed, he held an almost contrary view—but Coleridge thought that philosophy had encroached upon and destroyed his own powers, and the critics who speculate on Wordsworth's artistic fate seem to prefer Coleridge's psychology to Wordsworth's own. Observing in the Ode a contrast drawn between something called "the visionary gleam" and something called "the philosophic mind," they leap to the conclusion that the Ode is Wordsworth's conscious farewell to his art, a dirge sung over departing powers.

I am so far from agreeing with this conclusion that I believe the Ode is not only not a dirge sung over departing powers but actually a dedication to new powers. Wordsworth did not, to be sure, realize his hopes for these new powers, but that is quite another matter.

II

As with many poems, it is hard to understand any part of the Ode until we first understand the whole of it. I will therefore say at once what I think the poem is chiefly about. It is a poem about growing; some say it is a poem about growing old, but I believe it is about growing up. It is incidentally a poem about optics and then, inevitably, about epistemology; it is concerned with ways of seeing and then with ways of knowing. Ultimately it is concerned with ways of acting, for, as usual with Wordsworth, knowledge implies liberty and power. In only a limited sense is the Ode a poem about immortality.

Both formally and in the history of its composition

the poem is divided into two main parts. The first part, consisting of four stanzas, states an optical phenomenon and asks a question about it. The second part, consisting of seven stanzas, answers that question and is itself divided into two parts, of which the first is despairing, the second hopeful. Some time separates the composition of the question from that of the answer; the evidence most recently adduced by Professor de Selincourt seems to indicate that the interval was two years.

The question which the first part asks is this:

> Whither is fled the visionary gleam?
> Where is it now, the glory and the dream?

All the first part leads to this question, but although it moves in only one direction it takes its way through more than one mood. There are at least three moods before the climax of the question is reached.

The first stanza makes a relatively simple statement. "There was a time" when all common things seemed clothed in "celestial light," when they had "the glory and the freshness of a dream." In a poem ostensibly about immortality we ought perhaps to pause over the word "celestial," but the present elaborate title was not given to the poem until much later, and conceivably at the time of the writing of the first part the idea of immortality was not in Wordsworth's mind at all. Celestial light probably means only something different from ordinary, earthly, scientific light; it is a light of the mind, shining even in darkness—"by night or day"—and it is perhaps similar to the light which is praised in the invocation to the third book of *Paradise Lost*.

The second stanza goes on to develop this first mood, speaking of the ordinary, physical kind of vision and suggesting further the meaning of "celestial." We must remark that in this stanza Wordsworth is so far from observing a diminution of his physical senses that he explicitly affirms their strength. He is at pains to tell us how vividly he sees the rainbow, the rose, the moon, the stars, the water and the sunshine. I emphasize this because some of those who find the Ode a dirge over the

poetic power maintain that the poetic power failed with
the failure of Wordsworth's senses. It is true that Wordsworth, who lived to be eighty, was said in middle life
to look much older than his years. Still, thirty-two, his
age at the time of writing the first part of the Ode, is
an extravagantly early age for a dramatic failure of the
senses. We might observe here, as others have observed
elsewhere, that Wordsworth never did have the special
and perhaps modern sensibility of his sister or of Coleridge, who were so aware of exquisite particularities.
His finest passages are moral, emotional, subjective;
whatever visual intensity they have comes from his response to the object, not from his close observation of it.

And in the second stanza Wordsworth not only confirms his senses but he also confirms his ability to perceive beauty. He tells us how he responds to the loveliness of the rose and of the stars reflected in the water.
He can deal, in the way of Fancy, with the delight of
the moon when there are no competing stars in the sky.
He can see in Nature certain moral propensities. He
speaks of the sunshine as a "glorious birth." But here he
pauses to draw distinctions from that fascinating word
"glory": despite his perception of the sunshine as a glorious birth, he knows "That there hath past away a glory
from the earth."

Now, with the third stanza, the poem begins to com-
plicate itself. It is *while* Wordsworth is aware of the
"optical" change in himself, the loss of the "glory," that
there comes to him "a thought of grief." I emphasize
the word "while" to suggest that we must understand
that for some time he had been conscious of the "optical"
change *without* feeling grief. The grief, then, would
seem to be coincidental with but not necessarily caused
by the change. And the grief is not of long duration,
for we learn that

> A timely utterance gave that thought relief,
>   And I again am strong.

It would be not only interesting but also useful to know
what that "timely utterance" was, and I shall hazard a

guess; but first I should like to follow the development of the Ode a little further, pausing only to remark that the reference to the timely utterance seems to imply that, although the grief is not of long duration, still we are not dealing with the internal experiences of a moment, or of a morning's walk, but of a time sufficient to allow for development and change of mood; that is, the dramatic time of the poem is not exactly equivalent to the emotional time.

Stanza IV goes on to tell us that the poet, after gaining relief from the timely utterance, whatever that was, felt himself quite in harmony with the joy of Nature in spring. The tone of this stanza is ecstatic, and in a way that some readers find strained and unpleasant and even of doubtful sincerity. Twice there is a halting repetition of words to express a kind of painful intensity of response: "I feel—I feel it all," and "I hear, I hear, with joy I hear!" Wordsworth sees, hears, feels—and with that "joy" which both he and Coleridge felt to be so necessary to the poet. But despite the response, despite the joy, the ecstasy changes to sadness in a wonderful modulation which quite justifies the antecedent shrillness of affirmation:

> —But there's a Tree, of many, one,
> A single Field which I have looked upon.
> Both of them speak of something that is gone:
> The Pansy at my feet
> Doth the same tale repeat.

And what they utter is the terrible question:

> Whither is fled the visionary gleam?
> Where is it now, the glory and the dream?

III

Now, the interpretation which makes the Ode a dirge over departing powers and a conscious farewell to art takes it for granted that the visionary gleam, the glory, and the dream, are Wordsworth's names for the power by which he made poetry. This interpretation gives to the Ode a place in Wordsworth's life exactly analogous to the place that "Dejection: An Ode" has in Coleridge's life. It is well known how intimately the two poems are connected; the circumstances of their composition makes them symbiotic. Coleridge in his poem most certainly does say that his poetic powers are gone or going; he is very explicit, and the language he uses is very close to Wordsworth's own. He tells us that upon "the inanimate cold world" there must issue from the soul "a light, a glory, a fair luminous cloud," and that this glory *is* Joy, which he himself no longer possesses. But Coleridge's poem, although it responds to the first part of Wordsworth's, is not a recapitulation of it. On the contrary, Coleridge is precisely contrasting his situation with Wordsworth's. As Professor de Selincourt says in his comments on the first version of "Dejection," this contrast "was the root idea" of Coleridge's ode.[2] In April of 1802 Wordsworth was a month away from his marriage to Mary Hutchinson, on the point of establishing his life in a felicity and order which became his genius, while Coleridge was at the nadir of despair over his own unhappy marriage and his hopeless love for Sara, the sister of Wordsworth's fiancée. And the difference between the situations of the two friends stands in Coleridge's mind for the difference in the states of health of their respective poetic powers.

Coleridge explicitly ascribes the decay of his poetic power to his unhappiness, which worked him harm in two ways—by forcing him to escape from the life of emotion to find refuge in intellectual abstraction and by destroying the Joy which, issuing as "a light, a glory, a fair luminous cloud," so irradiated the world as to make it a fit object of the shaping power of imagination. But Wordsworth tells us something quite different about himself. He tells us that he has strength, that he has Joy, but still he has not the glory. In short, we have no reason to assume that, when he asks the question at the end of the fourth stanza, he means, "Where has my creative power gone?" Wordsworth tells us how he made poetry;

[2] *Wordsworthian and Other Studies*, Oxford, 1947.

he says he made it out of the experience of his senses as
worked upon by his contemplative intellect, but he nowhere tells us that he made poetry out of visionary
gleams, out of glories, or out of dreams.

To be sure, he writes very often about gleams. The
word "gleam" is a favorite one with him, and a glance
at the Lane Cooper concordance will confirm our impression that Wordsworth, whenever he has a moment
of insight or happiness, talks about it in the language of
light. His great poems are about moments of enlightenment, in which the metaphoric and the literal meaning
of the word are at one—he uses "glory" in the abstract
modern sense, but always with an awareness of the old
concrete iconographic sense of a visible nimbus.[3] But
this momentary and special light is the subject matter
of his poetry, not the power of making it. The moments
are moments of understanding, but Wordsworth does
not say that they make writing poetry any easier. Indeed, in lines 59–131 of the first book of The Prelude
he expressly says that the moments of clarity are by no
means always matched by poetic creativity.

As for dreams and poetry, there is some doubt about
the meaning that Wordsworth gave to the word "dream"
used as a metaphor. In "Expostulation and Reply" he
seems to say that dreaming—"dream my time away"—is
a good thing, but he is ironically using his interlocutor's
depreciatory word, and he really does not mean "dream"
at all. In the Peele Castle verses, which have so close a
connection with the Immortality Ode, he speaks of the
"poet's dream" and makes it synonymous with "gleam,"
with "the light that never was, on sea or land," and with
the "consecration." But the beauty of the famous lines
often makes us forget to connect them with what follows, for Wordsworth says that gleam, light, consecra-

[3] We recall that in The Varieties of Religious Experience
William James speaks of the "hallucinatory or pseudo-
hallucinatory luminous phenomena, photisms, to use the
term of the psychologists," the "floods of light and glory,"
which characterize so many moments of revelation. James
mentions one person who, experiencing the light, was uncertain of its externality.

tion, and dream would have made an "illusion," or, in the 1807 version, a "delusion." Professor Beatty reminds us that in the 1820 version Wordsworth destroyed the beauty of the lines in order to make his intention quite clear. He wrote:

> and add a gleam
> Of lustre known to neither sea nor land,
> But borrowed from the youthful Poet's Dream.

That is, according to the terms of Wordsworth's conception of the three ages of man, the youthful Poet was, as he had a right to be, in the service of Fancy and therefore saw the sea as calm. But Wordsworth himself can now no longer see in the way of Fancy; he has, he says, "submitted to a new control." This seems to be at once a loss and a gain. The loss: "A power is gone, which nothing can restore." The gain: "A deep distress hath humanized my Soul"; this is gain because happiness without "humanization" "is to be pitied, for 'tis surely blind"; to be "housed in a dream" is to be "at distance from the kind" (i.e., mankind). In the "Letter to Mathetes" he speaks of the Fancy as "dreaming"; and the Fancy is, we know, a lower form of intellect in Wordsworth's hierarchy, and peculiar to youth.

But although, as we see, Wordsworth uses the word "dream" to mean illusion, we must remember that he thought illusions might be very useful. They often led him to proper attitudes and allowed him to deal successfully with reality. In *The Prelude* he tells us how his reading of fiction made him able to look at the disfigured face of the drowned man without too much horror; how a kind of superstitious conviction of his own powers was useful to him; how, indeed, many of the most critical moments of his boyhood education were moments of significant illusion; and in *The Excursion* he is quite explicit about the salutary effects of superstition. But he was interested in dreams not for their own sake but for the sake of reality. Dreams may *perhaps* be associated with poetry, but reality *certainly* is; and reality for Wordsworth comes fullest with Imagination, the faculty of maturity. The loss of the "dream" may be painful, but it does not necessarily mean the end of poetry.

IV

And now for a moment I should like to turn back to the "timely utterance," because I think an understanding of it will help get rid of the idea that Wordsworth was saying farewell to poetry. Professor Garrod believes that this "utterance" was "My heart leaps up when I behold," which was written the day before the Ode was begun. Certainly this poem is most intimately related to the Ode—its theme, the legacy left by the child to the man, is a dominant theme of the Ode, and Wordsworth used its last lines as the Ode's epigraph. But I should like to suggest that the "utterance" was something else. In line 43 Wordsworth says, "Oh evil day! if I were sullen," and the word "sullen" leaps out at us as a striking and carefully chosen word. Now there is one poem in which Wordsworth says that he was sullen; it is "Resolution and Independence."

We know that Wordsworth was working on the first part of the Ode on the 27th of March, the day after the composition of the rainbow poem. On the 17th of June he added a little to the Ode, but what he added we do not know. Between these two dates Wordsworth and Dorothy had paid their visit to Coleridge, who was sojourning at Keswick; during this visit Coleridge, on April 4, had written "Dejection: an Ode," very probably after he had read what was already in existence of the Immortality Ode. Coleridge's mental state was very bad—still, not so bad as to keep him from writing a great poem—and the Wordsworths were much distressed. A month later, on May 3, Wordsworth began to compose "The Leech-Gatherer," later known as "Resolution and Independence." It is this poem that is, I think, the timely utterance.[4]

[4] I follow Professor Garrod in assuming that the "utterance" was a poem, but of course it may have been a letter or a spoken word. And if indeed the "utterance" does refer to

"Resolution and Independence" is a poem about the fate of poets. It is also a poem about sullenness, in the sense that the people in the Fifth Circle are said by Dante to be sullen: "'Sullen were we in the sweet air, that is gladdened by the sun, carrying lazy smoke within our hearts; now lie sullen here in the black mire!' This hymn they gurgle in their throats, for they cannot speak it in full words"[5]—that is, they cannot now have relief by timely utterance, as they would not on earth. And "sullenness" I take to be the creation of difficulties where none exist, the working of a self-injuring imagination such as a modern mental physician would be quick to recognize as a neurotic symptom. Wordsworth's poem is about a sudden unmotivated anxiety after a mood of great exaltation. He speaks of this reversal of feeling as something experienced by himself before and known to all. In this mood he is the prey of "fears and fancies," of "dim sadness" and "blind thoughts." These feelings have reference to two imagined catastrophes. One of them—natural enough in a man under the stress of approaching marriage, for Wordsworth was to be married in October—is economic destitution. He reproaches himself for his past indifference to the means of getting a living and thinks of what may follow from this carefree life: "solitude, pain of heart, distress, and poverty." His black thoughts are led to the fate of poets "in their misery dead," among them Chatterton and Burns. The second specific fear is of mental distress:

We Poets in our youth begin in gladness;
But thereof come in the end despondency and madness.

"Resolution and Independence," it may not refer to the poem itself—as Jacques Barzun has suggested to me, it may refer to what the Leech-gatherer in the poem says to the poet, for certainly it is what the old man "utters" that gives the poet "relief."

[5] The Carlyle-Wicksteed translation. Dante's word is *"tristi"*; in "Resolution and Independence" Wordsworth speaks of "dim sadness." I mention Dante's sinners simply to elucidate the emotion that Wordsworth speaks of, not to suggest an influence.

Coleridge, we must suppose, was in his thoughts after the depressing Keswick meeting, but he is of course thinking chiefly of himself. It will be remembered how the poem ends, how with some difficulty of utterance the poet brings himself to speak with an incredibly old leech-gatherer, and, taking heart from the man's resolution and independence, becomes again "strong."

This great poem is not to be given a crucial meaning in Wordsworth's life. It makes use of a mood to which everyone, certainly every creative person, is now and again a victim. It seems to me more likely that it, rather than the rainbow poem, is the timely utterance of which the Ode speaks because in it, and not in the rainbow poem, a sullen feeling occurs and is relieved. But whether or not it is actually the timely utterance, it is an autobiographical and deeply felt poem written at the time the Ode was being written and seeming to have an emotional connection with the first part of the Ode. (The meeting with the old man had taken place two years earlier and it is of some significance that it should have come to mind as the subject of a poem at just this time.) It is a very precise and hardheaded account of a mood of great fear and it deals in a very explicit way with the dangers that beset the poetic life. But although Wordsworth urges himself on to think of all the bad things that can possibly happen to a poet, and mentions solitude, pain of heart, distress and poverty, cold, pain and labor, all fleshly ills, and then even madness, he never says that a poet stands in danger of losing his talent. It seems reasonable to suppose that if Wordsworth were actually saying farewell to his talent in the Ode, there would be some hint of an endangered or vanishing talent in "Resolution and Independence." But there is none; at the end of the poem Wordsworth is resolute in poetry.

Must we not, then, look with considerable skepticism at such interpretations of the Ode and suppose without question that the "gleam," the "glory," and the "dream" constitute the power of making poetry?—especially when we remember that at a time still three years distant Wordsworth in *The Prelude* will speak of himself as be-

coming a *"creative* soul" (book XII, line 207; the italics
are Wordsworth's own) despite the fact that, as he says
(book XII, line 281), he "sees by glimpses now."

V

The second half of the Ode is divided into two large
movements, each of which gives an answer to the question with which the first part ends. The two answers
seem to contradict each other. The first issues in despair,
the second in hope; the first uses a language strikingly
supernatural, the second is entirely naturalistic. The two
parts even differ in the statement of fact, for the first
says that the gleam is gone, whereas the second says that
it is not gone, but only transmuted. It is necessary to
understand this contradiction, but it is not necessary to
resolve it, for from the circuit between its two poles
comes much of the power of the poem.

The first of the two answers (stanzas V–VIII) tells us
where the visionary gleam has gone by telling us where
it came from. It is a remnant of a pre-existence in which
we enjoyed a way of seeing and knowing now almost
wholly gone from us. We come into the world, not
with minds that are merely *tabulae rasae,* but with a
kind of attendant light, the vestige of an existence otherwise obliterated from our memories. In infancy and
childhood the recollection is relatively strong, but it
fades as we move forward into earthly life. Maturity,
with its habits and its cares and its increase of distance
from our celestial origin, wears away the light of recollection. Nothing could be more poignantly sad than the
conclusion of this part with the heavy sonority of its last
line as Wordsworth addresses the child in whom the
glory still lives:

> Full soon thy Soul shall have her earthly freight,
> And custom lie upon thee with a weight,
> Heavy as frost, and deep almost as life!

Between this movement of despair and the following
movement of hope there is no clear connection save that

of contradiction. But between the question itself and the movement of hope there is an explicit verbal link, for the question is: "Whither has *fled* the visionary gleam?" and the movement of hope answers that "nature yet remembers/What was so *fugitive*."

The second movement of the second part of the Ode tells us again what has happened to the visionary gleam: it has not wholly fled, for it is remembered. This possession of childhood has been passed on as a legacy to the child's heir, the adult man; for the mind, as the rainbow epigraph also says, is one and continuous, and what was so intense a light in childhood becomes "the fountain-light of all our day" and a "master-light of all our seeing," that is, of our adult day and our mature seeing. The child's recollection of his heavenly home exists in the recollection of the adult.

But what exactly is this fountain-light, this master-light? I am sure that when we understand what it is we shall see that the glory that Wordsworth means is very different from Coleridge's glory, which is Joy. Wordsworth says that what he holds in memory as the guiding heritage of childhood is exactly not the Joy of childhood. It is not "delight," not "liberty," not even "hope"—not for these, he says, "I raise/The song of thanks and praise." For what then does he raise the song? For this particular experience of childhood:

> . . . those obstinate questionings
> Of sense and outward things,
> Fallings from us, vanishings;
> Blank misgivings of a Creature
> Moving about in worlds not realised.

He mentions other reasons for gratitude, but here for the moment I should like to halt the enumeration.

We are told, then, that light and glory consist, at least in part, of "questionings," "fallings from us," "vanishings," and "blank misgivings" in a world not yet *made real*, for surely Wordsworth uses the word "realised" in its most literal sense. In his note on the poem he has this to say of the experience he refers to:

> . . . I was often unable to think of external things
> as having external existence, and I communed with
> all that I saw as something not apart from, but in-
> herent in, my own material nature. Many times
> while going to school have I grasped at a wall or
> tree to recall myself from this abyss of idealism to
> the reality. At this time I was afraid of such proc-
> esses.

He remarks that the experience is not peculiar to himself, which is of course true, and he says that it was
connected in his thoughts with a potency of spirit which
made him believe that he could never die.

The precise and naturalistic way in which Wordsworth talks of this experience of his childhood must cast
doubt on Professor Garrod's statement that Wordsworth
believed quite literally in the notion of pre-existence, with
which the "vanishings" experience is connected. Wordsworth is very careful to delimit the extent of his belief;
he says that it is "too shadowy a notion to be recommended to faith" as an evidence of immortality. He says
that he is using the idea to illuminate another idea—
using it, as he says, "for my purpose" and "as a poet."
It has as much validity for him as any "popular" religious
idea might have, that is to say, a kind of suggestive
validity. We may regard pre-existence as being for
Wordsworth a very serious conceit, vested with relative
belief, intended to give a high value to the natural experience of the "vanishings."[6]

The naturalistic tone of Wordsworth's note suggests
that we shall be doing no violence to the experience of
the "vanishings" if we consider it scientifically. In a well-
known essay, "Stages in the Development of the Sense
of Reality," the distinguished psychoanalyst Ferenczi
speaks of the child's reluctance to distinguish between
himself and the world and of the slow growth of objec-

---

[6] In his *Studies in the Poetry of Henry Vaughan*, a Cam-
bridge University dissertation, Andrew Chiappe makes a
similar judgment of the quality and degree of belief in
the idea of pre-existence in the poetry of Vaughan and
Traherne.

tivity which differentiates the self from external things. And Freud himself, dealing with the "oceanic" sensation of "being at one with the universe," which a literary friend had supposed to be the source of all religious emotions, conjectures that it is a vestige of the infant's state of feeling before he has learned to distinguish between the stimuli of his own sensations and those of the world outside. In *Civilization and Its Discontents* he writes:

> Originally the ego includes everything, later it detaches from itself the outside world. The ego-feeling we are aware of now is thus only a shrunken vestige of a more extensive feeling—a feeling which embraced the universe and expressed an inseparable connection of the ego with the external world. If we may suppose that this primary ego-feeling has been preserved in the minds of many people— to a greater or lesser extent—it would co-exist like a sort of counterpart with the narrower and more sharply outlined ego-feeling of maturity, and the ideational content belonging to it would be precisely the notion of limitless extension and oneness with the universe—the same feeling as that described by my friend as "oceanic."

This has its clear relation to Wordsworth's "worlds not realised." Wordsworth, like Freud, was preoccupied by the idea of reality, and, again like Freud, he knew that the child's way of apprehension was but a stage which, in the course of nature, would give way to another. If we understand that Wordsworth is speaking of a period common to the development of everyone, we are helped to see that we cannot identify the vision of that period with his peculiar poetic power.

But in addition to the experience of the "vanishings" there is another experience for which Wordsworth is grateful to his childhood and which, I believe, goes with the "vanishings" to make up the "master-light," the "fountain-light." I am not referring to the

> High instincts before which our mortal Nature
> Did tremble like a guilty Thing surprised,

but rather to what Wordsworth calls "those first affections."

I am inclined to think that with this phrase Wordsworth refers to a later stage in the child's development which, like the earlier stage in which the external world is included within the ego, leaves vestiges in the developing mind. This is the period described in a well-known passage in Book II of *The Prelude,* in which the child learns about the world in his mother's arms:

> Blest the infant Babe,
> (For with my best conjecture I would trace
> Our Being's earthly progress), blest the Babe,
> Nursed in his Mother's arms, who sinks to sleep,
> Rocked on his Mother's breast; who with his soul
> Drinks in the feelings of his Mother's eye!
> For him, in one dear Presence, there exists
> A virtue which irradiates and exalts
> Objects through widest intercourse of sense.
> No outcast he, bewildered and depressed:
> Along his infant veins are interfused
> The gravitation and the filial bond
> Of nature that connect him with the world.
> Is there a flower, to which he points with hand
> Too weak to gather it, already love
> Drawn from love's purest earthly fount for him
> Hath beautified that flower; already shades
> Of pity cast from inward tenderness
> Do fall around him upon aught that bears
> Unsightly marks of violence or harm.
> Emphatically such a Being lives,
> Frail creature as he is, helpless as frail,
> An inmate of this active universe:
> For feeling has to him imparted power
> That through the growing faculties of sense,
> Doth like an agent of the one great Mind
> Create, creator and receiver both,
> Working but in alliance with the works
> Which it beholds.—Such, verily, is the first
> Poetic[7] spirit of our human life,

[7] The use here of the word "poetic" is either metaphorical and general, or it is entirely literal, that is, it refers to the root-meaning of the word, which is "to make"—Wordsworth

By uniform control of after years,
In most, abated or suppressed; in some,
Through every change of growth and of decay
Pre-eminent till death.

The child, this passage says, does not perceive things
merely as objects; he first sees them, because maternal
love is a condition of his perception, as objects-and-judg-
ments, as valued objects. He does not learn about a
flower, but about the pretty-flower, the flower that-I-
want-and-that-mother-will-get-for-me; he does not
learn about the bird and a broken wing but about the
poor-bird-whose-wing-was-broken. The safety, warmth,
and good feeling of his mother's conscious benevolence
is a circumstance of his first learning. He sees, in short,
with "glory"; not only is he himself not in "utter nakedness" as the Ode puts it, but the objects he sees are not
in utter nakedness. The passage from *The Prelude* says
in naturalistic language what stanza v of the Ode expresses by a theistical metaphor. Both the *Prelude*
passage and the Ode distinguish a state of exile from a
state of security and comfort, of at-homeness; there is
(as the *Prelude* passage puts it) a "filial bond," or (as
in stanza x of the Ode) a "primal sympathy," which keeps
man from being an "outcast . . . bewildered and de-
pressed."

The Ode and *The Prelude* differ about the source of
this primal sympathy of filial bond. The Ode makes
heavenly pre-existence the source, *The Prelude* finds the
source in maternal affection. But the psychologists tell
us that notions of heavenly pre-existence figure commonly as representations of physical prenatality—the
womb is the environment which is perfectly adapted to
its inmate and compared to it all other conditions of life
may well seem like "exile" to the (very literal) "outcast."[8] Even the security of the mother's arms, although

---

has in mind the creative nature of right human perception
and not merely poetry.
[8] "Before born babe bliss had. Within womb won he worship. Whatever in that one case done commodiously done
was."—James Joyce, *Ulysses*. The myth of Eden is also in-

it is an effort to re-create for the child the old environment, is but a diminished comfort. And if we think of the experience of which Wordsworth is speaking, the "vanishings," as the child's recollection of a condition in which it was very nearly true that he and his environment were one, it will not seem surprising that Wordsworth should compound the two experiences and figure them in the single metaphor of the glorious heavenly pre-existence.[9]

I have tried to be as naturalistic as possible in speaking of Wordsworth's childhood experiences and the more-or-less Platonic notion they suggested to him. I believe that naturalism is in order here, for what we must now see is that Wordsworth is talking about something common to us all, the development of the sense of reality. To have once had the visionary gleam of the perfect union of the self and the universe is essential to and definitive of our human nature, and it is in that sense connected with the making of poetry. But the visionary gleam is not in itself the poetry-making power, and its diminution is right and inevitable.

That there should be ambivalence in Wordsworth's response to this diminution is quite natural, and the two answers, that of stanzas v–viii and that of stanzas ix–xi, comprise both the resistance to and the acceptance of growth. Inevitably we resist change and turn back with passionate nostalgia to the stage we are leaving. Still, we fulfill ourselves by choosing what is painful and

terpreted as figuring either childhood or the womb—see below Wordsworth's statement of the connection of the notion of pre-existence with Adam's fall.

[9] Readers of Ferenczi's remarkable study, *Thalassa*, a discussion, admittedly speculative but wonderfully fascinating, of unconscious racial memories of the ocean as the ultimate source of life, will not be able to resist giving an added meaning to Wordsworth's lines about the "immortal sea/ Which brought us hither" and of the unborn children who "Sport upon the shore." The recollection of Samuel Butler's delightful fantasy of the Unborn and his theory of unconscious memory will also serve to enrich our reading of the Ode by suggesting the continuing force of the Platonic myth.

difficult and necessary, and we develop by moving toward death. In short, organic development is a hard paradox which Wordsworth is stating in the discrepant answers of the second part of the Ode. And it seems to me that those critics who made the Ode refer to some particular and unique experience of Wordsworth's and who make it relate only to poetical powers have forgotten their own lives and in consequence conceive the Ode to be a lesser thing than it really is, for it is not about poetry, it is about life. And having made this error, they are inevitably led to misinterpret the meaning of the "philosophic mind" and also to deny that Wordsworth's ambivalence is sincere. No doubt it would not be a sincere ambivalence if Wordsworth were really saying farewell to poetry, it would merely be an attempt at self-consolation. But he is not saying farewell to poetry, he is saying farewell to Eden, and his ambivalence is much what Adam's was, and Milton's, and for the same reasons.[10]

To speak naturalistically of the quasi-mystical experiences of his childhood does not in the least bring into question the value which Wordsworth attached to them, for, despite its dominating theistical metaphor, the Ode is largely naturalistic in its intention. We can begin to see what that intention is by understanding the force of the word "imperial" in stanza VI. This stanza is the second of the four stanzas in which Wordsworth states and de-

---

[10] Milton provides a possible gloss to several difficult points in the poem. In stanza VIII, the Child is addressed as "thou Eye among the blind," and to the Eye are applied the epithets "deaf and silent"; Coleridge objected to these epithets as irrational, but his objection may be met by citing the brilliant precedent of "blind mouths" of "Lycidas." Again, Coleridge's question of the propriety of making a master *brood* over a slave is in part answered by the sonnet "On His Being Arrived at the Age of Twenty-three," in which Milton expresses his security in his development as it shall take place in his "great Task-master's eye." Between this sonnet and the Ode there are other significant correspondences of thought and of phrase; there are also correspondences to the Ode in the sonnet "On His Blindness."

velops the theme of the reminiscence of the light of heaven and its gradual evanescence through the maturing years. In stanza v we are told that the infant inhabits it; the Boy beholds it, seeing it "in his joy"; the Youth is still attended by it; "the Man perceives it die away,/ And fade into the light of common day." Stanza vi speaks briefly of the efforts made by earthly life to bring about the natural and inevitable amnesia:

> Earth fills her lap with pleasures of her own;
> Yearnings she hath in her own natural kind,
> And even with something of a Mother's mind,
> And no unworthy aim,
> The homely Nurse doth all she can
> To make her Foster-child, her Inmate Man,
> Forget the glories he hath known,
> And that imperial palace whence he came.

"Imperial" suggests grandeur, dignity, and splendor, everything that stands in opposition to what, in *The Excursion,* Wordsworth was to call "littleness." And "littleness" is the result of having wrong notions about the nature of man and his connection with the universe; its outcome is "deadness." The melancholy and despair of the Solitary in *The Excursion* are the signs of the deadness which resulted from his having conceived of man as something less than imperial. Wordsworth's idea of splendid power is his protest against all views of the mind that would limit and debase it. By conceiving, as he does, an intimate connection between mind and universe, by seeing the universe fitted to the mind and the mind to the universe, he bestows upon man a dignity which cannot be derived from looking at him in the actualities of common life, from seeing him engaged in business, in morality and politics.

Yet here we must credit Wordsworth with the double vision. Man must be conceived of as "imperial," but he must also be seen as he actually is in the field of life. The earth is not an environment in which the celestial or imperial qualities can easily exist. Wordsworth, who spoke of the notion of imperial pre-existence as being adumbrated by Adam's fall, uses the words "earth" and "earthly" in the common quasi-religious sense to refer to the things of this world. He does not make Earth synonymous with Nature, for although Man may be the true child of Nature, he is the "Foster-child" of Earth. But it is to be observed that the foster mother is a kindly one, that her disposition is at least quasi-maternal, that her aims are at least not unworthy; she is, in short, the foster mother who figures so often in the legend of the Hero, whose real and unknown parents are noble or divine.[11]

Wordsworth, in short, is looking at man in a double way, seeing man both in his ideal nature and in his earthly activity. The two views do not so much contradict as supplement each other. If in stanzas v–viii Wordsworth tells us that we live by decrease, in stanzas ix–xi he tells us of the everlasting connection of the diminished person with his own ideal personality. The child hands on to the hampered adult the imperial nature, the "primal sympathy/Which having been must ever be," the mind fitted to the universe, the universe to the mind. The sympathy is not so pure and intense in maturity as in childhood, but only because another relation grows up beside the relation of man to Nature—the relation of man to his fellows in the moral world of difficulty and pain. Given Wordsworth's epistemology the new relation is bound to change the very aspect of Nature itself: the clouds will take a sober coloring from an eye that hath kept watch o'er man's mortality, but a sober color is a color still.

There is sorrow in the Ode, the inevitable sorrow of giving up an old habit of vision for a new one. In shifting the center of his interest from Nature to man in the field of morality Wordsworth is fulfilling his own conception of the three ages of man which Professor Beatty has ex-

---

[11] Carlyle makes elaborate play with this idea in his account of Teufelsdröckh, and see the essay on *The Princess Casamassima* in this volume, page 65. The fantasy that their parents are really foster parents is a common one with children, and it is to be associated with the various forms of the belief that the world is not real.

pounded so well. The shift in interest he called the coming of "the philosophic mind," but the word "philosophic" does not have here either of two of its meanings in common usage—it does not mean abstract and it does not mean apathetic. Wordsworth is not saying, and it is sentimental and unimaginative of us to say, that he has become less a feeling man and less a poet. He is only saying that he has become less a youth. Indeed, the Ode is so little a farewell to art, so little a dirge sung over departing powers, that it is actually the very opposite—it is a welcome of new powers and a dedication to a new poetic subject. For if sensitivity and responsiveness be among the poetic powers, what else is Wordsworth saying at the end of the poem except that he has a greater sensitivity and responsiveness than ever before? The "philosophic mind" has not decreased but, on the contrary, increased the power to feel.

> The clouds that gather round the setting sun
> Do take a sober colouring from an eye
> That hath kept watch o'er man's mortality;
> Another race hath been and other palms are won.
> Thanks to the human heart by which we live,
> Thanks to its tenderness, its joys, and fears,
> To me the meanest flower that blows can give
> Thoughts that do often lie too deep for tears.

The meanest flower is significant now not only because, like the small celandine, it speaks of age, suffering, and death, but because to a man who is aware of man's mortality the world becomes significant and precious. The knowledge of man's mortality—this must be carefully noted in a poem presumably about immortality—now replaces the "glory" as the agency which makes things significant and precious. We are back again at optics, which we have never really left, and the Ode in a very honest fashion has come full circle.

The new poetic powers of sensitivity and responsiveness are new not so much in degree as in kind; they would therefore seem to require a new poetic subject matter for their exercise. And the very definition of the new powers seems to imply what the new subject matter must be—thoughts that lie too deep for tears are ideally the thoughts which are brought to mind by tragedy. It would be an extravagant but not an absurd reading of the Ode that found it to be Wordsworth's farewell to the characteristic mode of his poetry, the mode that Keats called the "egotistical sublime" and a dedication to the mode of tragedy. But the tragic mode could not be Wordsworth's. He did not have the "negative capability" which Keats believed to be the source of Shakespeare's power, the gift of being able to be "content with half-knowledge," to give up the "irritable reaching after fact and reason," to remain "in uncertainties, mysteries, doubts." In this he was at one with all the poets of the Romantic Movement and after—negative capability was impossible for them to come by and tragedy was not for them. But although Wordsworth did not realize the new kind of art which seems implied by his sense of new powers, yet his bold declaration that he had acquired a new way of feeling makes it impossible for us to go on saying that the Ode was his "conscious farewell to his art, a dirge sung over his departing powers."

Still, was there not, after the composition of the Ode, a great falling off in his genius which we are drawn to connect with the crucial changes the Ode records? That there was a falling off is certain, although we must observe that it was not so sharp as is commonly held and also that it did not occur immediately or even soon after the composition of the first four stanzas with their statement that the visionary gleam had gone; on the contrary, some of the most striking of Wordsworth's verse was written at this time. It must be remembered too that another statement of the loss of the visionary gleam, that made in "Tintern Abbey," had been followed by all the superb production of the "great decade"—an objection which is sometimes dealt with by saying that Wordsworth wrote his best work from his near memories of the gleam, and that, as he grew older and moved farther from it, his recollection dimmed and thus he lost his power: it is an explanation which suggests that mechanical and simple notions of the mind and of the poetic process are all too tempting to those who speculate on Wordsworth's decline. Given the fact of the great power, the desire to explain its relative deterioration will no doubt always be irresistible. But we must be aware, in any attempt to make this explanation, that an account of why Wordsworth ceased to write great poetry must at the same time be an account of how he once did write great poetry. And this latter account, in our present state of knowledge, we cannot begin to furnish.

Ode: Intimations of Immortality
from Recollections of Early Childhood

by WILLIAM WORDSWORTH

The Child is father of the Man;
And I could wish my days to be
Bound each to each by natural piety.

I

There was a time when meadow, grove, and stream
The earth, and every common sight,
                    To me did seem
                Apparelled in celestial light,
The glory and the freshness of a dream.
It is not now as it hath been of yore;—
            Turn wheresoe'er I may,
                By night or day,
The things which I have seen I now can see no more.

II

            The Rainbow comes and goes,
                And lovely is the Rose,
                The Moon doth with delight
Look round her when the heavens are bare,
            Waters on a starry night
                Are beautiful and fair;
    The sunshine is a glorious birth;
    But yet I know, where'er I go,
That there hath past away a glory from the earth.

III

Now, while the birds thus sing a joyous song,
   And while the young lambs bound
     As to the tabor's sound,
To me alone there came a thought of grief:
A timely utterance gave that thought relief,
     And I again am strong:
The cataracts blow their trumpets from the steep;
No more shall grief of mine the season wrong;
I hear the Echoes through the mountains throng,
The Winds come to me from the fields of sleep,
     And all the earth is gay;
      Land and sea
    Give themselves up to jollity,
     And with the heart of May
   Doth every Beast keep holiday;—
      Thou Child of Joy,
Shout round me, let me hear thy shouts, thou happy
   Shepherd boy!

IV

Ye blessèd Creatures, I have heard the call
   Ye to each other make; I see
The heavens laugh with you in your jubilee;
   My heart is at your festival,
   My head hath its coronal,
The fulness of your bliss, I feel—I feel it all.
     Oh evil day! if I were sullen
    While Earth herself is adorning,
     This sweet May-morning,
    And the Children are culling
     On every side,
   In a thousand valleys far and wide,
   Fresh flowers; while the sun shines warm,
And the Babe leaps up on his Mother's arm:—
    I hear, I hear, with joy I hear!
    —But there's a Tree, of many, one,
A single Field which I have looked upon,
Both of them speak of something that is gone:
    The Pansy at my feet

Doth the same tale repeat:
Whither is fled the visionary gleam?
Where is it now, the glory and the dream?

V

Our birth is but a sleep and a forgetting:
The Soul that rises with us, our life's Star,
    Hath had elsewhere its setting,
      And cometh from afar:
    Not in entire forgetfulness,
    And not in utter nakedness,
But trailing clouds of glory do we come
    From God, who is our home:
Heaven lies about us in our infancy!
Shades of the prison-house begin to close
    Upon the growing Boy,
But He beholds the light, and whence it flows,
    He sees it in his joy;
The Youth, who daily farther from the east
    Must travel, still is Nature's Priest,
    And by the vision splendid
    Is on his way attended;
At length the Man perceives it die away,
And fade into the light of common day.

VI

Earth fills her lap with pleasures of her own;
Yearnings she hath in her own natural kind,
And, even with something of a Mother's mind,
    And no unworthy aim,
    The homely Nurse doth all she can
To make her Foster-child, her Inmate Man,
    Forget the glories he hath known,
And that imperial palace whence he came.

VII

Behold the Child among his new-born blisses,
A six years' Darling of a pigmy size!
See, where 'mid work of his own hand he lies,
Fretted by sallies of his mother's kisses,
With light upon him from his father's eyes!
See, at his feet, some little plan or chart,

Some fragment from his dream of human life,
Shaped by himself with newly-learned art;
    A wedding or a festival,
    A mourning or a funeral;
        And this hath now his heart,
        And unto this he frames his song:
        Then will he fit his tongue
To dialogues of business, love, or strife;
        But it will not be long
        Ere this be thrown aside,
        And with new joy and pride
The little Actor cons another part;
Filling from time to time his "humorous stage"
With all the Persons, down to palsied Age,
That Life brings with her in her equipage;
        As if his whole vocation
        Were endless imitation.

VIII

Thou, whose exterior semblance doth belie
        Thy Soul's immensity;
Thou best Philosopher, who yet dost keep
Thy heritage, thou Eye among the blind,
That, deaf and silent, read'st the eternal deep,
Haunted for ever by the eternal mind,—
        Mighty Prophet! Seer blest!
        On whom those truths do rest,
Which we are toiling all our lives to find,
In darkness lost, the darkness of the grave;
Thou, over whom thy Immortality
Broods like the Day, a Master o'er a Slave,
A Presence which is not to be put by;
Thou little Child, yet glorious in the might
Of heaven-born freedom on thy being's height,
Why with such earnest pains dost thou provoke
The years to bring the inevitable yoke,
Thus blindly with thy blessedness at strife?
Full soon thy Soul shall have her earthly freight,
And custom lie upon thee with a weight,
Heavy as frost, and deep almost as life!

IX

O joy! that in our embers
Is something that doth live,
That nature yet remembers
What was so fugitive!
The thought of our past years in me doth breed
Perpetual benediction: not indeed
For that which is most worthy to be blest;
Delight and liberty, the simple creed
Of Childhood, whether busy or at rest,
With new-fledged hope still fluttering in his breast:—
　　Not for these I raise
　　The song of thanks and praise;
　But for those obstinate questionings
　Of sense and outward things,
　Fallings from us, vanishings;
　Blank misgivings of a Creature
Moving about in worlds not realised,
High instincts before which our mortal Nature
Did tremble like a guilty Thing surprised:
　　But for those first affections,
　　Those shadowy recollections,
　　Which, be they what they may,
Are yet the fountain-light of all our day,
Are yet a master-light of all our seeing;
　Uphold us, cherish, and have power to make
Our noisy years seem moments in the being
Of the eternal Silence: truths that wake,
　　To perish never:
Which neither listlessness, nor mad endeavour,
　　Nor Man nor Boy,
Nor all that is at enmity with joy,
Can utterly abolish or destroy.
　　Hence in a season of calm weather
　　Though inland far we be,
Our Souls have sight of that immortal sea
　　Which brought us hither,
　　Can in a moment travel thither,
And see the Children sport upon the shore,
And hear the mighty waters rolling evermore.

X

Then sing, ye Birds, sing, sing a joyous song!
  And let the young Lambs bound
  As to the tabor's sound!
We in thought will join your throng,
  Ye that pipe and ye that play,
  Ye that through your hearts to-day
  Feel the gladness of the May!
What though the radiance which was once so bright
Be now for ever taken from my sight,
  Though nothing can bring back the hour
Of splendour in the grass, of glory in the flower;
  We will grieve not, rather find
  Strength in what remains behind;
  In the primal sympathy
  Which having been must ever be;
  In the soothing thoughts that spring
  Out of human suffering;
  In the faith that looks through death,
In years that bring the philosophic mind.

XI

And O, ye Fountains, Meadows, Hills, and Groves,
Forebode not any severing of our loves!
Yet in my heart of hearts I feel your might;
I only have relinquished one delight
To live beneath your more habitual sway.
I love the Brooks which down their channels fret,
Even more than when I tripped lightly as they;
The innocent brightness of a new-born Day
  Is lovely yet;
The Clouds that gather round the setting sun
Do take a sober colouring from an eye
That hath kept watch o'er man's mortality;
Another race hath been, and other palms are won.
 Thanks to the human heart by which we live,
 Thanks to its tenderness, its joys, and fears,
 To me the meanest flower that blows can give
 Thoughts that do often lie too deep for tears.

Art and Neurosis

The question of the mental health of the artist has engaged the attention of our culture since the beginning of the Romantic Movement. Before that time it was commonly said that the poet was "mad," but this was only a manner of speaking, a way of saying that the mind of the poet worked in different fashion from the mind of the philosopher; it had no real reference to the mental hygiene of the man who was the poet. But in the early nineteenth century, with the development of a more elaborate psychology and a stricter and more literal view of mental and emotional normality, the statement was more strictly and literally intended. So much so, indeed, that Charles Lamb, who knew something about madness at close quarters and a great deal about art, undertook to refute in his brilliant essay, "On the Sanity of True Genius," the idea that the exercise of the imagination was a kind of insanity. And some eighty years later, the idea having yet further entrenched itself, Bernard Shaw felt called upon to argue the sanity of art, but his cogency was of no more avail than Lamb's. In recent years the connection between art and mental illness has been formulated not only by those who are openly or covertly hostile to art, but also and more significantly by those who are most intensely partisan to it. The latter willingly and even eagerly accept the idea that the artist is mentally ill and go on to make his illness a condition of his power to tell the truth.

This conception of artistic genius is indeed one of the characteristic notions of our culture. I should like to bring it into question. To do so is to bring also into question certain early ideas of Freud's and certain conclusions which literary laymen have drawn from the whole tendency of the Freudian psychology. From the very start it was recognized that psychoanalysis was likely to have important things to say about art and artists. Freud himself thought so, yet when he first addressed himself to the subject he said many clumsy and misleading things. I have elsewhere and at length tried to separate the useful from the useless and even dangerous statements about art that Freud has made.[1] To put it briefly here, Freud had some illuminating and even beautiful insights into certain particular works of art which made complex use of the element of myth. Then, without specifically undertaking to do so, his "Beyond the Pleasure Principle" offers a brilliant and comprehensive explanation of our interest in tragedy. And what is of course most important of all—it is a point to which I shall return—Freud, by the whole tendency of his psychology, establishes the *naturalness* of artistic thought. Indeed, it is possible to say of Freud that he ultimately did more for our understanding of art than any other writer since Aristotle; and this being so, it can only be surprising that in his early work he should have made the error of treating the artist as a neurotic who escapes from reality by means of "substitute gratifications."

As Freud went forward he insisted less on this simple formulation. Certainly it did not have its original force with him when, at his seventieth birthday celebration, he disclaimed the right to be called the discoverer of the unconscious, saying that whatever he may have done for the systematic understanding of the unconscious, the credit for its discovery properly belonged to the literary masters. And psychoanalysis has inherited from him a tenderness for art which is real although sometimes clumsy, and nowadays most psychoanalysts of any personal sensitivity are embarrassed by occasions which seem to lead them to reduce art to a formula of mental illness. Nevertheless Freud's early belief in the essential

[1] See "Freud and Literature."

neuroticism of the artist found an all too fertile ground—found, we might say, the very ground from which it first sprang, for, when he spoke of the artist as a neurotic, Freud was adopting one of the popular beliefs of his age. Most readers will see this belief as the expression of the industrial rationalization and the bourgeois philistinism of the nineteenth century. In this they are partly right. The nineteenth century established the basic virtue of "getting up at eight, shaving close at a quarter-past, breakfasting at nine, going to the City at ten, coming home at half-past five, and dining at seven." The Messrs. Podsnap who instituted this scheduled morality inevitably decreed that the arts must celebrate it and nothing else. "Nothing else to be permitted to these . . . vagrants the Arts, on pain of excommunication. Nothing else To Be—anywhere!" We observe that the virtuous day ends with dinner—bed and sleep are naturally not part of the Reality that Is, and nothing must be set forth which will, as Mr. Podsnap put it, bring a Blush to the Cheek of a Young Person.

The excommunication of the arts, when it was found necessary, took the form of pronouncing the artist mentally degenerate, a device which eventually found its theorist in Max Nordau. In the history of the arts this is new. The poet was always known to belong to a touchy tribe—*genus irritabile* was a tag anyone would know—and ever since Plato the process of the inspired imagination, as we have said, was thought to be a special one of some interest, which the similitude of madness made somewhat intelligible. But this is not quite to say that the poet was the victim of actual mental aberration. The eighteenth century did not find the poet to be less than other men, and certainly the Renaissance did not. If he was a professional, there might be condescension to his social status, but in a time which deplored all professionalism whatever, this was simply a way of asserting the high value of poetry, which ought not to be compromised by trade. And a certain good nature marked even the snubbing of the professional. At any rate, no one was likely to identify the poet with the weakling.

Indeed, the Renaissance ideal held poetry to be, like arms or music, one of the signs of manly competence.

The change from this view of things cannot be blamed wholly on the bourgeois or philistine public. Some of the "blame" must rest with the poets themselves. The Romantic poets were as proud of their art as the vaunting poets of the sixteenth century, but one of them talked with an angel in a tree and insisted that Hell was better than Heaven and sexuality holier than chastity; another told the world that he wanted to lie down like a tired child and weep away this life of care; another asked so foolish a question as "Why did I laugh tonight?"; and yet another explained that he had written one of his best poems in a drugged sleep. The public took them all at their word—they were not as other men. Zola, in the interests of science, submitted himself to examination by fifteen psychiatrists and agreed with their conclusion that his genius had its source in the neurotic elements of his temperament. Baudelaire, Rimbaud, Verlaine found virtue and strength in their physical and mental illness and pain. W. H. Auden addresses his "wound" in the cherishing language of a lover, thanking it for the gift of insight it has bestowed. "Knowing you," he says, "has made me understand." And Edmund Wilson in his striking phrase, "the wound and the bow," has formulated for our time the idea of the characteristic sickness of the artist, which he represents by the figure of Philoctetes, the Greek warrior who was forced to live in isolation because of the disgusting odor of a suppurating wound and who yet had to be sought out by his countrymen because they had need of the magically unerring bow he possessed.

The myth of the sick artist, we may suppose, has established itself because it is of advantage to the various groups who have one or another relation with art. To the artist himself the myth gives some of the ancient powers and privileges of the idiot and the fool, half-prophetic creatures, or of the mutilated priest. That the artist's neurosis may be but a mask is suggested by Thomas Mann's pleasure in representing his untried youth as "sick" but his successful maturity as senatorially robust. By means of his belief in his own sickness, the artist may the more easily fulfill his chosen, and assigned, function of putting himself into connection with the forces of spirituality and morality; the artist sees as insane the "normal" and "healthy" ways of established society, while aberration and illness appear as spiritual and moral health if only because they controvert the ways of respectable society.

Then too, the myth has its advantage for the philistine —a double advantage. On the one hand, the belief in the artist's neuroticism allows the philistine to shut his ears to what the artist says. But on the other hand it allows him to listen. For we must not make the common mistake—the contemporary philistine does want to listen, at the same time that he wants to shut his ears. By supposing that the artist has an interesting but not always reliable relation to reality, he is able to contain (in the military sense) what the artist tells him. If he did not want to listen at all, he would say "insane"; with "neurotic," which hedges, he listens when he chooses.

And in addition to its advantage to the artist and to the philistine, we must take into account the usefulness of the myth to a third group, the group of "sensitive" people, who, although not artists, are not philistines either. These people form a group by virtue of their passive impatience with philistinism, and also by virtue of their awareness of their own emotional pain and uncertainty. To these people the myth of the sick artist is the institutional sanction of their situation; they seek to approximate or acquire the character of the artist, sometimes by planning to work or even attempting to work as the artist does, always by making a connection between their own powers of mind and their consciousness of "difference" and neurotic illness.

The early attempts of psychoanalysis to deal with art went on the assumption that, because the artist was neurotic, the content of his work was also neurotic, which is to say that it did not stand in a correct relation to reality. But nowadays, as I have said, psychoanalysis is not likely to be so simple in its transactions with art. A good example of the psychoanalytical development in this respect is Dr. Saul Rosenzweig's well-known essay, "The Ghost of Henry James."[2] This is an admirable piece of work, marked by accuracy in the reporting of the literary fact and by respect for the value of the literary object. Although Dr. Rosenzweig explores the element of neurosis in James's life and work, he nowhere suggests that this element in any way lessens James's value as an artist or moralist. In effect he says that neurosis is a way of dealing with reality which, in real life, is uncomfortable and uneconomical, but that this judgment of neurosis in life cannot mechanically be transferred to works of art upon which neurosis has had its influence. He nowhere implies that a work of art in whose genesis a neurotic element may be found is for that reason irrelevant or in any way diminished in value. Indeed, the manner of his treatment suggests, what is of course the case, that every neurosis deals with a real emotional situation of the most intensely meaningful kind.

Yet as Dr. Rosenzweig brings his essay to its close, he makes use of the current assumption about the causal connection between the psychic illness of the artist and his power. His investigation of James, he says, "reveals the aptness of the Philoctetes pattern." He accepts the idea of "the sacrificial roots of literary power" and speaks of "the unhappy sources of James's genius." "The broader application of the inherent pattern," he says, "is familiar to readers of Edmund Wilson's recent volume *The Wound and the Bow*. . . . Reviewing the experience and work of several well-known literary masters, Wilson discloses the sacrificial roots of their power on the model of the Greek legend. In the case of Henry James, the present account . . . provides a similar insight into the unhappy sources of his genius. . . ."

This comes as a surprise. Nothing in Dr. Rosenzweig's theory requires it. For his theory asserts no more than

[2] First published in *Character and Personality*, December 1943, and reprinted in *Partisan Review*, Fall, 1944.

that Henry James, predisposed by temperament and
family situation to certain mental and emotional qualities, was in his youth injured in a way which he believed
to be sexual; that he unconsciously invited the injury in
the wish to identify himself with his father, who himself
had been similarly injured—"castrated": a leg had been
amputated—and under strikingly similar circumstances;
this resulted for the younger Henry James in a certain
pattern of life and in a preoccupation in his work with
certain themes which more or less obscurely symbolize
his sexual situation. For this I think Dr. Rosenzweig
makes a sound case. Yet I submit that this is not the same
thing as disclosing the roots of James's power or discovering the sources of his genius. The essay which gives
Edmund Wilson's book its title and cohering principle
does not explicitly say that the roots of power are sacrificial and that the source of genius is unhappy. Where
it is explicit, it states only that "genius and disease, like
strength and mutilation, may be inextricably bound up
together," which of course, on its face, says no more than
that personality is integral and not made up of detach-
able parts; and from this there is no doubt to be drawn
the important practical and moral implication that we
cannot judge or dismiss a man's genius and strength because of our awareness of his disease or mutilation. The
Philoctetes legend in itself does not suggest anything beyond this. It does not suggest that the wound is the price
of the bow, or that without the wound the bow may not
be possessed or drawn. Yet Dr. Rosenzweig has accurately summarized the force and, I think, the intention
of Mr. Wilson's whole book; its several studies do seem
to say that effectiveness in the arts does depend on sickness.

An examination of this prevalent idea might well begin with the observation of how pervasive and deeply
rooted is the notion that power may be gained by suffering. Even at relatively high stages of culture the mind
seems to take easily to the primitive belief that pain and
sacrifice are connected with strength. Primitive beliefs
must be treated with respectful alertness to their possible

truth and also with the suspicion of their being magical and irrational, and it is worth noting on both sides of the question, and in the light of what we have said about the ambiguous relation of the neurosis to reality, that the whole economy of the neurosis is based exactly on this idea of the *quid pro quo* of sacrificial pain: the neurotic person unconsciously subscribes to a system whereby he gives up some pleasure or power, or inflicts pain on himself in order to secure some other power or some other pleasure.

In the ingrained popular conception of the relation between suffering and power there are actually two distinct although related ideas. One is that there exists in the individual a fund of power which has outlets through various organs or faculties, and that if its outlet through one organ or faculty be prevented, it will flow to increase the force or sensitivity of another. Thus it is popularly believed that the sense of touch is intensified in the blind not so much by the will of the blind person to adapt himself to the necessities of his situation as, rather, by a sort of mechanical redistribution of power. And this idea would seem to explain, if not the origin of the ancient mutilation of priests, then at least a common understanding of their sexual sacrifice.

The other idea is that a person may be taught by, or proved by, the endurance of pain. There will easily come to mind the ritual suffering that is inflicted at the tribal initiation of youths into full manhood or at the admission of the apprentice into the company of journeyman adepts. This idea in sophisticated form found its way into high religion at least as early as Aeschylus, who held that man achieves knowledge of God through suffering, and it was from the beginning an important element of Christian thought. In the nineteenth century the Christianized notion of the didactic suffering of the artist went along with the idea of his mental degeneration and even served as a sort of countermyth to it. Its doctrine was that the artist, a man of strength and health, experienced and suffered, and thus learned both the facts of life and his artistic craft. "I am the man, I suffered, I was there," ran his boast, and he derived his authority from the knowledge gained through suffering.

There can be no doubt that both these ideas represent a measure of truth about mental and emotional power. The idea of didactic suffering expresses a valuation of experience and of steadfastness. The idea of natural compensation for the sacrifice of some faculty also says something that can be rationally defended: one cannot be and do everything and the wholehearted absorption in any enterprise, art for example, means that we must give up other possibilities, even parts of ourselves. And there is even a certain validity to the belief that the individual has a fund of undifferentiated energy which presses the harder upon what outlets are available to it when it has been deprived of the normal number.

Then, in further defense of the belief that artistic power is connected with neurosis, we can say that there is no doubt that what we call mental illness may be the source of psychic knowledge. Some neurotic people, because they are more apprehensive than normal people, are able to see more of certain parts of reality and to see them with more intensity. And many neurotic or psychotic patients are in certain respects in closer touch with the actualities of the unconscious than are normal people. Further, the expression of a neurotic or psychotic conception of reality is likely to be more intense than a normal one.

Yet when we have said all this, it is still wrong, I believe, to find the root of the artist's power and the source of his genius in neurosis. To the idea that literary power and genius spring from pain and neurotic sacrifice there are two major objections. The first has to do with the assumed uniqueness of the artist as a subject of psychoanalytical explanation. The second has to do with the true meaning of power and genius.

One reason why writers are considered to be more available than other people to psychoanalytical explanation is that they tell us what is going on inside them. Even when they do not make an actual diagnosis of their malaises or describe "symptoms," we must bear it in mind that it is their profession to deal with fantasy in some form or other. It is in the nature of the writer's job that he exhibit his unconscious. He may disguise it in various ways, but disguise is not concealment. Indeed, it may be said that the more a writer takes pains with his work to remove it from the personal and subjective, the more—and not the less—he will express his true unconscious, although not what passes with most for the unconscious.

Further, the writer is likely to be a great hand at personal letters, diaries, and autobiographies: indeed, almost the only good autobiographies are those of writers. The writer is more aware of what happens to him or goes on in him and often finds it necessary or useful to be articulate about his inner states, and prides himself on telling the truth. Thus, only a man as devoted to the truth of the emotions as Henry James was would have informed the world, despite his characteristic reticence, of an accident so intimate as his. We must not of course suppose that a writer's statements about his intimate life are equivalent to true statements about his unconscious, which, by definition, he doesn't consciously know; but they may be useful clues to the nature of an entity about which we can make statements of more or less cogency, although never statements of certainty; or they at least give us what is surely related to a knowledge of his unconscious—that is, an insight into his personality.[3]

[3] I am by no means in agreement with the statements of Dr. Edmund Bergler about "the" psychology of the writer, but I think that Dr. Bergler has done good service in warning us against taking at their face value a writer's statements about himself, the more especially when they are "frank." Thus, to take Dr. Bergler's notable example, it is usual for biographers to accept Stendhal's statements about his open sexual feelings for his mother when he was a little boy, feelings which went with an intense hatred of his father. But Dr. Bergler believes that Stendhal unconsciously used his consciousness of his love of his mother and of his hatred of his father to mask an unconscious love of his father, which frightened him. ("Psychoanalysis of Writers and of Literary Productivity" in *Psychoanalysis and the Social Sciences*, vol. I.)

But while the validity of dealing with the writer's intellectual life in psychoanalytical terms is taken for granted, the psychoanalytical explanation of the intellectual life of scientists is generally speaking not countenanced. The old myth of the mad scientist, with the exception of an occasional mad psychiatrist, no longer exists. The social position of science requires that it should cease, which leads us to remark that those partisans of art who insist on explaining artistic genius by means of psychic imbalance are in effect capitulating to the dominant mores which hold that the members of the respectable professions are, however dull they may be, free from neurosis. Scientists, to continue with them as the best example of the respectable professions, do not usually give us the clues to their personalities which writers habitually give. But no one who has ever lived observantly among scientists will claim that they are without an unconscious or even that they are free from neurosis. How often, indeed, it is apparent that the devotion to science, if it cannot be called a neurotic manifestation, at least can be understood as going very cozily with neurotic elements in the temperament, such as, for example, a marked compulsiveness. Of scientists as a group we can say that they are less concerned with the manifestations of personality, their own or others', than are writers as a group. But this relative indifference is scarcely a sign of normality—indeed, if we choose to regard it with the same sort of eye with which the characteristics of writers are regarded, we might say the indifference to matters of personality is in itself a suspicious evasion.

It is the basic assumption of psychoanalysis that the acts of *every* person are influenced by the forces of the unconscious. Scientists, bankers, lawyers, or surgeons, by reason of the traditions of their professions, practice concealment and conformity; but it is difficult to believe that an investigation according to psychoanalytical principles would fail to show that the strains and imbalances of their psyches are not of the same frequency as those of writers, and of similar kind. I do not mean that everybody has the same troubles and identical psyches, but only that there is no special category for writers.[4]

If this is so, and if we still want to relate the writer's power to his neurosis, we must be willing to relate all intellectual power to neurosis. We must find the roots of Newton's power in his emotional extravagances, and the roots of Darwin's power in his sorely neurotic temperament, and the roots of Pascal's mathematical genius in the impulses which drove him to extreme religious masochism—I choose but the classic examples. If we make the neurosis-power equivalence at all, we must make it in every field of endeavor. Logician, economist, botanist, physicist, theologian—no profession may be so respectable or so remote or so rational as to be exempt from the psychological interpretation.[5]

---

[4] Dr. Bergler believes that there is a particular neurosis of writers, based on an oral masochism which makes them the enemy of the respectable world, courting poverty and persecution. But a later development of Dr. Bergler's theory of oral masochism makes it *the* basic neurosis, not only of writers but of everyone who is neurotic.

[5] In his interesting essay, "Writers and Madness" (*Partisan Review*, January–February 1947), William Barrett has taken issue with this point and has insisted that a clear distinction is to be made between the relation that exists between the scientist and his work and the relation that exists between the artist and his work. The difference, as I understand it, is in the claims of the ego. The artist's ego makes a claim upon the world which is personal in a way that the scientist's is not, for the scientist, although he does indeed want prestige and thus "responds to one of the deepest urges of his ego, it is only that his prestige may come to attend his person through the public world of other men; and it is not in the end his own being that is exhibited or his own voice that is heard in the learned report to the Academy." Actually, however, as is suggested by the sense which mathematicians have of the *style* of mathematical thought, the creation of the abstract thinker is as deeply involved as the artist's—see *An Essay on the Psychology of Invention in the Mathematical Field* by Jacques Hadamard, Princeton University Press, 1945—and he quite as much as the artist seeks to impose *himself*, to *express* himself. I am of course not maintaining that the processes of scientific thought are the same as those of

Further, not only power but also failure or limitation must be accounted for by the theory of neurosis, and not merely failure or limitation in life but even failure or limitation in art. Thus it is often said that the warp of Dostoevski's mind accounts for the brilliance of his psychological insights. But it is never said that the same warp of Dostoevski's mind also accounted for his deficiency in insight. Freud, who greatly admired Dostoevski, although he did not like him, observed that "his insight was entirely restricted to the workings of the abnormal psyche. Consider his astounding helplessness before the phenomenon of love; he really only understands either crude, instinctive desire or masochistic submission or love from pity."[6] This, we must note, is not merely Freud's comment on the extent of the province which Dostoevski chose for his own, but on his failure to understand what, given the province of his choice, he might be expected to understand.

And since neurosis can account not only for intellec-

---

artistic thought, or even that the scientist's creation is involved with his total personality *in the same way* that the artist's is—I am maintaining only that the scientist's creation is as *deeply* implicated with his total personality as is the artist's.

This point of view seems to be supported by Freud's monograph on Leonardo. One of the problems that Freud sets himself is to discover why an artist of the highest endowment should have devoted himself more and more to scientific investigation, with the result that he was unable to complete his artistic enterprises. The particular reasons for this that Freud assigns need not be gone into here; all that I wish to suggest is that Freud understands these reasons to be the working out of an inner conflict, the attempt to deal with the difficulties that have their roots in the most primitive situations. Leonardo's scientific investigations were as necessary and "compelled" and they constituted as much of a claim on the whole personality as anything the artist undertakes; and so far from being carried out for the sake of public prestige, they were largely private and personal, and were thought by the public of his time to be something very like insanity.

[6] From a letter quoted in Theodor Reik's *From Thirty Years With Freud*, p. 175.

tual success and for failure or limitation but also for
mediocrity, we have most of society involved in neurosis.
To this I have no objection—I think most of society is
indeed involved in neurosis. But with neurosis accounting for so much, it cannot be made exclusively to account for one man's literary power.

We have now to consider what is meant by genius
when its source is identified as the sacrifice and pain of
neurosis.

In the case of Henry James, the reference to the neurosis of his personal life does indeed tell us something
about the latent intention of his work and thus about the
reason for some large part of its interest for us. But if
genius and its source are what we are dealing with, we
must observe that the reference to neurosis tells us nothing about James's passion, energy, and devotion, nothing
about his architectonic skill, nothing about the other
themes that were important to him which are not connected with his unconscious concern with castration.
We cannot, that is, make the writer's inner life exactly
equivalent to his power of expressing it. Let us grant
for the sake of argument that the literary genius, as distinguished from other men, is the victim of a "mutilation" and that his fantasies are neurotic.[7] It does not then
follow as the inevitable next step that his ability to express these fantasies and to impress us with them is
neurotic, for that ability is what we mean by his genius.
Anyone might be injured as Henry James was, and even
respond within himself to the injury as James is said to
have done, and yet not have his literary power.

The reference to the artist's neurosis tells us something about the material on which the artist exercises his
powers, and even something about his reasons for bring-

[7] I am using the word *fantasy*, unless modified, in a neutral
sense. A fantasy, in this sense, may be distinguished from
the representation of something that actually exists, but it
is not opposed to "reality" and not an "escape" from reality.
Thus the idea of a rational society, or the image of a good
house to be built, as well as the story of something that
could never really happen, is a fantasy. There may be
neurotic or non-neurotic fantasies.

ing his powers into play, but it does not tell us anything about the source of his power, it makes no causal connection between them and the neurosis. And if we look into the matter, we see that there is in fact no causal connection between them. For, still granting that the poet is uniquely neurotic, what is surely not neurotic, what indeed suggests nothing but health, is his power of using his neuroticism. He shapes his fantasies, he gives them social form and reference. Charles Lamb's way of putting this cannot be improved. Lamb is denying that genius is allied to insanity; for "insanity" the modern reader may substitute "neurosis." "The ground of the mistake," he says, "is, that men, finding in the raptures of the higher poetry a condition of exaltation, to which they have no parallel in their own experience, besides the spurious resemblance of it in dreams and fevers, impute a state of dreaminess and fever to the poet. But the true poet dreams being awake. He is not possessed by his subject but has dominion over it. . . . Where he seems most to recede from humanity, he will be found the truest to it. From beyond the scope of nature if he summon possible existences, he subjugates them to the law of her consistency. He is beautifully loyal to that sovereign directress, when he appears most to betray and desert her. . . . Herein the great and the little wits are differenced; that if the latter wander ever so little from nature or natural existence, they lose themselves and their readers. . . . They do not create, which implies shaping and consistency. Their imaginations are not active—for to be active is to call something into act and form—but passive as men in sick dreams."

The activity of the artist, we must remember, may be approximated by many who are themselves not artists. Thus, the expressions of many schizophrenic people have the intense appearance of creativity and an inescapable interest and significance. But they are not works of art, and although Van Gogh may have been schizophrenic he was in addition an artist. Again, as I have already suggested, it is not uncommon in our society for certain kinds of neurotic people to imitate the artist in his life and even in his ideals and ambitions. They follow the artist in everything except successful performance. It was, I think, Otto Rank who called such people half-artists and confirmed the diagnosis of their neuroticism at the same time that he differentiated them from true artists.

Nothing is so characteristic of the artist as his power of shaping his work, of subjugating his raw material, however aberrant it be from what we call normality, to the consistency of nature. It would be impossible to deny that whatever disease or mutilation the artist may suffer is an element of his production which has its effect on every part of it, but disease and mutilation are available to us all—life provides them with prodigal generosity. What marks the artist is his power to shape the material of pain we all have.

At this point, with our recognition of life's abundant provision of pain, we are at the very heart of our matter, which is the meaning we may assign to neurosis and the relation we are to suppose it to have with normality. Here Freud himself can be of help, although it must be admitted that what he tells us may at first seem somewhat contradictory and confusing.

Freud's study of Leonardo da Vinci is an attempt to understand why Leonardo was unable to pursue his artistic enterprises, feeling compelled instead to advance his scientific investigations. The cause of this Freud traces back to certain childhood experiences not different in kind from the experiences which Dr. Rosenzweig adduces to account for certain elements in the work of Henry James. And when he has completed his study Freud makes this *caveat*: "Let us expressly emphasize that we have never considered Leonardo as a neurotic. . . . We no longer believe that health and disease, normal and nervous, are sharply distinguished from each other. We know today that neurotic symptoms are substitutive formations for certain repressive acts which must result in the course of our development from the child to the cultural man, that we all produce such substitutive formations, and that only the amount, intensity, and distribution of these substitutive formations justify the practical conception of illness. . . ." The statement becomes the more striking when we remember that in the course of his study Freud has had occasion to observe that Leonardo was both homosexual and sexually inactive. I am not sure that the statement that Leonardo was not a neurotic is one that Freud would have made at every point in the later development of psychoanalysis, yet it is in conformity with his continuing notion of the genesis of culture. And the *practical,* the quantitative or economic, conception of illness he insists on in a passage in the *Introductory Lectures.* "The neurotic symptoms," he says, ". . . are activities which are detrimental, or at least useless, to life as a whole; the person concerned frequently complains of them as obnoxious to him or they involve suffering and distress for him. The principal injury they inflict lies in the expense of energy they entail, and, besides this, in the energy needed to combat them. Where the symptoms are extensively developed, these two kinds of effort may exact such a price that the person suffers a very serious impoverishment in available mental energy which consequently disables him for all the important tasks of life. This result depends principally upon the amount of energy taken up in this way; therefore you will see that 'illness' is essentially a practical conception. But if you look at the matter from a theoretical point of view and ignore this question of degree, you can very well see that we are all ill, i.e., neurotic; for the conditions required for symptom-formation are demonstrable also in normal persons."

We are all ill: the statement is grandiose, and its implications—the implications, that is, of understanding the totality of human nature in the terms of disease—are vast. These implications have never been properly met (although I believe that a few theologians have responded to them), but this is not the place to attempt to meet them. I have brought forward Freud's statement of the essential sickness of the psyche only because it stands as the refutation of what is implied by the literary use of the theory of neurosis to account for genius. For if we are all ill, and if, as I have said, neurosis can account for everything, for failure and mediocrity—"a very serious impoverishment of available mental energy"—as well as for genius, it cannot uniquely account for genius.

This, however, is not to say that there is no connection between neurosis and genius, which would be tantamount, as we see, to saying that there is no connection between human nature and genius. But the connection lies wholly in a particular and special relation which the artist has to neurosis.

In order to understand what this particular and special connection is we must have clearly in mind what neurosis is. The current literary conception of neurosis as a *wound* is quite misleading. It inevitably suggests passivity, whereas, if we follow Freud, we must understand a neurosis to be an *activity,* and activity with a purpose, and a particular kind of activity, a *conflict.* This is not to say that there are no abnormal mental states which are not conflicts. There are; the struggle between elements of the unconscious may never be instituted in the first place, or it may be called off. As Freud says in a passage which follows close upon the one I last quoted, "If regressions do not call forth a prohibition on the part of the ego, no neurosis results; the libido succeeds in obtaining a real, although not a normal, satisfaction. But if the ego . . . is not in agreement with these regressions, conflict ensues." And in his essay on Dostoevski, Freud says that "there are no neurotic complete masochists," by which he means that the ego which gives way completely to masochism (or to any other pathological excess) has passed beyond neurosis; the conflict has ceased, but at the cost of the defeat of the ego, and now some other name than that of neurosis must be given to the condition of the person who thus takes himself beyond the pain of the neurotic conflict. To understand this is to become aware of the curious complacency with which literary men regard mental disease. The psyche of the neurotic is not equally complacent; it regards with the greatest fear the chaotic and destructive forces it contains, and it struggles fiercely to keep them at bay.[8]

We come then to a remarkable paradox: we are all ill, but we are ill in the service of health, or ill in the service of life, or, at the very least, ill in the service of life-in-culture. The form of the mind's dynamics is that of the neurosis, which is to be understood as the ego's struggle against being overcome by the forces with which it coexists, and the strategy of this conflict requires that the ego shall incur pain and make sacrifices of itself, at the same time seeing to it that its pain and sacrifice be as small as they may.

But this is characteristic of all minds: no mind is exempt except those which refuse the conflict or withdraw from it; and we ask wherein the mind of the artist is unique. If he is not unique in neurosis, is he then unique in the significance and intensity of his neurosis? I do not believe that we shall go more than a little way toward a definition of artistic genius by answering this question affirmatively. A neurotic conflict cannot ever be either meaningless or merely personal; it must be understood as exemplifying cultural forces of great moment, and this

[8] In the article to which I refer in the note on page 169, William Barrett says that he prefers the old-fashioned term "madness" to "neurosis." But it is not quite for him to choose—the words do not differ in fashion but in meaning. Most literary people, when they speak of mental illness, refer to neurosis. Perhaps one reason for this is that the neurosis is the most benign of the mental ills. Another reason is surely that psychoanalytical literature deals chiefly with the neurosis, and its symptomatology and therapy have become familiar; psychoanalysis has far less to say about psychosis, for which it can offer far less therapeutic hope. Further, the neurosis is easily put into a causal connection with the social maladjustments of our time. Other forms of mental illness of a more severe and degenerative kind are not so widely recognized by the literary person and are often assimilated to neurosis with a resulting confusion. In the present essay I deal only with the conception of neurosis, but this should not be taken to imply that I believe that other pathological mental conditions, including actual madness, do not have relevance to the general matter of the discussion.

is true of any neurotic conflict at all. To be sure, some neuroses may be more interesting than others, perhaps because they are fiercer or more inclusive; and no doubt the writer who makes a claim upon our interest is a man who by reason of the energy and significance of the forces in struggle within him provides us with the largest representation of the culture in which we, with him, are involved; his neurosis may thus be thought of as having a connection of concomitance with his literary powers. As Freud says in the Dostoevski essay, "the neurosis . . . comes into being all the more readily the richer the complexity which has to be controlled by his ego." Yet even the rich complexity which his ego is doomed to control is not the definition of the artist's genius, for we can by no means say that the artist is pre-eminent in the rich complexity of elements in conflict within him. The slightest acquaintance with the clinical literature of psychoanalysis will suggest that a rich complexity of struggling elements is no uncommon possession. And that same literature will also make it abundantly clear that the devices of art—the most extreme devices of poetry, for example—are not particular to the mind of the artist but are characteristic of mind itself.

But the artist is indeed unique in one respect, in the respect of his relation to his neurosis. He is what he is by virtue of his successful objectification of his neurosis, by his shaping it and making it available to others in a way which has its effect upon their own egos in struggle. His genius, that is, may be defined in terms of his faculties of perception, representation, and realization, and in these terms alone. It can no more be defined in terms of neurosis than can his power of walking and talking, or his sexuality. The use to which he puts his power, or the manner and style of his power, may be discussed with reference to his particular neurosis, and so may such matters as the untimely diminution or cessation of its exercise. But its essence is irreducible. It is, as we say, a gift.

We are all ill: but even a universal sickness implies an idea of health. Of the artist we must say that whatever elements of neurosis he has in common with his fellow mortals, the one part of him that is healthy, by any conceivable definition of health, is that which gives him the power to conceive, to plan, to work, and to bring his work to a conclusion. And if we are all ill, we are ill by a universal accident, not by a universal necessity, by a fault in the economy of our powers, not by the nature of the powers themselves. The Philoctetes myth, when it is used to imply a causal connection between the fantasy of castration and artistic power, tells us no more about the source of artistic power than we learn about the source of sexuality when the fantasy of castration is adduced, for the fear of castration may explain why a man is moved to extravagant exploits of sexuality, but we do not say that his sexual power itself derives from his fear of castration; and further the same fantasy may also explain impotence or homosexuality. The Philoctetes story, which has so established itself among us as explaining the source of the artist's power, is not really an explanatory myth at all; it is a moral myth having reference to our proper behavior in the circumstances of the universal accident. In its juxtaposition of the wound and the bow, it tells us that we must be aware that weakness does not preclude strength nor strength weakness. It is therefore not irrelevant to the artist, but when we use it we will do well to keep in mind the other myths of the arts, recalling what Pan and Dionysius suggest of the relation of art to physiology and superabundance, remembering that to Apollo were attributed the bow and the lyre, two strengths together, and that he was given the lyre by its inventor, the baby Hermes—that miraculous infant who, the day he was born, left his cradle to do mischief: and the first thing he met with was a tortoise, which he greeted politely before scooping it from its shell, and, thought and deed being one with him, he contrived the instrument to which he sang "the glorious tale of his own begetting." These were gods, and very early ones, but their myths tell us something about the nature and source of art even in our grim, late human present.

The Sense of the Past

In recent years the study of literature in our universities has again and again been called into question, chiefly on the ground that what is being studied is not so much literature itself as the history of literature. John Jay Chapman was perhaps the first to state the case against the literary scholars when in 1927 he denounced the "archaeological, quasi-scientific, and documentary study of the fine arts" because, as he said, it endeavored "to express the fluid universe of many emotions in terms drawn from the study of the physical sciences." And since Chapman wrote, the issue in the universities has been clearly drawn in the form of an opposition of "criticism" to "scholarship." Criticism has been the aggressor, and its assault upon scholarship has been successful almost in proportion to the spiritedness with which it has been made; at the present time, although the archaeological and quasi-scientific and documentary study of literature is still the dominant one in our universities, it is clear to everyone that scholarship is on the defensive and is ready to share the rule with its antagonist.

This revision of the academic polity can be regarded only with satisfaction. The world seems to become less and less responsive to literature; we can even observe that literature is becoming something like an object of suspicion, and it is possible to say of the historical study of literature that its very existence is an evidence of this mistrust. De Quincey's categories of *knowledge* and *power* are most pertinent here; the traditional scholarship, in so far as it takes literature to be chiefly an object of knowledge, denies or obscures that active power by which literature is truly defined. All sorts of studies are properly ancillary to the study of literature. For example, the study of the intellectual conditions in which a work of literature was made is not only legitimate but sometimes even necessary to our perception of its power. Yet when Professor Lovejoy in his influential book, *The Great Chain of Being*, tells us that for the study of the history of ideas a really dead writer is better than one whose works are still enjoyed, we naturally pull up short and wonder if we are not in danger of becoming like the Edinburgh body-snatchers who *saw to it* that there were enough cadavers for study in the medical school.

Criticism made its attack on the historians of literature in the name of literature as power. The attack was the fiercer because literary history had all too faithfully followed the lead of social and political history, which, having given up its traditional connection with literature, had allied itself with the physical sciences of the nineteenth century and had adopted the assumption of these sciences that the world was reflected with perfect literalness in the will-less mind of the observer. The new history had many successes and it taught literary study what it had itself learned, that in an age of science prestige is to be gained by approximating the methods of science. Of these methods the most notable and most adaptable was the investigation of genesis, of how the work of art came into being. I am not concerned to show that the study of genesis is harmful to the right experience of the work of art: I do not believe it is. Indeed, I am inclined to suppose that whenever the genetic method is attacked we ought to suspect that special interests are being defended. So far is it from being true that the genetic method is in itself inimical to the work of art, that the very opposite is so; a work of art, or any human thing, studied in its genesis can take on an added value. Still, the genetic method can easily be vulgarized, and when it is used in its vulgar form, it can indeed reduce the value of a thing; in much genetic study the implication is clear that to the scholar the work of art is nothing but its conditions.

One of the attractions of the genetic study of art is that it seems to offer a high degree of certainty. Aristotle tells us that every study has its own degree of certainty and that the well-trained man accepts that degree and does not look for a greater one. We may add that there are different kinds as well as different degrees of certainty, and we can say that the great mistake of the scientific-historical scholarship is that it looks for a degree and kind of certainty that literature does not need and cannot allow.

The error that is made by literary scholars when they seek for a certainty analogous with the certainty of science has been so often remarked that at this date little more need be said of it. Up to a point the scientific study of art is legitimate and fruitful; the great thing is that we should recognize the terminal point and not try to push beyond it, that we should not expect that the scientific study of, say, literature will necessarily assure us of the experience of literature; and if we wish as teachers to help others to the experience of literature, we cannot do so by imparting the fruits of our scientific study. What the partisans of the so-called New Criticism revolted against was the scientific notion of the fact as transferred in a literal way to the study of literature. They wished to restore autonomy to the work of art, to see it as the agent of power rather than as the object of knowledge.

The faults of these critics we know. Perhaps their chief fault they share with the scientific-historical scholars themselves—they try too hard. No less than the scholars, the critics fall into an error that Chapman denounced, the great modern illusion "that anything whatever . . . can be discovered through hard intellectual work and concentration." We often feel of them that they make the elucidation of poetic ambiguity or irony a kind of intellectual calisthenic ritual. Still, we can forgive them their strenuousness, remembering that something has happened to our relation with language which seems to require that we make methodical and explicit what was once immediate and unformulated.

But there is another fault of the New Critics of which we must take notice. It is that in their reaction from the historical method they forget that the literary work is ineluctably a historical fact, and, what is more important, that its historicity is a fact in our aesthetic experience. Literature, we may say, must in some sense always be a historical study, for literature is a historical art. It is historical in three separate senses.

In the old days the poet was supposed to be himself a historian, a reliable chronicler of events. Thucydides said that he was likely to be an inaccurate historian, but Aristotle said that he was more accurate, because more general, than any mere annalist; and we, following Aristotle, suppose that a large part of literature is properly historical, the recording and interpreting of personal, national, and cosmological events.

Then literature is historical in the sense that it is necessarily aware of its own past. It is not always consciously aware of this past, but it is always practically aware of it. The work of any poet exists by reason of its connection with past work, both in continuation and in divergence, and what we call his originality is simply his special relation to tradition. The point has been fully developed by T. S. Eliot in his well-known essay "Tradition and the Individual Talent." And Mr. Eliot reminds us how each poet's relation to tradition changes tradition itself, so that the history of literature is never quiet for long and is never merely an additive kind of growth. Each new age makes the pattern over again, forgetting what was once dominant, finding new affinities; we read any work within a kaleidoscope of historical elements.

And in one more sense literature is historical, and it is with this sense that I am here chiefly concerned. In the existence of every work of literature of the past, its historicity, its *pastness*, is a factor of great importance. In certain cultures the pastness of a work of art gives it an extra-aesthetic authority which is incorporated into its aesthetic power. But even in our own culture with its

ambivalent feeling about tradition, there inheres in a
work of art of the past a certain quality, an element of its
aesthetic existence, which we can identify as its pastness.
Side by side with the formal elements of the work, and
modifying these elements, there is the element of history,
which, in any complete aesthetic analysis, must be taken
into account.

The New Critics exercised their early characteristic
method almost exclusively upon lyric poetry, a genre in
which the historical element, although of course present,
is less obtrusive than in the long poem, the novel, and the
drama. But even in the lyric poem the factor of historicity is part of the aesthetic experience; it is not merely a
negative condition of the other elements, such as prosody
or diction, which, if they are old enough, are likely to be
insufficiently understood—it is itself a positive aesthetic
factor with positive and pleasurable relations to the other
aesthetic factors. It is a part of the *given* of the work,
which we cannot help but respond to. The New Critics
imply that this situation *should* not exist, but it cannot
help existing, and we have to take it into account.

We are creatures of time, we are creatures of the historical sense, not only as men have always been but in a
new way since the time of Walter Scott. Possibly this
may be for the worse; we would perhaps be stronger if
we believed that Now contained all things, and that we
in our barbarian moment were all that had ever been.
Without the sense of the past we might be more certain,
less weighted down and apprehensive. We might also
be less generous, and certainly we would be less aware.
In any case, we have the sense of the past and must live
with it, and by it.

And we must read our literature by it. Try as we will,
we cannot be like Partridge at the play, wholly without
the historical sense. The leap of the imagination which
an audience makes when it responds to *Hamlet* is enormous, and it requires a comprehensive, although not
necessarily a highly instructed, sense of the past. This
sense does not, for most artistic purposes, need to be

highly instructed; it can consist largely of the firm belief that there really is such a thing as the past.

In the New Critics' refusal to take critical account of the historicity of a work there is, one understands, the impulse to make the work of the past more immediate and more real, to deny that between Now and Then there is any essential difference, the spirit of man being one and continuous. But it is only if we are aware of the reality of the past as past that we can feel it as alive and present. If, for example, we try to make Shakespeare literally contemporaneous, we make him monstrous. He is contemporaneous only if we know how much a man of his own age he was; he is relevant to us only if we see his distance from us. Or to take a poet closer to us in actual time, Wordsworth's Immortality Ode is acceptable to us only when it is understood to have been written at a certain past moment; if it had appeared much later than it did, if it were offered to us now as a contemporary work, we would not admire it; and the same is true of *The Prelude,* which of all works of the Romantic Movement is closest to our present interest. In the pastness of these works lies the assurance of their validity and relevance.

The question is always arising: What is the real poem? Is it the poem we now perceive? Is it the poem the author consciously intended? Is it the poem the author intended and his first readers read? Well, it is all these things, depending on the state of our knowledge. But in addition the poem is the poem as it has existed in history, as it has lived its life from Then to Now, as it is a thing which submits itself to one kind of perception in one age and another kind of perception in another age, as it exerts in each age a different kind of power. This makes it a thing we can never wholly understand—other things too, of course, help to make it that—and the mystery, the unreachable part of the poem, is one of its aesthetic elements.

To suppose that we can think like men of another time is as much of an illusion as to suppose that we can think in a wholly different way. But it is the first illusion that is exemplified in the attitude of the anti-historical critics. In the admirable poetry textbook of Cleanth Brooks and Robert Penn Warren, the authors disclaim all historical intention. Their purpose being what it is, they are right to do so, but I wonder if they are right in never asking in their aesthetic analysis the question: What effect is created by our knowledge that the language of a particular poem is not such as would be uttered by a poet writing now? To read a poem of even a hundred years ago requires as much translation of its historical circumstance as of its metaphors. This the trained and gifted critic is likely to forget; his own historical sense is often so deeply ingrained that he is not wholly conscious of it, and sometimes, for reasons of his own, he prefers to keep it merely implicit. Yet whether or not it is made conscious and explicit, the historical sense is one of the aesthetic and critical faculties.

What more apposite reminder of this can we have than the early impulse of the New Critics themselves to discover all poetic virtue in the poetry of the seventeenth century, the impulse, only lately modified, to find the essence of poetic error in the poetry of Romanticism? Their having given rein to this impulse is certainly not illegitimate. They were doing what we all do, what we all must and even should do: they were involving their aesthetics with certain cultural preferences, they were implying choices in religion, metaphysics, politics, manners. And in so far as they were doing this by showing a preference for a particular period of the past, which they brought into comparison with the present, they were exercising their historical sense. We cannot question their preference itself; we can only question the mere implicitness of their historical sense, their attitude of making the historical sense irrelevant to their aesthetic.

But if the historical sense is always with us, it must, for just that reason, be refined and made more exact. We have, that is, to open our minds to the whole question of what we mean when we speak of causation in culture. Hume, who so shook our notions of causation in the physical sciences, raises some interesting questions of causation in culture. "There is no subject," he says, "in which we must proceed with more caution than in tracing the history of the arts and sciences; lest we assign causes which never existed and reduce what is merely contingent to stable and universal principles." The cultivators of the arts, he goes on to say, are always few in number and their minds are delicate and "easily perverted." "Chance, therefore, or secret and unknown causes must have great influence on the rise and progress of all refined arts." But there is one fact, he continues, which gives us the license to speculate—this is the fact that the choice spirits arise from and are related to the mass of the people of their time. "The question, therefore, is not altogether concerning the taste, genius, and spirit of a few, but concerning those of a whole people; and may, therefore, be accounted for, in some measure, by general causes and principles." This gives us our charter to engage in cultural history and cultural criticism, but we must see that it is a charter to deal with a mystery.

The refinement of our historical sense chiefly means that we keep it properly complicated. History, like science and art, involves abstraction: we abstract certain events from others and we make this particular abstraction with an end in view, we make it to serve some purpose of our will. Try as we may, we cannot, as we write history, escape our purposiveness. Nor, indeed, should we try to escape, for purpose and meaning are the same thing. But in pursuing our purpose, in making our abstractions, we must be aware of what we are doing; we ought to have it fully in mind that our abstraction is not perfectly equivalent to the infinite complication of events from which we have abstracted. I should like to suggest a few ways in which those of us who are literary scholars can give to our notion of history an appropriate complication.

It ought to be for us a real question whether, and in what way, human nature is always the same. I do not mean that we ought to settle this question before we get to work, but only that we insist to ourselves that the question is a real one. What we certainly know has changed is the *expression* of human nature, and we must keep before our minds the problem of the relation which expression bears to feeling. E. E. Stoll, the well-known Shakespearean critic, has settled the matter out of hand by announcing the essential difference between what he calls "convention" and what he calls "life," and he insists that the two may have no truck with each other, that we cannot say of Shakespeare that he is psychologically or philosophically acute because these are terms we use of "life," whereas Shakespeare was dealing only with "convention." This has the virtue of suggesting how important is the relation of "convention" to "life," but it misses the point that "life" is always expressed through "convention" and in a sense always *is* "convention," and that convention has meaning only because of the intentions of life. Professor Stoll seems to go on the assumption that Shakespeare's audiences were conscious of convention; they were aware of it, but certainly not conscious of it; what they were conscious of was life, into which they made an instantaneous translation of all that took place on the stage. The problem of the interplay between the emotion and the convention which is available for it, and the reciprocal influence they exert on each other, is a very difficult one, and I scarcely even state its complexities, let alone pretend to solve them. But the problem with its difficulties should be admitted, and simplicity of solution should always be regarded as a sign of failure.

A very important step forward in the complication of our sense of the past was made when Whitehead and after him Lovejoy taught us to look not for the expressed but for the assumed ideas of an age, what Whitehead describes as the "assumptions which appear so obvious that people do not know that they are assuming them because no other way of putting things has ever occurred to them."

But a regression was made when Professor Lovejoy, in that influential book of his, assured us that "the ideas in serious reflective literature are, of course, in great part philosophical ideas in dilution." To go fully into the error of this common belief would need more time than we have now at our disposal. It is part of our suspiciousness of literature that we undertake thus to make it a dependent art. Certainly we must question the assumption which gives the priority in ideas to the philosopher and sees the movement of thought as always from the systematic thinker, who thinks up the ideas in, presumably, a cultural vacuum, to the poet who "uses" the ideas "in dilution." We must question this even if it means a reconstruction of what we mean by "ideas."

And this leads to another matter about which we may not be simple, the relation of the poet to his environment. The poet, it is true, is an effect of environment, but we must remember that he is no less a cause. He may be used as the barometer, but let us not forget that he is also part of the weather. We have been too easily satisfied by a merely elementary meaning of environment; we have been content with a simple quantitative implication of the word, taking a large and literally environing thing to be always the environment of a smaller thing. In a concert room the audience and its attitude are of course the environment of the performer, but also the performer and his music make the environment of the audience. In a family the parents are no doubt the chief factors in the environment of the child; but also the child is a factor in the environment of the parents and himself conditions the actions of his parents toward him.

Corollary to this question of environment is the question of influence, the influence which one writer is said to have had on another. In its historical meaning, from which we take our present use, *influence* was a word intended to express a mystery. It means a flowing-in, but not as a tributary river flows into the main stream at a certain observable point; historically the image is an astrological one and the meanings which the Oxford Dictionary gives all suggest "producing effects by *insensible* or *invisible* means"—"the infusion of any kind of divine, spiritual, moral, immaterial, or *secret* power or principle." Before the idea of influence we ought to be far more puzzled than we are; if we find it hard to be puzzled enough, we may contrive to induce the proper state of uncertainty by turning the word upon ourselves, asking, "What have been the influences that made me the person I am, and to whom would I entrust the task of truly discovering what they were?"

Yet another thing that we have not understood with sufficient complication is the nature of ideas in their relation to the conditions of their development and in relation to their transmission. Too often we conceive of an idea as being like the baton that is handed from runner to runner in a relay race. But an idea as a transmissible thing is rather like the sentence that in the parlor game is whispered about in a circle; the point of the game is the amusement that comes when the last version is compared with the original. As for the origin of ideas, we ought to remember that an idea is the formulation of a response to a situation; so, too, is the modification of an existing idea. Since the situations in which people or cultures find themselves are limited in number, and since the possible responses are also limited, ideas certainly do have a tendency to recur, and because people think habitually ideas also have a tendency to persist when the situation which called them forth is no longer present; so that ideas do have a certain limited autonomy, and sometimes the appearance of a complete autonomy. From this there has grown up the belief in the actual perfect autonomy of ideas. It is supposed that ideas think themselves, create themselves and their descendants, have a life independent of the thinker and the situation. And from this we are often led to conclude that ideas, systematic ideas, are directly responsible for events.

A similar feeling is prevalent among our intellectual classes in relation to words. Semantics is not now the lively concern that it was a few years ago, but the mythology of what we may call political semantics has become established in our intellectual life, the belief that we are betrayed by words, that words push us around against our will. "The tyranny of words" became a popular phrase and is still in use, and the semanticists offer us an easier world and freedom from war if only we assert our independence from words. But nearly a century ago Dickens said that he was tired of hearing about "the tyranny of words" (he used that phrase); he was, he said, less concerned with the way words abuse us than with the way we abuse words. It is not words that make our troubles, but our own wills. Words cannot control us unless we desire to be controlled by them. And the same is true of the control of systematic ideas. We have come to believe that some ideas can betray us, others save us. The educated classes are learning to blame ideas for our troubles, rather than blaming what is a very different thing—our own bad thinking. This is the great vice of academicism, that it is concerned with ideas rather than with thinking, and nowadays the errors of academicism do not stay in the academy; they make their way into the world, and what begins as a failure of perception among intellectual specialists finds its fulfillment in policy and action.

In time of war, when two different cultures, or two extreme modifications of the same culture, confront each other with force, this belief in the autonomy of ideas becomes especially strong and therefore especially clear. In any modern war there is likely to be involved a conflict of ideas which is in part factitious but which is largely genuine. But this conflict of ideas, genuine as it may be, suggests to both sides the necessity of believing in the fixed, immutable nature of the ideas to which each side owes allegiance. What gods were to the ancients at war, ideas are to us. Thus, in the last war, an eminent American professor of philosophy won wide praise for demonstrating that Nazism was to be understood as the inevitable outcome of the ideas of Schopenhauer and Nietzsche, while the virtues of American democracy were to be explained by tracing a direct line of descent from Plato and the Athenian polity. Or consider a few sentences from a biography of Byron, written when, not so long ago, the culture of Nazism was at its height. The author, a truly admirable English biographer, is making an estimate of the effort of the Romantic Movement upon our time. He concludes that the Romantic Movement failed. Well, we have all heard that before, and perhaps it is true, although I for one know less and less what it means. Indeed, I know less and less what is meant by the ascription of failure to any movement in literature. All movements fail, and perhaps the Romantic Movement failed more than most because it attempted more than most; possibly it attempted too much. To say that a literary movement failed seems to suggest a peculiar view of both literature and history; it implies that literature ought to settle something for good and all, that life ought to be progressively completed. And according to our author, not only did the Romantic Movement fail —it left a terrible legacy:

> Nationalism was essentially a Romantic movement, and from nationalism springs the half-baked racial theorist with his romantic belief in the superiority of "Aryan" blood and his romantic distrust of the use of reason. So far-reaching were the effects of the Romantic Revival that they still persist in shapes under which they are no longer recognized. . . . For Romantic literature appeals to that strain of anarchism which inhabits a dark corner of every human mind and is continually advancing the charms of extinction against the claims of life—the beauty of all that is fragmentary and youthful and half-formed as opposed to the compact achievement of adult genius.

It is of course easy enough to reduce the argument to absurdity—we have only to ask why Germany and not ourselves responded so fiercely to the romantic ideas which, if they be indeed the romantic ideas, were certainly available to everybody. The failure of logic is not however what concerns us, but rather what the logic is intended to serve: the belief that ideas generate events, that they have an autonomous existence, and that they can seize upon the minds of some men and control their actions independently of circumstance and will.

Needless to say, these violations of historical principle

require a violation of historical fact. The Schopenhauer and the Nietzsche of the first explanation have no real reference to two nineteenth-century philosophers of the same names; the Plato is imaginary, the Athens out of a storybook, and no attempt is made to reconcile this fanciful Athens with the opinion of the real Athens held by the real Plato. As for the second explanation, how are we to connect anarchism, and hostility to the claims of life, and the fragmentary, and the immature, and the half-formed, with Kant, or Goethe, or Wordsworth, or Beethoven, or Berlioz, or Delacroix? And how from these men, who *are* Romanticism, dare we derive the iron rigidity and the desperate centralization which the New Order of the Nazis involved, or the systematic cruelty or the elaborate scientism with which the racial doctrine was implicated?

The two books to which I refer are of course in themselves harmless and I don't wish to put upon them a weight which they should not properly be made to bear. But they do suggest something of the low estate into which history has fallen among our educated classes, and they are of a piece with the depreciation of the claims of history which a good many literary people nowadays make, a depreciation which has had the effect of leading young students of literature, particularly the more gifted ones, to incline more and more to resist historical considerations, justifying themselves, as it is natural they should, by pointing to the dullness and deadness and falsifications which have resulted from the historical study of literature. Our resistance to history is no doubt ultimately to be accounted for by nothing less than the whole nature of our life today. It was said by Nietzsche—the real one, not the lay figure of cultural propaganda—that the historical sense was an actual faculty of the mind, "a sixth sense," and that the credit for the recognition of its status must go to the nineteenth century. What was uniquely esteemed by the nineteenth century is not likely to stand in high favor with us: our coldness to historical thought may in part be explained by our feeling that it is precisely the past that caused all our troubles, the nineteenth century being the most blameworthy of all the culpable centuries. Karl Marx, for whom history was indeed a sixth sense, expressed what has come to be the secret hope of our time, that man's life in politics, which is to say, man's life in history, shall come to an end. History, as we now understand it, envisions its own extinction—that is really what we nowadays mean by "progress"—and with all the passion of a desire kept secret even from ourselves, we yearn to elect a way of life which shall be satisfactory once and for all, time without end, and we do not want to be reminded by the past of the considerable possibility that our present is but perpetuating mistakes and failures and instituting new troubles.

And yet, when we come to think about it, the chances are all in favor of our having to go on making our choices and so of making our mistakes. History, in its meaning of a continuum of events, is not really likely to come to an end. There may therefore be some value in bringing explicitly to mind what part in culture is played by history in its other meaning of an ordering and understanding of the continuum of events. There is no one who is better able to inform us on this point than Nietzsche. We can perhaps listen to him with the more patience because he himself would have had considerable sympathy for our impatience with history, for although he thought that the historical sense brought certain virtues, making men "unpretentious, unselfish, modest, brave, habituated to self-control and self-renunciation," he also thought that it prevented them from having the ability to respond to the very highest and noblest developments of culture, making them suspicious of what is wholly completed and fully matured. This ambivalent view of the historical sense gives him a certain authority when he defines what the historical sense is and does. It is, he said, "the capacity for divining quickly the order of the rank of the valuation according to which a people, a community, or an individual has lived." In the case of a people or of a community, the valuations are those which are expressed not only by the gross institutional facts of their life, what Nietzsche called "the operating forces," but also and more significantly by their morals and manners, by their philosophy and art. And the historical sense, he goes on to say, is "the 'divining instinct' for the relationships of these valuations, for the relation of the valuations to the operating forces." The historical sense, that is, is to be understood as the critical sense, as the sense which life uses to test itself. And since there never was a time when the instinct for divining—and "quickly"! —the order of rank of cultural expressions was so much needed, our growing estrangement from history must be understood as the sign of our desperation.

Nietzsche's own capacity for quickly divining the order of rank of cultural things was, when he was at his best, more acute than that of any other man of his time or since. If we look for the explanation of his acuity, we find it in the fact that it never occurred to him to separate his historical sense from his sense of art. They were not two senses but one. And the merit of his definition of the historical sense, especially when it is taken in conjunction with the example of himself, is that it speaks to the historian and to the student of art as if they were one person. To that person Nietzsche's definition prescribes that culture be studied and judged as life's continuous evaluation of itself, the evaluation being understood as never finding full expression in the "operating forces" of a culture, but as never finding expression at all without reference to these gross, institutional facts.

Tacitus Now

The histories of Tacitus have been put to strange uses. The princelings of Renaissance Italy consulted the *Annals* on how to behave with the duplicity of Tiberius. The German racists overlooked all the disagreeable things which Tacitus observed of their ancestors, took note only of his praise of the ancient chastity and independence, and thus made of the *Germania* their anthropological primer. But these are the aberrations; the influence of Tacitus in Europe has been mainly in the service of liberty, as he intended it to be. Perhaps this influence has been most fully felt in France, where, under the dictatorships both of the Jacobins and of Napoleon, Tacitus was regarded as a dangerously subversive writer. In America, however, he has never meant a great deal. James Fenimore Cooper is an impressive exception to our general indifference, but Cooper was temperamentally attracted by the very one of all the qualities of Tacitus which is likely to alienate most American liberals, the aristocratic color of his libertarian ideas. Another reason for our coolness to Tacitus is that, until recently, our political experience gave us no ground to understand what he is talking about. Dictatorship and repression, spies and political informers, blood purges and treacherous dissension have not been part of our political tradition as they have been of Europe's. But Europe has now come very close to us, and our political education of the last decades fits us to understand the historian of imperial Rome.

It is the mark of a great history that sooner or later

we become as much aware of the historian as of the events he relates. In reading Tacitus we are aware of him from the first page: we are aware of him as one of the few great writers who are utterly without hope. He is always conscious of his own despair; it is nearly a fault in him; the attitude sometimes verges on attitudinizing. Yet the great fact about Tacitus is that he never imposes or wishes to impose his despair upon the reader. He must, he says, be always telling of "the merciless biddings of a tyrant, incessant prosecution, faithless friendships, the ruin of innocence, the same causes issuing in the same results," and he complains of "the wearisome monotony" of his subject matter. But the reader never feels the monotony; despite the statements which seem to imply the contrary, Tacitus never becomes the victim of what he writes about—he had too much power of mind for that.

His power of mind is not like that of Thucydides; it is not really political and certainly not military. It is, on a grand scale, psychological. We are irresistibly reminded of Proust when Tacitus sets about creating the wonderful figure of Tiberius and, using a hundred uncertainties and contradictions, tries to solve this great enigma of a man, yet always avoids the solution because the enigma is the character. In writing of political events his real interest is not in their political meaning but rather in what we would now call their cultural meaning, in what they tell us of the morale and morals of the nation; it is an interest that may profitably be compared with Flaubert's in *L'Education Sentimentale*, and perhaps it has been remarked that that novel, and *Salammbô* as well, have elements of style and emotion which reinforce our sense of Flaubert as a Tacitean personality.

Tacitus's conception of history was avowedly personal and moral. "This I regard as history's highest function," he says, "to let no worthy action be uncommemorated, and to hold out the reprobation of posterity to evil words and deeds." This moral preoccupation finds expression in a moral sensibility which is not ours and which in many respects we find it hard to understand. It has often been pointed out that slaves, Christians, Jews, and barbarians are outside the circle of his sympathies; he rather despised the Stoic humanitarianism of Seneca. Yet, as he says, half his historical interest is in the discovery of good deeds, and perhaps nothing in literature has a greater impact of astonishment, a more sudden sense of illumination, than the occurrence of a good deed in the pages of his histories. He represents the fabric of society as so loosened that we can scarcely credit the account of any simple human relationship, let alone a noble action. Yet the simple human relationships exist—a soldier weeps at having killed his brother in the civil war, the aristocrats open their houses to the injured thousands when the great amphitheater falls down; and the noble actions take place—the freedwoman Epicharis, when Piso's enormous conspiracy against Nero was discovered, endured the torture and died, implicating no one, "screening strangers and those whom she hardly knew." But the human relationship and the noble deed exist in the midst of depravity and disloyalty so great that we are always surprised by the goodness before we are relieved by it; what makes the fortitude of Epicharis so remarkable and so puzzling is that the former slave screened strangers and those whom she hardly knew "when freeborn men, Roman knights and senators, yet unscathed by the torture, betrayed, every one, his dearest kinsfolk." From these pages we learn really to understand those well-worn lines of Portia's about the beam of the candle, for we discover what Portia meant by a naughty world, literally a world of naught, a moral vacancy so great and black that in it the beam of a candle seems a flash of lightning.

The moral and psychological interests of Tacitus are developed at the cost of what nowadays is believed to be the true historical insight. The French scholar Boissier remarks that it is impossible to read the *History* and the *Annals* without wondering how the Roman Empire could possibly have held together through the eighty years of mutiny, infamy, intrigue, riot, expenditure, and irresponsibility which the two books tell us of. At any moment, we think, the political structure must collapse under this unnatural weight. Yet almost any modern account of the post-Augustan Empire suggests that we are wrong to make this supposition and seems to imply a radical criticism of Tacitus's methods. Breasted, for example, includes the period from Tiberius to Vespasian in a chapter which he calls "The First of Two Centuries of Peace." And Rostovtzeff in his authoritative work gives us to understand that Rome, despite the usual minor troubles, was a healthy, developing society. Yet Tacitus finds it worthy of comment that at this time a certain man died a natural death—"a rare incident in so high a rank," he says.

It is not, as I gather, that Tacitus lacks veracity. What he lacks is what in the thirties used to be called "the long view" of history. But to minds of a certain sensitivity "the long view" is the falsest historical view of all, and indeed the insistence on the length of perspective is intended precisely to overcome sensitivity—seen from sufficient distance, it says, the corpse and the hacked limbs are not so very terrible, and eventually they even begin to compose themselves into a "meaningful pattern." Tacitus had no notions of historical development to comfort him; nor did he feel it his duty to look at present danger and pain with the remote, objective eyes of posterity. The knowledge, if he had it, that trade with the East was growing or that a more efficient bureaucracy was evolving by which well-trained freedmen might smoothly administer affairs at home and in the provinces could not have consoled him for what he saw as the degradation of his class and nation. He wrote out of his feelings of the present and did not conceive the consolations of history and the future.

What for many modern scholars is the vice of history was for Tacitus its virtue—he thought that history should be literature and that it should move the minds of men through their feelings. And so he contrived his narrative with the most elaborate attention to its dramatic effects. Yet something more than a scrupulous concern for lit-

erary form makes Tacitus so impressive in a literary
way; some essential poise of his mind allowed him to
see events with both passion and objectivity, and one
cannot help wondering if the bitter division which his
mind had to endure did not reinforce this quality. For
Tacitus hated the Rome of the emperors, all his feelings
being for the vanished republic; yet for the return of
the republic he had no hope whatever. "It is easy to
commend," he said, "but not to produce; or if it is produced, it cannot be lasting." He served the ideal of the
republic in his character of historian; the actuality of the
empire he served as praetor, consul, and proconsul, and
complied with the wishes of the hated Domitian. The
more he saw of the actuality, the more he despaired of
his ideal—and the more he loved it. And perhaps this
secret tension of love and despair accounts for the poise
and energy of his intellect.

We can see this poise and energy in almost all his
judgments. For example, he despised the Jews, but he
would not repress his wry appreciation of their stubborn
courage and his intense admiration for their conception
of God. The one phrase of his that everyone knows,
"They make a solitude and call it peace," he put into
the mouth of a British barbarian, the leader of a revolt
against Roman rule; it will always be the hostile char-
acterization of imperialist domination, yet Tacitus himself measured Roman virtue by imperialist success. He
makes no less than four successive judgments of Otho:
scorns him as Nero's courtier and cuckold, admires him
as a provincial governor, despises him as emperor, and
praises him for choosing to die and end the civil war.
Much as he loved the republican character, he knew
that its day was past, and he ascribes Galba's fall to his
old-fashioned inflexibility in republican virtue.

The poise and energy of Tacitus's mind manifests itself
in his language, and Professor Hadas in his admirable
introduction to the useful Modern Library edition tells
us how much we must lose in translation. Yet even a
reader of the translation cannot help being aware of the
power of the writing. When Tacitus remarks that Tibe-

rius was an emperor "who feared freedom while he
hated sycophancy" or that the name of Lucius Volusius
was made glorious by his ninety-three years, his honorable wealth, and his "wide avoidance of the malignity of
so many emperors" or that "perhaps a sense of weariness
steals over princes when they have bestowed everything,
or over favorites when there is nothing left to them to
desire," we catch a glimpse of the force of the original
because the thought itself is so inherently dramatic.
Sometimes we wonder, no doubt foolishly, if we really
need the original, so striking is the effect in translation,
as when Sabinus is being led to his death through the
streets and the people flee from his glance, fearing that
it will implicate them: "Wherever he turned, wherever
his eyes fell, there was flight and solitude"; or when the
soldiers undertake to "absolve" themselves of a mutiny
by the ferocity with which they slaughter their leaders;
or when, in that greatest of street scenes, the debauchees
look out of their brothel doors to observe with casual
interest the armies fighting for the possession of Rome.

Tacitus is not a tragic writer as, in some strict use of
the word, Thucydides is often said to be. It has been
conjectured of Thucydides that he conceived his *Pelo-
ponnesian War* on the model of actual tragic drama, Athens being his hero; and certainly the downfall of Athens,
which Thucydides himself witnessed, makes a fable with
the typical significance of tragedy. But Tacitus had no
such matter for his histories. The republic had died before his grandfather was born and he looked back at it
through a haze of idealization—the tragedy had ended
long ago; what he observed was the aftermath which
had no end, which exactly lacked the coherence of tragedy. His subject is not Rome at all, not Rome the political entity, but rather the grotesque career of the
human spirit in a society which, if we may summarize
the whole tendency of his thought, appeared to him to
endure for no other purpose than to maintain the long
and lively existence of anarchy. From this it is easy, and
all too easy, to discover his relevance to us now, but the

relevance does not account for the strange invigoration of his pages, which is rather to be explained by his power of mind and his stubborn love of virtue maintained in desperate circumstances.

Manners, Morals, and
the Novel

The invitation that was made to me to address you this evening[1] was couched in somewhat uncertain terms. Time, place, and cordiality were perfectly clear, but when it came to the subject our hosts were not able to specify just what they wanted me to talk about. They wanted me to consider literature in its relation to manners—by which, as they relied on me to understand, they did not really mean *manners*. They did not mean, that is, the rules of personal intercourse in our culture; and yet such rules were by no means irrelevant to what they did mean. Nor did they quite mean manners in the sense of *mores*, customs, although, again, these did bear upon the subject they had in mind.

I understood them perfectly, as I would not have understood them had they been more definite. For they were talking about a nearly indefinable subject.

Somewhere below all the explicit statements that a people makes through its art, religion, architecture, legislation, there is a dim mental region of intention of which it is very difficult to become aware. We now and then get a strong sense of its existence when we deal with the past, not by reason of its presence in the past but by reason of its absence. As we read the great formulated monuments of the past, we notice that we are

[1] This essay was read at the Conference on the Heritage of the English-speaking Peoples and Their Responsibilities, at Kenyon College, September 1947.

reading them without the accompaniment of something that always goes along with the formulated monuments of the present. The voice of multifarious intention and activity is stilled, all the buzz of implication which always surrounds us in the present, coming to us from what never gets fully stated, coming in the tone of greetings and the tone of quarrels, in slang and humor and popular songs, in the way children play, in the gesture the waiter makes when he puts down the plate, in the nature of the very food we prefer.

Some of the charm of the past consists of the quiet—the great distracting buzz of implication has stopped and we are left only with what has been fully phrased and precisely stated. And part of the melancholy of the past comes from our knowledge that the huge, unrecorded hum of implication was once there and left no trace—we feel that because it is evanescent it is especially human. We feel, too, that the truth of the great preserved monuments of the past does not fully appear without it. From letters and diaries, from the remote, unconscious corners of the great works themselves, we try to guess what the sound of the multifarious implication was and what it meant.

Or when we read the conclusions that are drawn about our own culture by some gifted foreign critic—or by some stupid native one—who is equipped only with a knowledge of our books, when we try in vain to say what is wrong, when in despair we say that he has read the books "out of context," then we are aware of the matter I have been asked to speak about tonight.

What I understand by manners, then, is a culture's hum and buzz of implication. I mean the whole evanescent context in which its explicit statements are made. It is that part of a culture which is made up of half-uttered or unuttered or unutterable expressions of value. They are hinted at by small actions, sometimes by the arts of dress or decoration, sometimes by tone, gesture, emphasis, or rhythm, sometimes by the words that are used with a special frequency or a special meaning. They are the things that for good or bad draw the peo-

ple of a culture together and that separate them from
the people of another culture. They make the part of a
culture which is not art, or religion, or morals, or politics,
and yet it relates to all these highly formulated depart-
ments of culture. It is modified by them; it modifies
them; it is generated by them; it generates them. In this
part of culture assumption rules, which is often so much
stronger than reason.

The right way to begin to deal with such a subject is
to gather together as much of its detail as we possibly
can. Only by doing so will we become fully aware of
what the gifted foreign critic or the stupid native one is
not aware of, that in any complex culture there is not a
single system of manners but a conflicting variety of
manners, and that one of the jobs of a culture is the
adjustment of this conflict.

But the nature of our present occasion does not permit
this accumulation of detail and so I shall instead try to
drive toward a generalization and in hypothesis which,
however wrong they turn out to be, may at least permit
us to circumscribe the subject. I shall try to generalize
the subject of American manners by talking about the
attitude of Americans toward the subject of manners itself. And since in a complex culture there are, as I say,
many different systems of manners and since I cannot
talk about them all, I shall select the manners and the
attitude toward manners of the literate, reading, responsible middle class of people who are ourselves. I specify
that they be reading people because I shall draw my
conclusions from the novels they read. The hypothesis
I propose is that our attitude toward manners is the expression of a particular conception of reality.

All literature tends to be concerned with the question
of reality—I mean quite simply the old opposition between reality and appearance, between what really is
and what merely seems. "Don't you *see*?" is the question
we want to shout at Oedipus as he stands before us and
before fate in the pride of his rationalism. And at the
end of *Oedipus Rex* he demonstrates in a particularly
direct way that he now sees what he did not see before.

"Don't you *see?*" we want to shout again at Lear and Gloucester, the two deceived, self-deceiving fathers: blindness again, resistance to the clear claims of reality, the seduction by mere appearance. The same with Othello—reality is right under your stupid nose, how *dare* you be such a gull? So with Molière's Orgon—my good man, my honest citizen, merely *look* at Tartuffe and you will know what's what. So with Milton's Eve—"Woman, watch out! Don't you see—anyone can see—that's a *snake!*"

The problem of reality is central, and in a special way, to the great forefather of the novel, the great book of Cervantes, whose four-hundredth birthday was celebrated in 1947. There are two movements of thought in *Don Quixote,* two different and opposed notions of reality. One is the movement which leads toward saying that the world of ordinary practicality *is* reality in its fullness. It is the reality of the present moment in all its powerful immediacy of hunger, cold, and pain, making the past and the future, and all ideas, of no account. When the conceptual, the ideal, and the fanciful come into conflict with this, bringing their notions of the past and the future, then disaster results. For one thing, the ordinary proper ways of life are upset—the chained prisoners are understood to be good men and are released, the whore is taken for a lady. There is general confusion. As for the ideal, the conceptual, the fanciful, or romantic—whatever you want to call it—it fares even worse: it is shown to be ridiculous.

Thus one movement of the novel. But Cervantes changed horses in midstream and found that he was riding Rosinante. Perhaps at first not quite consciously—although the new view is latent in the old from the very beginning—Cervantes begins to show that the world of tangible reality is not the real reality after all. The real reality is rather the wildly conceiving, the madly fantasying mind of the Don: people change, practical reality changes, when they come into its presence.

In any genre it may happen that the first great example contains the whole potentiality of the genre. It has been said that all philosophy is a footnote to Plato. It can be said that all prose fiction is a variation on the theme of *Don Quixote*. Cervantes sets for the novel the problem of appearance and reality: the shifting and conflict of social classes becomes the field of the problem of knowledge, of how we know and of how reliable our knowledge is, which at that very moment of history is vexing the philosophers and scientists. And the poverty of the Don suggests that the novel is born with the appearance of money as a social element—money, the great solvent of the solid fabric of the old society, the great generator of illusion. Or, which is to say much the same thing, the novel is born in response to snobbery.

Snobbery is not the same thing as pride of class. Pride of class may not please us but we must at least grant that it reflects a social function. A man who exhibited class pride—in the day when it was possible to do so—may have been puffed up about what he *was*, but this ultimately depended on what he *did*. Thus, aristocratic pride was based ultimately on the ability to fight and administer. No pride is without fault, but pride of class may be thought of as today we think of pride of profession, toward which we are likely to be lenient.

Snobbery is pride in status without pride in function. And it is an uneasy pride of status. It always asks, "Do I belong—do I really belong? And does he belong? And if I am observed talking to him, will it make me seem to belong or not to belong?" It is the peculiar vice not of aristocratic societies which have their own appropriate vices, but of bourgeois democratic societies. For us the legendary strongholds of snobbery are the Hollywood studios, where two thousand dollars a week dare not talk to three hundred dollars a week for fear he be taken for nothing more than fifteen hundred dollars a week. The dominant emotions of snobbery are uneasiness, self-consciousness, self-defensiveness, the sense that one is not quite real but can in some way acquire reality.

Money is the medium that, for good or bad, makes for a fluent society. It does not make for an equal society but for one in which there is a constant shifting of classes, a frequent change in the personnel of the dominant class. In a shifting society great emphasis is put on appearance—I am using the word now in the common meaning, as when people say that "a good appearance is very important in getting a job." To appear to be established is one of the ways of becoming established. The old notion of the solid merchant who owns far more than he shows increasingly gives way to the ideal of signalizing status by appearance, by showing more than you have: status in a democratic society is presumed to come not with power but with the tokens of power. Hence the development of what Tocqueville saw as a mark of democratic culture, what he called the "hypocrisy of luxury"—instead of the well-made peasant article and the well-made middle-class article, we have the effort of all articles to appear as the articles of the very wealthy.

And a shifting society is bound to generate an interest in appearance in the philosophical sense. When Shakespeare lightly touched on the matter that so largely preoccupies the novelist—that is, the movement from one class to another—and created Malvolio, he immediately involved the question of social standing with the problem of appearance and reality. Malvolio's daydreams of bettering his position present themselves to him as reality, and in revenge his enemies conspire to convince him that he is literally mad and that the world is not as he sees it. The predicament of the characters in *A Midsummer Night's Dream* and of Christopher Sly seems to imply that the meeting of social extremes and the establishment of a person of low class in the privileges of a high class always suggested to Shakespeare's mind some radical instability of the senses and the reason.

The characteristic work of the novel is to record the illusion that snobbery generates and to try to penetrate to the truth which, as the novel assumes, lies hidden beneath all the false appearances. Money, snobbery, the ideal of status, these become in themselves the objects of fantasy, the support of the fantasies of love, freedom, charm, power, as in *Madame Bovary*, whose heroine is the sister, at a three-centuries' remove, of Don Quixote.

The greatness of *Great Expectations* begins in its title: modern society bases itself on great expectations which, if ever they are realized, are found to exist by reason of a sordid, hidden reality. The real thing is not the gentility of Pip's life but the hulks and the murder and the rats and decay in the cellarage of the novel.

An English writer, recognizing the novel's central concern with snobbery, recently cried out half-ironically against it. "Who cares whether Pamela finally exasperates Mr. B. into marriage, whether Mr. Elton is more or less than moderately genteel, whether it is sinful for Pendennis nearly to kiss the porter's daughter, whether young men from Boston can ever be as truly refined as middle-aged women in Paris, whether the District Officer's fiancée ought to see so much of Dr. Aziz, whether Lady Chatterley ought to be made love to by the gamekeeper, even if he was an officer during the war? Who cares?"

The novel, of course, tells us much more about life than this. It tells us about the look and feel of things, how things are done and what things are worth and what they cost and what the odds are. If the English novel in its special concern with class does not, as the same writer says, explore the deeper layers of personality, then the French novel in exploring these layers must start and end in class, and the Russian novel, exploring the ultimate possibilities of spirit, does the same—every situation in Dostoevski, no matter how spiritual, starts with a point of social pride and a certain number of rubles. The great novelists knew that manners indicate the largest intentions of men's souls as well as the smallest and they are perpetually concerned to catch the meaning of every dim implicit hint.

The novel, then, is a perpetual quest for reality, the field of its research being always the social world, the material of its analysis being always manners as the indication of the direction of man's soul. When we understand this we can understand the pride of profession that moved D. H. Lawrence to say, "Being a novelist, I consider myself superior to the saint, the scientist, the philosopher and the poet. The novel is the one bright book of life."

Now the novel as I have described it has never really established itself in America. Not that we have not had very great novels but that the novel in America diverges from its classic intention, which, as I have said, is the investigation of the problem of reality beginning in the social field. The fact is that American writers of genius have not turned their minds to society. Poe and Melville were quite apart from it; the reality they sought was only tangential to society. Hawthorne was acute when he insisted that he did not write novels but romances—he thus expressed his awareness of the lack of social texture in his work. Howells never fulfilled himself because, although he saw the social subject clearly, he would never take it with full seriousness. In America in the nineteenth century, Henry James was alone in knowing that to scale the moral and aesthetic heights in the novel one had to use the ladder of social observation.

There is a famous passage in James's life of Hawthorne in which James enumerates the things which are lacking to give the American novel the thick social texture of the English novel—no state; barely a specific national name; no sovereign; no court; no aristocracy; no church; no clergy; no army; no diplomatic service; no country gentlemen; no palaces; no castles; no manors; no old country houses; no parsonages; no thatched cottages; no ivied ruins; no cathedrals; no great universities; no public schools; no political society; no sporting class—no Epsom, no Ascot! That is, no sufficiency of means for the display of a variety of manners, no opportunity for the novelist to do his job of searching out reality, not enough complication of appearance to make the job interesting. Another great American novelist of very different temperament had said much the same thing some decades before: James Fenimore Cooper found that American manners were too simple and dull to nourish the novelist.

This is cogent but it does not explain the condition of the American novel at the present moment. For life in

America has increasingly thickened since the nineteenth century. It has not, to be sure, thickened so much as to permit our undergraduates to understand the characters of Balzac, to understand, that is, life in a crowded country where the competitive pressures are great, forcing intense passions to express themselves fiercely and yet within the limitations set by a strong and complicated tradition of manners. Still, life here has become more complex and more pressing. And even so we do not have the novel that touches significantly on society, on manners. Whatever the virtues of Dreiser may be, he could not report the social fact with the kind of accuracy it needs. Sinclair Lewis is shrewd, but no one, however charmed with him as a social satirist, can believe that he does more than a limited job of social understanding. John Dos Passos sees much, sees it often in the great way of Flaubert, but can never use social fact as more than either backdrop or "condition." Of our novelists today perhaps only William Faulkner deals with society as the field of tragic reality and he has the disadvantage of being limited to a provincial scene.

It would seem that Americans have a kind of resistance to looking closely at society. They appear to believe that to touch accurately on the matter of class, to take full note of snobbery, is somehow to demean themselves. It is as if we felt that one cannot touch pitch without being defiled—which, of course, may possibly be the case. Americans will not deny that we have classes and snobbery, but they seem to hold it to be indelicate to take precise cognizance of these phenomena. Consider that Henry James is, among a large part of our reading public, still held to be at fault for noticing society as much as he did. Consider the conversation that has, for some interesting reason, become a part of our literary folklore. Scott Fitzgerald said to Ernest Hemingway, "The very rich are different from us." Hemingway replied, "Yes, they have more money." I have seen the exchange quoted many times and always with the intention of suggesting that Fitzgerald was infatuated by wealth and had received a salutary rebuke from his democratic friend. But the truth is that after a certain point quantity of money does indeed change into quality of personality: in an important sense the very rich *are* different from us. So are the very powerful, the very gifted, the very poor. Fitzgerald was right, and almost for that remark alone he must surely have been received in Balzac's bosom in the heaven of novelists.

It is of course by no means true that the American reading class has no interest in society. Its interest fails only before society as it used to be represented by the novel. And if we look at the commercially successful serious novels of the last decade, we see that almost all of them have been written from an intense social awareness —it might be said that our present definition of a serious book is one which holds before us some image of society to consider and condemn. What is the situation of the dispossessed Oklahoma farmer and whose fault it is, what situation the Jew finds himself in, what it means to be a Negro, how one gets a bell for Adano, what is the advertising business really like, what it means to be insane and how society takes care of you or fails to do so— these are the matters which are believed to be most fertile for the novelist, and certainly they are the subjects most favored by our reading class.

The public is probably not deceived about the quality of most of these books. If the question of quality is brought up, the answer is likely to be: no, they are not great, they are not imaginative, they are not "literature." But there is an unexpressed addendum: and perhaps they are all the better for not being imaginative, for not being literature—they are not literature, they are reality, and *in a time like this* what we need is reality in large doses.

When, generations from now, the historian of our times undertakes to describe the assumptions of our culture, he will surely discover that the word *reality* is of central importance in his understanding of us. He will observe that for some of our philosophers the meaning of the word was a good deal in doubt, but that for our political writers, for many of our literary critics, and for most of our reading public, the word did not open discussion but, rather, closed it. Reality, as conceived by us, is whatever is external and hard, gross, unpleasant. Involved in its meaning is the idea of power conceived in a particular way. Some time ago I had occasion to remark how, in the critical estimates of Theodore Dreiser, it is always being said that Dreiser has many faults but that it cannot be denied that he has great power. No one ever says "a kind of power." Power is assumed to be always "brute" power, crude, ugly, and undiscriminating, the way an elephant appears to be. It is seldom understood to be the way an elephant actually is, precise and discriminating; or the way electricity is, swift and absolute and scarcely embodied.

The word *reality* is a honorific word and the future historian will naturally try to discover our notion of its pejorative opposite, appearance, mere appearance. He will find it in our feeling about the internal; whenever we detect evidences of style and thought we suspect that reality is being a little betrayed, that "mere subjectivity" is creeping in. There follows from this our feeling about complication, modulation, personal idiosyncrasy, and about social forms, both the great and the small.

Having gone so far, our historian is then likely to discover a puzzling contradiction. For we claim that the great advantage of reality is its hard, bedrock, concrete quality, yet everything we say about it tends toward the abstract and it almost seems that what we want to find in reality is abstraction itself. Thus we believe that one of the unpleasant bedrock facts is social class, but we become extremely impatient if ever we are told that social class is indeed so real that it produces actual difference of personality. The very people who talk most about class and its evils think that Fitzgerald was bedazzled and Hemingway right. Or again, it might be observed that in the degree that we speak in praise of the "individual" we have contrived that our literature should have no individuals in it—no people, that is, who are shaped by our liking for the interesting and memorable and special and precious.

Here, then, is our generalization: that in proportion as we have committed ourselves to our particular idea of reality we have lost our interest in manners. For the novel this is a definitive condition because it is inescapably true that in the novel manners make men. It does not matter in what sense the word manners is taken—it is equally true of the sense which so much interested Proust or of the sense which interested Dickens or, indeed, of the sense which interested Homer. The Duchesse de Guermantes unable to delay departure for the dinner party to receive properly from her friend Swann the news that he is dying but able to delay to change the black slippers her husband objects to; Mr. Pickwick and Sam Weller; Priam and Achilles—they exist by reason of their observed manners.

So true is this, indeed, so creative is the novelist's awareness of manners, that we may say that it is a function of his love. It is some sort of love that Fielding has for Squire Western that allows him to note the great, gross details which bring the insensitive sentient man into existence for us. If that is true, we are forced to certain conclusions about our literature and about the particular definition of reality which has shaped it. The reality we admire tells us that the observation of manners is trivial and even malicious, that there are things much more important for the novel to consider. As a consequence our social sympathies have indeed broadened, but in proportion as they have done so we have lost something of our power of love, for our novels can never create characters who truly exist. We make public demands for love, for we know that broad social feeling should be infused with warmth, and we receive a kind of public product which we try to believe is not cold potatoes. The reviewers of Helen Howe's novel of a few years ago, *We Happy Few,* thought that its satiric first part, an excellent comment on the manners of a small but significant segment of society, was ill-natured and unsatisfactory, but they approved the second part, which is the record of the heroine's self-accusing effort to come into communication with the great soul of America. Yet it should have been clear that the satire had its source in a kind of affection, in a real community of feeling, and told the truth, while the second part, said to be so "warm," was mere abstraction, one more example of our public idea of ourselves and our national life. John Steinbeck is generally praised both for his reality and his warmheartedness, but in *The Wayward Bus* the lower-class characters receive a doctrinaire affection in proportion to the suffering and sexuality which define their existence, while the ill-observed middle-class characters are made to submit not only to moral judgment but to the withdrawal of all fellow-feeling, being mocked for their very misfortunes and almost for their susceptibility to death. Only a little thought or even less feeling is required to perceive that the basis of his creation is the coldest response to abstract ideas.

Two novelists of the older sort had a prevision of our present situation. In Henry James's *The Princess Casamassima* there is a scene in which the heroine is told about the existence of a conspiratorial group of revolutionaries pledged to the destruction of all existing society. She has for some time been drawn by a desire for social responsibility; she has wanted to help "the people," she has longed to discover just such a group as she now hears about, and she exclaims in joy, "Then it's real, it's solid!" We are intended to hear the Princess's glad cry with the knowledge that she is a woman who despises herself, "that in the darkest hour of her life she sold herself for a title and a fortune. She regards her doing so as such a terrible piece of frivolity that she can never for the rest of her days be serious enough to make up for it." She seeks out poverty, suffering, sacrifice, and death because she believes that these things alone are real; she comes to believe that art is contemptible; she withdraws her awareness and love from the one person of her acquaintance who most deserves them, and she increasingly scorns whatever suggests variety and modulation, and is more and more dissatisfied with the humanity of the present in her longing for the more perfect humanity of the future. It is one of the great points that the novel makes that with each passionate step that she takes toward what she calls the real, the solid, she in fact moves further away from the life-giving reality.

In E. M. Forster's *The Longest Journey* there is a young man named Stephen Wonham who, although a gentleman born, has been carelessly brought up and has no real notion of the responsibilities of his class. He has a friend, a country laborer, a shepherd, and on two occasions he outrages the feelings of certain intelligent, liberal, democratic people in the book by his treatment of this friend. Once, when the shepherd reneges on a bargain, Stephen quarrels with him and knocks him down; and in the matter of the loan of a few shillings he insists that the money be paid back to the last farthing. The intelligent, liberal, democratic people know that this is not the way to act to the poor. But Stephen cannot think of the shepherd as the poor nor, although he is a country laborer, as an object of research by J. L. and Barbara Hammond; he is rather a reciprocating subject in a relationship of affection—as we say, a friend—and therefore liable to anger and required to pay his debts. But this view is held to be deficient in intelligence, liberalism, and democracy.

In these two incidents we have the premonition of our present cultural and social situation, the passionate self-reproachful addiction to a "strong" reality which must limit its purview to maintain its strength, the replacement by abstraction of natural, direct human feeling. It is worth noting, by the way, how clear is the line by which the two novels descend from *Don Quixote*—how their young heroes come into life with large preconceived ideas and are knocked about in consequence; how both are concerned with the problem of appearance and reality, *The Longest Journey* quite explicitly, *The Princess Casamassima* by indirection; how both evoke the question of the nature of reality by contriving a meeting and conflict of diverse social classes and take scrupulous note of the differences of manners. Both have as their leading characters people who are specifically and passionately concerned with social injustice and both agree in saying that to act against social injustice is right and noble but that to choose to act so does not settle all moral problems but on the contrary generates new ones of an especially difficult sort.

I have elsewhere given the name of moral realism to the perception of the dangers of the moral life itself. Perhaps at no other time has the enterprise of moral realism ever been so much needed, for at no other time have so many people committed themselves to moral righteousness. We have the books that point out the bad conditions, that praise us for taking progressive attitudes. We have no books that raise questions in our minds not only about conditions but about ourselves, that lead us to refine our motives and ask what might lie behind our good impulses.

There is nothing so very terrible in discovering that something does lie behind. Nor does it need a Freud to make the discovery. Here is a publicity release sent out by one of our oldest and most respectable publishing houses. Under the heading "What Makes Books Sell?" it reads, "Blank & Company reports that the current interest in horror stories has attracted a great number of readers to John Dash's novel . . . because of its depiction of Nazi brutality. Critics and readers alike have commented on the stark realism of Dash's handling of the torture scenes in the book. The publishers originally envisaged a woman's market because of the love story, now find men reading the book because of the other angle." This does not suggest a more than usual depravity in the male reader, for "the other angle" has always had a fascination, no doubt a bad one, even for those who would not themselves commit or actually witness an act of torture. I cite the extreme example only to suggest that something may indeed lie behind our sober intelligent interest in moral politics. In this instance the pleasure in the cruelty is protected and licensed by moral indignation. In other instances moral indignation, which has been said to be the favorite emotion of the middle class, may be in itself an exquisite pleasure. To understand this does not invalidate moral indignation but only sets up the conditions on which it ought to be entertained, only says when it is legitimate and when not.

But, the answer comes, however important it may be for moral realism to raise questions in our minds about our motives, is it not at best a matter of secondary importance? Is it not of the first importance that we be given a direct and immediate report on the reality that is daily being brought to dreadful birth? The novels that have done this have effected much practical good, bringing to consciousness the latent feelings of many people, making it harder for them to be unaware or indifferent, creating an atmosphere in which injustice finds it harder to thrive. To speak of moral realism is all very well. But it is an elaborate, even fancy, phrase and it is to be suspected of having the intention of sophisticating the simple reality that is easily to be conceived. Life presses us so hard, time is so short, the suffering of the world is so huge, simple, unendurable—anything that complicates our moral fervor in dealing with reality as we immediately see it and wish to drive headlong upon it must be regarded with some impatience.

True enough: and therefore any defense of what I have called moral realism must be made not in the name of some highflown fineness of feeling but in the name of simple social practicality. And there is indeed a simple social fact to which moral realism has a simple practical relevance, but it is a fact very difficult for us nowadays to perceive. It is that the moral passions are even more willful and imperious and impatient than the self-seeking passions. All history is at one in telling us that their tendency is to be not only liberating but also restrictive.

It is probable that at this time we are about to make great changes in our social system. The world is ripe for such changes and if they are not made in the direction of greater social liberality, the direction forward, they will almost of necessity be made in the direction backward, of a terrible social niggardliness. We all know which of those directions we want. But it is not enough to want it, not even enough to work for it—we must want it and work for it with intelligence. Which means that we must be aware of the dangers which lie in our most generous wishes. Some paradox of our natures leads us, when once we have made our fellow men the objects of our enlightened interest, to go on to make them the objects of our pity, then of our wisdom, ultimately of our coercion. It is to prevent this corruption, the most ironic and tragic that man knows, that we stand in need of the moral realism which is the product of the free play of the moral imagination.

For our time the most effective agent of the moral imagination has been the novel of the last two hundred years. It was never, either aesthetically or morally, a perfect form and its faults and failures can be quickly enumerated. But its greatness and its practical usefulness lay in its unremitting work of involving the reader himself in the moral life, inviting him to put his own motives under examination, suggesting that reality is not as his conventional education has led him to see it. It taught us, as no other genre ever did, the extent of human variety and the value of this variety. It was the literary form to which the emotions of understanding and forgiveness were indigenous, as if by the definition of the form itself. At the moment its impulse does not seem strong, for there never was a time when the virtues of its greatness were so likely to be thought of as weaknesses. Yet there never was a time when its particular activity was so much needed, was of so much practical, political, and social use—so much so that if its impulse does not respond to the need, we shall have reason to be sad not only over a waning form of art but also over our waning freedom.

The Kinsey Report

By virtue of its intrinsic nature and also because of its dramatic reception, the Kinsey Report,[1] as it has come to be called, is an event of great importance in our culture. It is an event which is significant in two separate ways, as symptom and as therapy. The therapy lies in the large permissive effect the Report is likely to have, the long way it goes toward establishing the *community* of sexuality. The symptomatic significance lies in the fact that the Report was felt to be needed at all, that the community of sexuality requires now to be established in explicit quantitative terms. Nothing shows more clearly the extent to which modern society has atomized itself than the isolation in sexual ignorance which exists among us. We have censored the folk knowledge of the most primal things and have systematically dried up the social affections which might naturally seek to enlighten and release. Many cultures, the most primitive and the most complex, have entertained sexual fears of an irrational sort, but probably our culture is unique in strictly isolating the individual in the fears that society has devised. Now, having become somewhat aware of what we have perpetrated at great cost and with little gain, we must assure ourselves by statistical science that the solitude is imaginary. The Report will surprise one part of the population with some facts and another part with other facts, but really all that it says to society as a

[1] *Sexual Behavior in the Human Male*, by Alfred C. Kinsey, Wardell B. Pomeroy, and Clyde E. Martin. Philadelphia: Saunders, 1948.

whole is that there is an almost universal involvement in the sexual life and therefore much variety of conduct. This was taken for granted in any comedy that Aristophanes put on the stage.

There is a further diagnostic significance to be found in the fact that our society makes this effort of self-enlightenment through the agency of science. Sexual conduct is inextricably involved with morality, and hitherto it has been dealt with by those representatives of our cultural imagination which are, by their nature and tradition, committed to morality—it has been dealt with by religion, social philosophy, and literature. But now science seems to be the only one of our institutions which has the authority to speak decisively on the matter. Nothing in the Report is more suggestive in a large cultural way than the insistent claims it makes for its strictly scientific nature, its pledge of indifference to all questions of morality at the same time that it patently intends a moral effect. Nor will any science do for the job—it must be a science as simple and materialistic as the subject can possibly permit. It must be a science of statistics and not of ideas. The way for the Report was prepared by Freud, but Freud, in all the years of his activity, never had the currency or authority with the public that the Report has achieved in a matter of weeks.

The scientific nature of the Report must be taken in conjunction with the manner of its publication. The Report says of itself that it is only a "preliminary survey," a work intended to be the first step in a larger research; that it is nothing more than an "accumulation of scientific fact," a collection of "objective data," a "report on what people do, which raises no question of what they should do," and it is fitted out with a full complement of charts, tables, and discussions of scientific method. A work conceived and executed in this way is usually presented only to an audience of professional scientists; and the publishers of the Report, a medical house, pay their ritual respects to the old tradition which held that not all medical or quasi-medical knowledge was to be made easily available to the general lay reader, or at least not until it had been subjected to professional debate; they tell us in a foreword for what limited professional audience the book was primarily intended—physicians, biologists, and social scientists and "teachers, social workers, personnel officers, law enforcement groups, and others concerned with the direction of human behavior." And yet the book has been so successfully publicized that for many weeks it was a national best seller.

This way of bringing out a technical work of science is a cultural phenomenon that ought not to pass without some question. The public which receives this technical report, this merely preliminary survey, this accumulation of data, has never, even on its upper educational levels, been properly instructed in the most elementary principles of scientific thought. With this public, science is authority. It has been trained to accept heedlessly "what science says," which it conceives to be a unitary utterance. To this public nothing is more valuable, more precisely "scientific," and more finally convincing than raw data without conclusions; no disclaimer of conclusiveness can mean anything to it—it has learned that the disclaimer is simply the hallmark of the scientific attitude, science's way of saying "thy unworthy servant."

So that if the Report were really, as it claims to be, only an accumulation of objective data, there would be some question of the cultural wisdom of dropping it in a lump on the general public. But in point of fact it is full of assumption and conclusion; it makes very positive statements on highly debatable matters and it editorializes very freely. This preliminary survey gives some very conclusive suggestions to a public that is quick to obey what science says, no matter how contradictory science may be, which is most contradictory indeed. This is the public that, on scientific advice, ate spinach in one generation and avoided it in the next, that in one decade trained its babies to rigid Watsonian schedules and believed that affection corrupted the infant character, only to learn in the next decade that rigid discipline was harmful and that cuddling was as scientific as induction. Then there is the question of whether the Report does not do harm by encouraging people in their commitment to mechanical attitudes toward life. The tendency to divorce sex from the other manifestations of life is already a strong one. This truly absorbing study of sex in charts and tables, in data and quantities, may have the effect of strengthening the tendency still more with people who are by no means trained to invert the process of abstraction and to put the fact back into the general life from which it has been taken. And the likely mechanical implications of a statistical study are in this case supported by certain fully formulated attitudes which the authors strongly hold despite their protestations that they are scientific to the point of holding no attitudes whatever.

These, I believe, are valid objections to the book's indiscriminate circulation. And yet I also believe that there is something good about the manner of publication, something honest and right. Every complex society has its agencies which are "concerned with the direction of human behavior," but we today are developing a new element in that old activity, the element of scientific knowledge. Whatever the Report claims for itself, the social sciences in general no longer pretend that they can merely describe what people do; they now have the clear consciousness of their power to manipulate and adjust. First for industry and then for government, sociology has shown its instrumental nature. A government which makes use of social knowledge still suggests benignity; and in an age that daily brings the proliferation of government by police methods it may suggest the very spirit of rational liberalism. Yet at least one sociologist has expressed the fear that sociology may become the instrument of a bland tyranny—it is the same fear that Dostoevski gave immortal expression to in "The Grand Inquisitor." And indeed there is something repulsive in the idea of men being studied for their own good. The paradigm of what repels us is to be found in the common situation of the child who is *understood* by its parents, hemmed in, anticipated and lovingly circumscribed, thoroughly taped, finding it easier and easier to conform internally and in the future to the parents' own interpretation of the external acts of the past, and so, yielding to understanding as never to coercion, does not develop the mystery and wildness of spirit which it is still our grace to believe is the mark of full humanness. The act of understanding becomes an act of control.

If, then, we are to live under the aspect of sociology, let us at least all be sociologists together—let us broadcast what every sociologist knows, and let us all have a share in observing one another, including the sociologists. The general indiscriminate publication of the Report makes sociology a little less the study of many men by a few men and a little more man's study of himself. There is something right in turning loose the Report on the American public—it turns the American public loose on the Report. It is right that the Report should be sold in stores that never before sold books and bought by people who never before bought books, and passed from hand to hand and talked about and also snickered at and giggled over and generally submitted to humor: American popular culture has surely been made the richer by the Report's gift of a new folk hero—he already is clearly the hero of the Report—the "scholarly and skilled lawyer" who for thirty years has had an orgasmic frequency of thirty times a week.

As for the objection to the involvement of sex with science, it may be said that if science, through the Report, serves in any way to free the physical and even the "mechanical" aspects of sex, it may by that much have acted to free the emotions it might seem to deny. And perhaps only science could effectively undertake the task of freeing sexuality from science itself. Nothing so much as science has reinforced the moralistic or religious prohibitions in regard to sexuality. At some point in the history of Europe, some time in the Reformation, masturbation ceased to be thought of as merely a sexual sin which could be dealt with like any other sexual sin, and, perhaps by analogy with the venereal diseases with which the sexual mind of Europe was obsessed, came to be thought of as the specific cause of mental and physical disease, of madness and decay.[2] The prudery of Victorian England went forward with scientific hygiene; and both in Europe and in America the sexual mind was haunted by the idea of *degeneration*, apparently by analogy with the second law of thermodynamics—here is enlightened liberal opinion in 1896: "The effects of venereal disease have been treated at length, but the amount of vitality burned out through lust has never been and, perhaps, never can be adequately measured." [3] The very word *sex*, which we now utter so casually, came into use for scientific reasons, to replace *love*, which had once been indiscriminately used but was now to be saved for ideal purposes, and *lust*, which came to seem both too pejorative and too human: *sex* implied scientific neutrality, then vague devaluation, for the word which neutralizes the mind of the observer also neuterizes the men and women who are being observed. Perhaps the Report is the superfetation of neutrality and objectivity which, in the dialectic of culture, was needed before sex could be free of their cold dominion.

Certainly it is a great merit of the Report that it brings to mind the earliest and best commerce between sex and science—the best thing about the Report is the quality that makes us remember Lucretius. The dialectic of culture has its jokes, and *alma Venus* having once been called to preside protectively over science, the situation is now reversed. The Venus of the Report does not, like the Venus of *De Rerum Natura*, shine in the light of the heavenly signs, nor does the earth put forth flowers for her. She is rather fusty and hole-in-the-corner and no doubt it does not help her charm to speak of her in terms of mean frequencies of 3.2. No *putti* attend her: although Dr. Gregg in his Preface refers to sex as the reproductive instinct, there is scarcely any further indication in the book that sex has any connection with propagation. Yet clearly all things still follow where she leads,

[2] See Abram Kardiner, *The Psychological Frontiers of Society*, p. 32 and the footnote on p. 441.
[3] Article "Degeneration" in *The Encyclopedia of Social Reform*.

and somewhere in the authors' assumptions is buried the genial belief that still without her "nothing comes forth into the shining borders of light, nothing joyous and lovely is made." Her pandemic quality is still here—it is one of the great points of the Report how much of every kind of desire there is, how early it begins, how late it lasts. Her well-known jealousy is not abated, and prodigality is still her characteristic virtue: the Report assures us that those who respond to her earliest continue to do so longest. The Lucretian flocks and herds are here too. Professor Kinsey is a zoologist and he properly keeps us always in mind of our animal kinship, even though he draws some very illogical conclusions from it; and those who are honest will have to admit that their old repulsion by the idea of human-animal contacts is somewhat abated by the chapter on this subject, which is, oddly, the only chapter in the book which hints that sex may be touched with tenderness. This large, recognizing, Lucretian sweep of the Report is the best thing about it and it makes up for much that is deficient and confused in its ideas.

But the Report is something more than a public and symbolic act of cultural revision in which, while the Heavenly Twins brood benignly over the scene in the form of the National Research Council and the Rockefeller Foundation, Professor Kinsey and his coadjutors drag forth into the light all the hidden actualities of sex so that they may lose their dark power and become domesticated among us. It is also an early example of science undertaking to deal head-on with a uniquely difficult matter that has traditionally been involved in valuation and morality. We must ask the question very seriously: how does science conduct itself in such an enterprise?

Certainly it does not conduct itself the way it says it does. I have already suggested that the Report overrates its own objectivity. The authors, who are enthusiastically committed to their method and to their principles, make the mistake of believing that, being scientists, they do not deal in assumptions, preferences, and conclusions.

Nothing comes more easily to their pens than the criticism of the subjectivity of earlier writers on sex, yet their own subjectivity is sometimes extreme. In the nature of the enterprise, a degree of subjectivity was inevitable. Intellectual safety would then seem to lie not only in increasing the number of mechanical checks or in more rigorously examining those assumptions which had been brought to conscious formulation, but also in straightforwardly admitting that subjectivity was bound to appear and inviting the reader to be on the watch for it. This would not have guaranteed an absolute objectivity, but it would have made for a higher degree of relative objectivity. It would have done a thing even more important—it would have taught the readers of the Report something about the scientific processes to which they submit their thought.

The first failure of objectivity occurs in the title of the Report, *Sexual Behavior in the Human Male*. That the behavior which is studied is not that of the human male but only that of certain North American males has no doubt been generally observed and does not need further comment.[4] But the intention of the word *behavior* requires notice. By *behavior* the Report means behavioristic behavior, only that behavior which is physical. "To a large degree the present study has been confined to securing a record of the individual's overt sexual experiences." This limitation is perhaps forced on the authors by considerations of method, because it will yield simpler data and more manageable statistics, but it is also a limitation which suits their notion of human nature and its effect is to be seen throughout the book.

The Report, then, is a study of sexual behavior in so far as it can be quantitatively measured. This is certainly very useful. But, as we might fear, the sexuality that is measured is taken to be the definition of sexuality itself. The authors are certainly not without interest in what

---

[4] The statistical method of the report lies, necessarily, outside my purview. Nor am I able to assess with any confidence the validity of the interviewing methods that were employed.

they call attitudes, but they believe that attitudes are best shown by "overt sexual experiences." We want to know, of course, what they mean by an experience and we want to know by what principles of evidence they draw their conclusions about attitudes.

We are led to see that their whole conception of a sexual experience is totally comprised by the physical act and that their principles of evidence are entirely quantitative and cannot carry them beyond the conclusion that the more the merrier. Quality is not integral to what they mean by experience. As I have suggested, the Report is partisan with sex, it wants people to have a good sexuality. But by good it means nothing else but frequent. "It seems safe to assume that daily orgasm would be within the capacity of the average male and that the more than daily rates which have been observed for some primate species could be matched by a large portion of the human population if sexual activity were unrestricted." The Report never suggests that a sexual experience is anything but the discharge of specifically sexual tension and therefore seems to conclude that frequency is always the sign of a robust sexuality. Yet masturbation in children may be and often is the expression not of sexuality only but of anxiety. In the same way, adult intercourse may be the expression of anxiety; its frequency may not be so much robust as compulsive.

The Report is by no means unaware of the psychic conditions of sexuality, yet it uses the concept almost always under the influence of its quantitative assumption. In a summary passage (p. 159) it describes the different intensities of orgasm and the various degrees of satisfaction, but disclaims any intention of taking these variations into account in its record of behavior. The Report holds out the hope to respectable males that they might be as frequent in performance as underworld characters if they were as unrestrained as this group. But before the respectable males aspire to this unwonted freedom they had better ascertain in how far the underworld characters are ridden by anxiety and in how far their sexuality is to be correlated with other ways of dealing with anxiety, such as dope, and in how far it is actually enjoyable. The Report's own data suggest that there may be no direct connection between on the one hand lack of restraint and frequency and on the other hand psychic health; they tell us of men in the lower social levels who in their sexual careers have intercourse with many hundreds of girls but who despise their sexual partners and cannot endure relations with the same girl more than once.

But the Report, as we shall see, is most resistant to the possibility of making any connection between the sexual life and the psychic structure. This strongly formulated attitude of the Report is based on the assumption that the whole actuality of sex is anatomical and physiological; the emotions are dealt with very much as if they were a "superstructure." "The subject's awareness of the erotic situation is summed up by this statement that he is 'emotionally' aroused; but the material sources of the emotional disturbance are rarely recognized, either by laymen or scientists, both of whom are inclined to think in terms of passion, or natural drive, or a libido, which partakes of the mystic[5] more than it does of solid anatomy and physiologic function." Now there is of course a clear instrumental advantage in being able to talk about psychic or emotional phenomena in terms of physiology, but to make a disjunction between the two descriptions of the same event, to make the anatomical and physiological description the "source" of the emotional and then to consider it as the more real of the

[5] We must observe how the scientific scorn of the "mystic" quite abates when the "mystic" suits the scientist's purpose. The Report is explaining why the interviews were not checked by means of narcosynthesis, lie-detectors, etc.: "In any such study which needs to secure quantities of data from human subjects, there is no way except to win their voluntary cooperation through the establishment of that intangible thing known as rapport." This intangible thing is established by looking the respondent squarely in the eye. It might be asked why a thing which is intangible but real enough to assure scientific accuracy should not be real enough to be considered as having an effect in sexual behavior.

two, is simply to commit not only the Reductive Fallacy but also what William James called the Psychologist's Fallacy. It must bring under suspicion any subsequent generalization which the Report makes about the nature of sexuality.[6]

The emphasis on the anatomical and physiological nature of sexuality is connected with the Report's strong reliance on animal behavior as a norm. The italics in the following quotation are mine. *"For those who like the term,* it is clear that there is a sexual drive which cannot be set aside for any large portion of the population, by any sort of social convention. *For those who prefer to think in simpler terms of action and reaction,* it is a picture of an animal who, however civilized or cultured, continues to respond to the constantly present sexual stimuli, albeit with some social and physical restraints." The Report obviously finds the second formulation to be superior to the first, and implies with a touch of irony that those who prefer it are on firmer ground.

Now there are several advantages in keeping in mind our own animal nature and our family connection with the other animals. The advantages are instrumental, moral, and poetic—I use the last word for want of a better to suggest the mere pleasure in finding kinship with some animals. But perhaps no idea is more difficult to use with precision than this one. In the Report it is

[6] The implications of the Reductive Fallacy may be seen by paraphrasing the sentence I have quoted in which Professor Kinsey commits it: "Professor Kinsey's awareness of the intellectual situation is summed up by his statement that he 'has had an idea' or 'has come to a conclusion'; but the material sources of his intellectual disturbances are rarely recognized, either by laymen or scientists, both of whom are inclined to think in terms of 'thought' or 'intellection' or 'cognition,' which partakes of the mystic more than it does of solid anatomy or physiologic function." The Psychologist's Fallacy is what James calls "the confusion of his own standpoint with that of the mental fact about which he is making a report." "Another variety of the psychologist's fallacy is the assumption that the mental fact studied must be conscious of itself as the psychologist is conscious of it." *Principles of Psychology,* vol. I, pp. 196-97.

used to establish a dominating principle of judgment, which is the Natural. As a concept of judgment this is notoriously deceptive and has been belabored for generations, but the Report knows nothing of its dangerous reputation and uses it with the naïvest confidence. And although the Report directs the harshest language toward the idea of the Normal, saying that it has stood in the way of any true scientific knowledge of sex, it is itself by no means averse to letting the idea of the Natural develop quietly into the idea of the Normal. The Report has in mind both a physical normality—as suggested by its belief that under optimal conditions men should be able to achieve the orgasmic frequency of the primates—and a moral normality, the acceptability, on the authority of animal behavior, of certain usually taboo practices.

It is inevitable that the concept of the Natural should haunt any discussion of sex. It is inevitable that it should make trouble, but most of all for a scientific discussion that bars judgments of value. Thus, in order to show that homosexuality is not a neurotic manifestation, as the Freudians say it is, the Report adduces the homosexual behavior of rats. But the argument *de animalibus* must surely stand by its ability to be inverted and extended. Thus, in having lost sexual periodicity, has the human animal lost naturalness? Again, the female mink, as we learn from the Report itself, fiercely resists intercourse and must be actually coerced into submission. Is it she who is unnatural or is her defense of her chastity to be taken as a comment on the females, animal or human, who willingly submit or who merely play at escape? Professor Kinsey is like no one so much as Sir Percival in Malory, who, seeing a lion and a serpent in battle with each other, decided to help the lion, "for he was the more natural beast of the two."

This awkwardness in the handling of ideas is characteristic of the Report. It is ill at ease with any idea that is in the least complex and it often tries to get rid of such an idea in favor of another that has the appearance of not going beyond the statement of physical fact. We see this especially in the handling of certain Freudian ideas. The Report acknowledges its debt to Freud with the generosity of spirit that marks it in other connections and it often makes use of Freudian concepts in a very direct and sensible way. Yet nothing could be clumsier than its handling of Freud's idea of pregenital generalized infantile sexuality. Because the Report can show, what is interesting and significant, that infants are capable of actual orgasm, although without ejaculation, it concludes that infantile sexuality is not generalized but specifically genital. But actually it has long been known, though the fact of orgasm had not been established, that infants can respond erotically to direct genital stimulation, and this knowledge does not contradict the Freudian idea that there is a stage in infant development in which sexuality is generalized throughout the body rather than specifically centered in the genital area; the fact of infant orgasm must be interpreted in conjunction with other and more complex manifestations of infant sexuality.[7]

The Report, we may say, has an extravagant fear of all ideas that do not seem to it to be, as it were, immediately dictated by simple physical fact. Another way of saying this is that the Report is resistant to any idea that seems to refer to a specifically human situation. An example is the position it takes on the matter of male potency. The folk feeling, where it is formulated on the question, and certainly where it is formulated by women, holds that male potency is not to be measured, as the Report measures it, merely by frequency, but by the ability to withhold orgasm long enough to bring the woman to climax. This is also the psychoanalytic view, which holds further that the inability to sustain intercourse is the result of unconscious fear or resentment. This view is very strongly resisted by the Report. The

[7] The Report also handles the idea of sublimation in a very clumsy way. It does not represent accurately what the Freudian theory of sublimation is. For this, however, there is some excuse in the change of emphasis and even in meaning in Freud's use of the word.

denial is based on mammalian behavior—"in many species" (but not in all?) ejaculation follows almost immediately upon intromission; in chimpanzees ejaculation occurs in ten to twenty seconds. The Report therefore concludes that the human male who ejaculates immediately upon intromission "is quite normal [here the word becomes suddenly permissible] among mammals and usual among his own species." Indeed, the Report finds it odd that the term "impotent" should be applied to such rapid responses. "It would be difficult to find another situation in which an individual who was quick and intense in his responses was labeled anything but superior, and that in most instances is exactly what the rapidly ejaculating male probably is, however inconvenient and unfortunate his qualities may be from the standpoint of the wife in the relationship."

But by such reasoning the human male who is quick and intense in his leap to the lifeboat is natural and superior, however inconvenient and unfortunate his speed and intensity may be to the wife he leaves standing on the deck, as is also the man who makes a snap judgment, who bites his dentist's finger, who kicks the child who annoys him, who bolts his—or another's—food, who is incontinent of his feces. Surely the problem of the natural in the human was solved four centuries ago by Rabelais, and in the simplest naturalistic terms; and it is sad to have the issue all confused again by the naïveté of men of science. Rabelais' solution lay in the simple perception of the *natural* ability and tendency of man to grow in the direction of organization and control. The young Gargantua in his natural infancy had all the quick and intense responses just enumerated; had his teachers confused the traits of his natural infancy with those of his natural manhood, he would not have been the more natural but the less; he would have been a monster.

In considering the Report as a major cultural document, we must not underestimate the significance of its petulant protest against the inconvenience to the male of the unjust demand that is made upon him. This protest is tantamount to saying that sexuality is not to be involved in specifically human situations or to be connected with desirable aims that are conceived of in specifically human terms. We may leave out of account any ideal reasons which would lead a man to solve the human situation of the discrepancy—arising from conditions of biology or of culture or of both—between his own orgasmic speed and that of his mate, and we can consider only that it might be hedonistically desirable for him to do so, for advantages presumably accrue to him in the woman's accessibility and responsiveness. Advantages of this kind, however, are precisely the matters of quality in experience that the Report ignores.[8]

And its attitude on the question of male potency is but one example of the Report's insistence on drawing sexuality apart from the general human context. It is striking how small a role woman plays in *Sexual Behavior in the Human Male.* We learn nothing about the connection of sex and reproduction; the connection, from the sexual point of view, is certainly not constant yet it is of great interest. The pregnancy or possibility of pregnancy of his mate has a considerable effect, sometimes one way, sometimes the other, on the sexual behavior of the male; yet in the index under *Pregnancy* there is but a single entry—*"fear of."* Again, the contraceptive devices which *Pregnancy, fear of,* requires have a notable influence on male sexuality; but the index lists only *Contraception, techniques.* Or again, menstruation has an elaborate mythos which men take very seriously; but the two indexed passages which refer to menstruation give no information about its relation to sexual conduct.

Then too the Report explicitly and stubbornly resists the idea that sexual behavior is involved with the whole

[8] It is hard not to make a connection between the Report's strong stand against any delay in the male orgasm and its equally strong insistence that there is no difference for the woman between a clitoral and vaginal orgasm, a view which surely needs more investigation before it is as flatly put as the Report puts it. The conjunction of the two ideas suggests the desirability of a sexuality which uses a minimum of sexual apparatus.

of the individual's character. In this it is strangely inconsistent. In the conclusion of its chapter on masturbation, after saying that masturbation does no physical harm and, if there are no conflicts over it, no mental harm, it goes on to raise the question of the effect of adult masturbation on the ultimate personality of the individual. With a certain confusion of cause and effect which we need not dwell on, it says: "It is now clear that masturbation is relied upon by the upper [social] level primarily because it has insufficient outlet through heterosexual coitus. This is, to a degree, an escape from reality, and the effect upon the ultimate personality of the individual is something that needs consideration." The question is of course a real one, yet the Report strenuously refuses to extend the principle of it to any other sexual activity. It summarily rejects the conclusions of psychoanalysis which make the sexual conduct an important clue to, even the crux of, character. It finds the psychoanalytical view unacceptable for two reasons: (1) The psychiatric practitioner misconceives the relation between sexual aberrancy and psychic illness because only those sexually aberrant people who are ill seek out the practitioner, who therefore never learns about the large incidence of mental health among the sexually aberrant. (2) The emotional illness which sends the sexually aberrant person to find psychiatric help is the result of no flaw in the psyche itself that is connected with the aberrancy but is the result only of the fear of social disapproval of his sexual conduct. And the Report instances the many men who are well adjusted socially and who yet break, among them, all the sexual taboos.

The quality of the argument which the Report here advances is as significant as the wrong conclusions it reaches. "It is not possible," the Report says, "to insist that any departure from the sexual mores, or any participation in socially taboo activities, always, or even usually, involves a neurosis or psychosis, for the case histories abundantly demonstrate that most individuals who engage in taboo activities make satisfactory social adjustments." In this context either "neuroses and psy-

choses" are too loosely used to stand for all psychic maladjustment, or "social adjustment" is too loosely used to
stand for emotional peace and psychic stability. When
the Report goes on to cite the "socially and intellectually significant persons," the "successful scientists, edu-
cators, physicians," etc., who have among them "accepted the whole range of the so-called abnormalities,"
we must keep in mind that very intense emotional disturbance, known only to the sufferer, can go along with
the efficient discharge of social duties, and that the psychoanalyst could counter with as long a list of distinguished and efficient people who do consult him.

Then, only an interest in attacking straw men could
have led the Report to insist that psychoanalysis is
wrong in saying that *any* departure from sexual mores,
or *any* participation in sexually taboo activities, involves
a neurosis or a psychosis, for psychoanalysis holds nothing like this view. It is just at this point that distinctions
are needed of a sort which the Report seems not to want
to make. For example: the Report comes out in a bold
and simple way for the naturalness and normality and
therefore for the desirability of mouth-genital contacts
in heterosexual love-making. This is a form of sexual expression which is officially taboo enough, yet no psychoanalyst would say that its practice indicated a neurosis
or psychosis. But a psychoanalyst would say that a person who disliked or was unable to practice any other
form of sexual contact thereby gave evidence of a
neurotic strain in his psychic constitution. His social adjustment, in the rather crude terms which the Report
conceives of it, might not be impaired, but certainly the
chances are that his psychic life would show signs of
disturbance, not from the practice itself but from the
psychic needs which made him insist on it. It is not the
breaking of the taboo but the emotional circumstance of
the breaking of the taboo that is significant.

The Report handles in the same oversimplified way
and with the same confusing use of absolute concepts
the sexual aberrancy which is, I suppose, the most complex and the most important in our cultural life, homo-

sexuality. It rejects the view that homosexuality is innate and that "no modification of it may be expected." But then it goes on also to reject the view that homosexuality provides evidence of a "psychopathic personality." "Psychopathic personality" is a very strong term which perhaps few analysts would wish to use in this connection. Perhaps even the term "neurotic" would be extreme in a discussion which, in the manner of the Report, takes "social adjustment," as indicated by status, to be the limit of its analysis of character. But this does not leave the discussion where the Report seems to want to leave it —at the idea that homosexuality is to be accepted as a form of sexuality like another and that it is as "natural" as heterosexuality, a judgment to which the Report is led in part because of the surprisingly large incidence of homosexuality it finds in the population. Nor does the practice of "an increasing proportion of the most skilled psychiatrists who make no attempt to redirect behavior, but who devote their attention to helping an individual accept himself" imply what the Report seems to want it to, that these psychiatrists have thereby judged homosexuality to be an unexceptionable form of sexuality; it is rather that, in many cases, they are able to effect no change in the psychic disposition and therefore do the sensible and humane next best thing. Their opinion of the etiology of homosexuality as lying in some warp—as our culture judges it—of the psychic structure has not, I believe, changed. And I think that they would say that the condition that produced the homosexuality also produced other character traits on which judgment could be passed. This judgment need by no means be totally adverse; as passed upon individuals it need not be adverse at all; but there can be no doubt that a society in which homosexuality was dominant or even accepted would be different in nature and quality from one in which it was censured.

That the Report refuses to hold this view of homosexuality, or any other view of at least equivalent complexity, leads us to take into account the motives that animate the work, and when we do, we see how very characteristically *American* a document the Report is. In speaking of its motives, I have in mind chiefly its impulse toward acceptance and liberation, its broad and generous desire for others that they be not harshly judged. Much in the Report is to be understood as having been dictated by a recoil from the crude and often brutal rejection which society has made of the persons it calls sexually aberrant. The Report has the intention of habituating its readers to sexuality in all its manifestations; it wants to establish, as it were, a democratic pluralism of sexuality. And this good impulse toward acceptance and liberation is not unique with the Report but very often shows itself in those parts of our intellectual life which are more or less official and institutionalized. It is, for example, far more established in the universities than most of us with our habits of criticism of America, particularly of American universities, will easily admit; and it is to a considerable extent an established attitude with the foundations that support intellectual projects.

That this generosity of mind is much to be admired goes without saying. But when we have given it all the credit it deserves as a sign of something good and enlarging in American life, we cannot help observing that it is often associated with an almost intentional intellectual weakness. It goes with a nearly conscious aversion from making intellectual distinctions, almost as if out of the belief that an intellectual distinction must inevitably lead to a social discrimination or exclusion. We might say that those who most explicitly assert and wish to practice the democratic virtues have taken it as their assumption that all social facts—with the exception of exclusion and economic hardship—must be *accepted*, not merely in the scientific sense but also in the social sense, in the sense, that is, that no judgment must be passed on them, that any conclusion drawn from them which perceives values and consequences will turn out to be "undemocratic."

The Report has it in mind to raise questions about the official restrictive attitudes toward sexual behavior, including those attitudes that are formulated on the statute books of most states. To this end it accumulates facts with the intention of showing that standards of judgment of sexual conduct as they now exist do not have real reference to the actual sexual behavior of the population. So far, so good. But then it goes on to imply that there can be only one standard for the judgment of sexual behavior—that is, sexual behavior as it actually exists; which is to say that sexual behavior is not to be judged at all, except, presumably, in so far as it causes pain to others. (But from its attitude to the "inconvenience" of the "wife in the relationship," we must presume that not all pain is to be reckoned with.) Actually the Report does not stick to its own standard of judgment; it is, as I have shown, sometimes very willing to judge among behaviors. But the preponderant weight of its argument is that a fact is a physical fact, to be considered only in its physical aspect and apart from any idea or ideal that might make it a social fact, as having no ascertainable personal or cultural meaning and no possible consequences—as being, indeed, not available to social interpretation at all. In short, the Report by its primitive conception of the nature of fact quite negates the importance and even the existence of sexuality as a social fact. That is why, although it is possible to say of the Report that it brings light, it is necessary to say of it that it spreads confusion.

F. Scott Fitzgerald

" 'So be it! I die content and my destiny is fulfilled,' said Racine's Orestes; and there is more in his speech than the insanely bitter irony that appears on the surface. Racine, fully conscious of this tragic grandeur, permits Orestes to taste for a moment before going mad with grief the supreme joy of a hero; to assume his *exemplary* role." The heroic awareness of which André Gide speaks in his essay on Goethe was granted to Scott Fitzgerald for whatever grim joy he might find in it. It is a kind of seal set upon his heroic quality that he was able to utter his vision of his own fate publicly and aloud and in *Esquire* with no lessening of his dignity, even with an enhancement of it. The several essays in which Fitzgerald examined his life in crisis have been gathered together by Edmund Wilson—who is for many reasons the most appropriate editor possible—and published, together with Fitzgerald's notebooks and some letters, as well as certain tributes and memorabilia, in a volume called, after one of the essays, *The Crack-Up*. It is a book filled with the grief of the lost and the might-have-been, with physical illness and torture of mind. Yet the heroic quality is so much here, Fitzgerald's assumption of the "exemplary role" is so proper and right that it occurs to us to say, and not merely as a piety but as the most accurate expression of what we really do feel, that

> Nothing is here for tears, nothing to wail
> Or knock the breast, no weakness, no contempt,
> Dispraise, or blame, nothing but well and fair,
> And what may quiet us in a death so noble.

This isn't what we may fittingly say on all tragic occasions, but the original occasion for these words has a striking aptness to Fitzgerald. Like Milton's Samson, he had the consciousness of having misused the power with which he had been endowed. "I had been only a mediocre caretaker . . . of my talent," he said. And the parallel carries further, to the sojourn among the Philistines and even to the maimed hero exhibited and mocked for the amusement of the crowd—on the afternoon of September 25, 1936, the New York *Evening Post* carried on its front page a feature story in which the triumphant reporter tells how he managed to make his way into the Southern nursing home where the sick and distracted Fitzgerald was being cared for and there "interviewed" him, taking all due note of the contrast between the present humiliation and the past glory. It was a particularly gratuitous horror, and yet in retrospect it serves to augment the moral force of the poise and fortitude which marked Fitzgerald's mind in the few recovered years that were left to him.

The root of Fitzgerald's heroism is to be found, as it sometimes is in tragic heroes, in his power of love. Fitzgerald wrote much about love, he was preoccupied with it as between men and women, but it is not merely where he is being explicit about it that his power appears. It is to be seen where eventually all a writer's qualities have their truest existence, in his style. Even in Fitzgerald's early, cruder books, or even in his commercial stories, and even when the style is careless, there is a tone and pitch to the sentences which suggest his warmth and tenderness, and, what is rare nowadays and not likely to be admired, his gentleness without softness. In the equipment of the moralist and therefore in the equipment of the novelist, aggression plays an important part, and although it is of course sanctioned by the novelist's moral intention and by whatever truth of moral vision he may have, it is often none the less fierce and sometimes even cruel. Fitzgerald was a moralist to the core and his desire to "preach at people in some acceptable form" is the reason he gives for not going the way of Cole Porter and Rodgers and Hart—we must always remember in judging him how many real choices he was free and forced to make—and he was gifted with the satiric eye; yet we feel that in his morality he was more drawn to celebrate the good than to denounce the bad. We feel of him, as we cannot feel of all moralists, that he did not attach himself to the good because this attachment would sanction his fierceness toward the bad—his first impulse was to love the good, and we know this the more surely because we perceive that he loved the good not only with his mind but also with his quick senses and his youthful pride and desire.

He really had but little impulse to blame, which is the more remarkable because our culture peculiarly honors the act of blaming, which it takes as the sign of virtue and intellect. "Forbearance, good word," is one of the jottings in his notebook. When it came to blame, he preferred, it seems, to blame himself. He even did not much want to blame the world. Fitzgerald knew where "the world" was at fault. He knew that it was the condition, the field, of tragedy. He is conscious of "what preyed on Gatsby, what foul dust floated in the wake of his dreams." But he never made out that the world imposes tragedy, either upon the heroes of his novels, whom he called his "brothers," or upon himself. When he speaks of his own fate, he does indeed connect it with the nature of the social world in which he had his early flowering, but he never finally lays it upon that world, even though at the time when he was most aware of his destiny it was fashionable with minds more pretentious than his to lay all personal difficulty whatever at the door of the "social order." It is, he feels, *his* fate—and as much as to anything else in Fitzgerald, we respond to the delicate tension he maintained between his idea of personal free will and his idea of circumstance: we respond to that moral and intellectual energy. "The test of a first-rate intelligence," he said, "is the ability to hold two opposed ideas in the mind, at the same time, and still retain the ability to function."

The power of love in Fitzgerald, then, went hand in

hand with a sense of personal responsibility and perhaps created it. But it often happens that the tragic hero can conceive and realize a love that is beyond his own prudence or beyond his powers of dominance or of self-protection, so that he is destroyed by the very thing that gives him his spiritual status and stature. From Proust we learn about a love that is destructive by a kind of corrosiveness, but from Fitzgerald's two mature novels, *The Great Gatsby* and *Tender Is the Night,* we learn about a love—perhaps it is peculiarly American—that is destructive by reason of its very tenderness. It begins in romance, sentiment, even "glamour"—no one, I think, has remarked how innocent of mere "sex," how charged with sentiment is Fitzgerald's description of love in the jazz age—and it takes upon itself reality, and permanence, and duty discharged with an almost masochistic scrupulousness of honor. In the bright dreams begins the responsibility which needs so much prudence and dominance to sustain; and Fitzgerald was anything but a prudent man and he tells us that at a certain point in his college career "some old desire for personal dominance was broken and gone." He connects that loss of desire for dominance with his ability to write; and he set down in his notebook the belief that "to record one must be unwary." Fitzgerald, we may say, seemed to feel that both love and art needed a sort of personal defenselessness.

The phrase from Yeats, the derivation of the "responsibility" from the "dreams," reminds us that we must guard against dismissing, with easy words about its immaturity, Fitzgerald's preoccupation with the bright charm of his youth. Yeats himself, a wiser man and wholly fulfilled in his art, kept to the last of his old age his connection with his youthful vanity. A writer's days must be bound each to each by his sense of his life, and Fitzgerald the undergraduate was father of the best in the man and the novelist.

His sojourn among the philistines is always much in the mind of everyone who thinks about Fitzgerald, and indeed it was always much in his own mind. Everyone

knows the famous exchange between Fitzgerald and
Ernest Hemingway—Hemingway refers to it in his story,
"The Snows of Kilimanjaro" and Fitzgerald records it in
his notebook—in which, to Fitzgerald's remark, "The very
rich are different from us," Hemingway replied, "Yes,
they have more money." It is usually supposed that
Hemingway had the better of the encounter and quite
settled the matter. But we ought not be too sure. The
novelist of a certain kind, if he is to write about social
life, may not brush away the reality of the differences
of class, even though to do so may have the momentary
appearance of a virtuous social avowal. The novel took
its rise and its nature from the radical revision of the class
structure in the eighteenth century, and the novelist must
still live by his sense of class differences, and must be absorbed by them, as Fitzgerald was, even though he
despised them, as Fitzgerald did.

No doubt there was a certain ambiguity in Fitzgerald's attitude toward the "very rich"; no doubt they were
for him something more than the mere object of his social
observation. They seem to have been the nearest thing
to an aristocracy that America could offer him, and we
cannot be too simple about what a critic has recently
noted, the artist's frequent "taste for aristocracy, his need
—often quite open—of a superior social class with which
he can make some fraction of common cause—enough, at
any rate, to account for his own distinction." Every
modern reader is by definition wholly immune from all
ignoble social considerations, and, no matter what his
own social establishment or desire for it may be, he
knows that in literature the interest in social position
must never be taken seriously. But not all writers have
been so simple and virtuous—what are we to make of
those risen gentlemen, Shakespeare and Dickens, or those
fabricators of the honorific "de," Voltaire and Balzac?
Yet their snobbery—let us call it that—is of a large and
generous kind and we are not entirely wrong in connect-
ing their peculiar energies of mind with whatever it was
they wanted from gentility or aristocracy. It is a common habit of writers to envision an actuality of personal

life which shall have the freedom and the richness of
detail and the order of form that they desire in art.
Yeats, to mention him again, spoke of the falseness of
the belief that the "inherited glory of the rich" really
holds richness of life. This, he said, was a mere dream;
and yet, he goes on, it is a necessary illusion—

> Yet Homer had not sung
> Had he not found it certain beyond dreams
> That out of life's own self-delight had sprung
> The abounding glittering jet. . . .

And Henry James, at the threshold of his career, allegorized in his story "Benvolio" the interplay that is necessary for some artists between their creative asceticism
and the bright, free, gay life of worldliness, noting at the
same time the desire of worldliness to destroy the asceticism.[1]

With a man like Goethe the balance between the
world and his asceticism is maintained, and so we forgive him his often absurd feelings—but perhaps absurd
as well as forgivable only in the light of our present
opinion of his assured genius—about aristocracy. Fitzgerald could not always keep the balance true; he was not,
as we know, a prudent man. And no doubt he deceived
himself a good deal in his youth, but certainly his self-
deception was not in the interests of vulgarity, for aristocracy meant to him a kind of disciplined distinction of
personal existence which, presumably, he was so humble
as not to expect from his art. What was involved in that
notion of distinction can be learned from the use which
Fitzgerald makes of the word "aristocracy" in one of
those serious moments which occur in his most frivolous *Saturday Evening Post* stories; he says of the life of
the young man of the story, who during the war was on
duty behind the lines, that "it was not so bad—except

---

[1] George Moore's comment on Æ's having spoken in re-
proof of Yeats's pride in a quite factitious family line is
apposite; "Æ, who is usually quick-witted, should have
guessed that Yeats's belief in his lineal descent from the
great Duke of Ormonde was part of his poetic equipment."

that when the infantry came limping back from the
trenches he wanted to be one of them. The sweat and
mud they wore seemed only one of those ineffable symbols of aristocracy that were forever eluding him." Fitzgerald was perhaps the last notable writer to affirm the
Romantic fantasy, descended from the Renaissance, of
personal ambition and heroism, of life committed to, or
thrown away for, some ideal of self. To us it will no
doubt come more and more to seem a merely boyish
dream; the nature of our society requires the young man
to find his distinction through cooperation, subordina-
tion, and an expressed piety of social usefulness, and although a few young men have made Fitzgerald into a
hero of art, it is likely that even to these admirers the
whole nature of his personal fantasy is not comprehen-
sible, for young men find it harder and harder to understand the youthful heroes of Balzac and Stendhal, they
increasingly find reason to blame the boy whose generosity is bound up with his will and finds its expression in
a large, strict, personal demand upon life.

I am aware that I have involved Fitzgerald with a
great many great names and that it might be felt by
some that this can do him no service, the disproportion
being so large. But the disproportion will seem large
only to those who think of Fitzgerald chiefly through
his early public legend of heedlessness. Those who have
a clear recollection of the mature work or who have read
The Crack-Up will at least not think of the disproportion as one of kind. Fitzgerald himself did not, and it is
by a man's estimate of himself that we must begin to
estimate him. For all the engaging self-depreciation
which was part of his peculiarly American charm, he
put himself, in all modesty, in the line of greatness, he
judged himself in a large way. When he writes of his
depression, of his "dark night of the soul" where "it is
always three o'clock in the morning," he not only derives
the phrase from St. John of the Cross but adduces the
analogous black despairs of Wordsworth, Keats, and
Shelley. A novel with Ernest Hemingway as the model
of its hero suggests to him Stendhal portraying the By-

ronic man, and he defends *The Great Gatsby* from some
critical remark of Edmund Wilson's by comparing it with
The Brothers Karamazov. Or again, here is the stuff of
his intellectual pride at the very moment that he speaks
of giving it up, as years before he had given up the
undergraduate fantasies of valor: "The old dream of being an entire man in the Goethe-Byron-Shaw tradition
. . . has been relegated to the junk heap of the shoulder
pads worn for one day on the Princeton freshman foot-
ball field and the overseas cap never worn overseas."
And was it, that old dream, unjustified? To take but one
great name, the one that on first thought seems the least
relevant of all—between Goethe at twenty-four the author
of *Werther,* and Fitzgerald, at twenty-four the author of
This Side of Paradise, there is not really so entire a difference as piety and textbooks might make us think;
both the young men so handsome, both winning immediate and notorious success, both rather more interested
in life than in art, each the spokesman and symbol of
his own restless generation.

It is hard to overestimate the benefit which came to
Fitzgerald from his having consciously placed himself in
the line of the great. He was a "natural," but he did not
have the contemporary American novelist's belief that if
he compares himself with the past masters, or if he
takes thought—which, for a writer, means really knowing what his predecessors have done—he will endanger
the integrity of his natural gifts. To read Fitzgerald's letters to his daughter—they are among the best and most
affecting letters I know—and to catch the tone in which
he speaks about the literature of the past, or to read the
notebooks he faithfully kept, indexing them as Samuel
Butler had done, and to perceive how continuously he
thought about literature, is to have some clue to the secret of the continuing power of Fitzgerald's work.

The Great Gatsby, for example, after a quarter-century is still as fresh as when it first appeared; it has even
gained in weight and relevance, which can be said of
very few American books of its time. This, I think, is to
be attributed to the specifically intellectual courage with

which it was conceived and executed, a courage which implies Fitzgerald's grasp—both in the sense of awareness and of appropriation—of the traditional resources available to him. Thus, *The Great Gatsby* has its interest as a record of contemporary manners, but this might only have served to date it, did not Fitzgerald take the given moment of history as something more than a mere circumstance, did he not, in the manner of the great French novelists of the nineteenth century, seize the given moment as a moral fact. The same boldness of intellectual grasp accounts for the success of the conception of its hero—Gatsby is said by some to be not quite credible, but the question of any literal credibility he may or may not have becomes trivial before the large significance he implies. For Gatsby, divided between power and dream, comes inevitably to stand for America itself. Ours is the only nation that prides itself upon a dream and gives its name to one, "the American dream." We are told that "the truth was that Jay Gatsby of West Egg, Long Island, sprang from his Platonic conception of himself. He was a son of God—a phrase which, if it means anything, means just that—and he must be about His Father's business, the service of a vast, vulgar, and meretricious beauty." Clearly it is Fitzgerald's intention that our mind should turn to the thought of the nation that has sprung from its "Platonic conception" of itself. To the world it is anomalous in America, just as in the novel it is anomalous in Gatsby, that so much raw power should be haunted by envisioned romance. Yet in that anomaly lies, for good or bad, much of the truth of our national life, as, at the present moment, we think about it.

Then, if the book grows in weight of significance with the years, we can be sure that this could not have happened had its form and style not been as right as they are. Its form is ingenious—with the ingenuity, however, not of craft but of intellectual intensity. The form, that is, is not the result of careful "plotting"—the form of a good novel never is—but is rather the result of the necessities of the story's informing idea, which require the sharpness of radical foreshortening. Thus, it will be observed, the characters are not "developed": the wealthy and brutal Tom Buchanan, haunted by his "scientific" vision of the doom of civilization, the vaguely guilty, vaguely homosexual Jordan Baker, the dim Wolfsheim, who fixed the World Series of 1919, are treated, we might say, as if they were ideographs, a method of economy that is reinforced by the ideographic use that is made of the Washington Heights flat, the terrible "valley of ashes" seen from the Long Island Railroad, Gatsby's incoherent parties, and the huge sordid eyes of the oculist's advertising sign. (It is a technique which gives the novel an affinity with *The Waste Land,* between whose author and Fitzgerald there existed a reciprocal admiration.) Gatsby himself, once stated, grows only in the understanding of the narrator. He is allowed to say very little in his own person. Indeed, apart from the famous "Her voice is full of money," he says only one memorable thing, but that remark is overwhelming in its intellectual audacity: when he is forced to admit that his lost Daisy did perhaps love her husband, he says, "In any case it was just personal." With that sentence he achieves an insane greatness, convincing us that he really is a Platonic conception of himself, really some sort of Son of God.

What underlies all success in poetry, what is even more important than the shape of the poem or its wit of metaphor, is the poet's voice. It either gives us confidence in what is being said or it tells us that we do not need to listen; and it carries both the modulation and the living form of what is being said. In the novel no less than in the poem, the voice of the author is the decisive factor. We are less consciously aware of it in the novel, and, in speaking of the elements of a novel's art, it cannot properly be exemplified by quotation because it is continuous and cumulative. In Fitzgerald's work the voice of his prose is of the essence of his success. We hear in it at once the tenderness toward human desire that modifies a true firmness of moral judgment. It is, I would venture to say, the normal or ideal voice of the novelist. It is characteristically modest, yet it has in it, without apology or self-consciousness, a largeness, even a stateliness, which derives from Fitzgerald's connection with tradition and with mind, from his sense of what has been done before and the demands which this past accomplishment makes. ". . . I became aware of the old island here that flowered once for Dutch sailors' eyes—a fresh green breast of the new world. Its vanished trees, the trees that had made way for Gatsby's house, had once pandered in whispers to the last and greatest of all human dreams; for a transitory and enchanted moment man must have held his breath in the presence of this continent, compelled into an aesthetic contemplation he neither understood nor desired, face to face for the last time in history with something commensurate to his capacity for wonder." Here, in the well-known passage, the voice is a little dramatic, a little *intentional*, which is not improper to a passage in climax and conclusion, but it will the better suggest in brief compass the habitual music of Fitzgerald's seriousness.

Fitzgerald lacked prudence, as his heroes did, lacked that blind instinct of self-protection which the writer needs and the American writer needs in double measure. But that is all he lacked—and it is the generous fault, even the heroic fault. He said of his Gatsby, "If personality is an unbroken series of successful gestures, there was something gorgeous about him, some heightened sensitivity to the promises of life, as if he were related to one of those intricate machines that register earthquakes ten thousand miles away. This responsiveness had nothing to do with that flabby impressionability which is dignified under the name of 'the creative temperament'—it was an extraordinary gift for hope, a romantic readiness such as I have never found in any other person and which it is not likely I shall ever find again." And it is so that we are drawn to see Fitzgerald himself as he stands in his exemplary role.

Art and Fortune

I

It is impossible to talk about the novel nowadays without having in our minds the question of whether or not the novel is still a living form. Twenty-five years ago T. S. Eliot said that the novel came to an end with Flaubert and James, and at about the same time Señor Ortega said much the same thing. This opinion is now heard on all sides. It is heard in conversation rather than read in formal discourse, for to insist on the death or moribundity of a great genre is an unhappy task which the critic will naturally avoid if he can, yet the opinion is now an established one and has a very considerable authority. Do we not see its influence in, for example, V. S. Pritchett's recent book, *The Living Novel?* Although Mr. Pritchett is himself a novelist and writes about the novel with the perception that comes of love, and even by the name he gives his book disputes the fact of the novel's death, yet still, despite these tokens of his faith, he deals with the subject under a kind of constraint, as if he had won the right to claim life for the novel only upon condition of not claiming for it much power.

I do not believe that the novel is dead. And yet particular forms of the creative imagination may indeed die —English poetic drama stands as the great witness of the possibility—and there might at this time be an advantage in accepting the proposition as an hypothesis which will lead us to understand under what conditions the novel may live.

If we consent to speak of the novel as dead, three

possible explanations of the fact spring at once to mind. The first is simply that the genre has been exhausted, worked out in the way that a lode of ore is worked out —it can no longer yield a valuable supply of its natural matter. The second explanation is that the novel was developed in response to certain cultural circumstances which now no longer exist but have given way to other circumstances which must be met by other forms of the imagination. The third explanation is that although the circumstances to which the novel was a response do still exist we either lack the power to use the form,[1] or no longer find value in the answers that the novel provides, because the continuing circumstances have entered a phase of increased intensity.

The first theory was put forward by Ortega in his essay "Notes on the Novel." It is an explanation which has its clear limitations, but it is certainly not without its cogency. We have all had the experience of feeling that some individual work of art, or some canon of art, or a whole idiom of art, has lost, temporarily or permanently, its charm and power. Sometimes we weary of the habitual or half-mechanical devices by which the artist warms up for his ideas or by which he bridges the gap between his ideas; this can happen even with Mozart. Sometimes it is the very essence of the man's thought that fatigues; we feel that his characteristic insights can too easily be foreseen and we become too much aware of how they exist at the expense of blindness to other truths; this can happen even with Dostoevski. And so with an entire genre of art—there may come a moment when it cannot satisfy one of our legitimate demands, which is that it shall surprise us. This demand, and the liability of our artistic interests to wear out, do not show us to be light-minded. Without them our use of art would be only ritualistic, or commemorative of our past experiences; and although there is nothing

[1] This might seem to beg the cultural question; yet certain technical abilities do deteriorate or disappear for reasons which although theoretically ascertainable are almost beyond practical determination.

wrong in using art for ritual and commemoration, still these are not the largest uses to which it can be put. Curiosity is as much an instinct as hunger and love, and curiosity about any particular thing may be satisfied.

Then we must consider that technique has its autonomy and that it dictates the laws of its own growth. Aristotle speaks of Athenian tragedy as seeking and finding its fulfillment, its entelechy, and it may be that we are interested in any art only just so long as it is in process of search; that what moves us is the mysterious energy of quest. At a certain point in the development of a genre, the practitioner looks back and sees all that has been done by others before him and knows that no ordinary effort can surpass or even match it; ordinary effort can only repeat. It is at this point that, as Ortega says, we get the isolated extraordinary effort which transcends the tradition and brings it to an end. This, no doubt, is what people mean when they speak of Joyce and Proust bringing the novel to its grave.

Here is the case, as strongly as I can put it, for the idea that a genre can exhaust itself simply by following the laws of its own development. As an explanation of the death of the novel it does not sufficiently exfoliate or sufficiently connect with the world. It can by no means be ignored, but of itself it cannot give an adequate answer to our question.

II

So we must now regard the novel as an art form contrived to do a certain kind of work, its existence conditioned by the nature of that work. In another essay[2] I undertook to say what the work of the novel was—I said that it was the investigation of reality and illusion. Of course the novel does not differ in this from all other highly developed literary forms; it differs, however, in at least one significant respect, that it deals with reality and illusion in relation to questions of social class, which in relatively recent times are bound up with money.

[2] "Manners, Morals, and the Novel."

In Western civilization the idea of money exercises a great fascination—it is the fascination of an actual thing which has attained a metaphysical ideality or of a metaphysical entity which has attained actual existence. Spirits and ghosts are beings in such a middling state of existence; and money is both real and not real, like a spook. We invented money and we use it, yet we cannot either understand its laws or control its actions. It has a life of its own which it properly should not have; Karl Marx speaks with a kind of horror of its indecent power to reproduce, as if, he says, love were working in its body. It is impious, being critical of existent social realities, and it has the effect of lessening their degree of reality. The social reality upon which it has its most devastating effect is of course that of class. And class itself is a social fact which, whenever it is brought into question, has like money a remarkable intimacy with metaphysics and the theory of knowledge—I have suggested how for Shakespeare any derangement of social classes seems always to imply a derangement of the senses in madness or dream, some elaborate joke about the nature of reality. This great joke is the matter of the book which we acknowledge as the ancestor of the modern novel, *Don Quixote;* and indeed no great novel exists which does not have the joke at its very heart.

In the essay to which I refer I also said that, in dealing with the questions of illusion and reality which were raised by the ideas of money and class, the novel characteristically relied upon an exhaustive exploitation of manners. Although I tried to give a sufficiently strong and complicated meaning to the word *manners,* I gather that my merely having used the word, or perhaps my having used it in a context that questioned certain political assumptions of a pious sort, has led to the belief that I am interested in establishing a new genteel tradition in criticism and fiction. Where misunderstanding serves others as an advantage, one is helpless to make oneself understood; yet to guard as well as I can against this imputation, I will say not only that the greatest exploitation of manners ever made is the *Iliad,* but also that *The Possessed* and *Studs Lonigan* are works whose concern with manners is of their very essence.

To these characteristics of the novel—the interest in illusion and reality as generated by class and money, this interest expressed by the observation of manners—we must add the unabashed interest in ideas. From its very beginning the novel made books the objects of its regard. Nowadays we are inclined to see the appearance of a literary fact in a novel as the sign of its "intellectuality" and specialness of appeal, and even as a sign of decadence. But Joyce's solemn literary discussions in *A Portrait of the Artist as a Young Man,* or his elaborate literary play in the later works, or Proust's critical excursions, are in the direct line of *Don Quixote* and *Tom Jones,* which are works of literary criticism before they are anything else. The Germans had a useful name for a certain kind of novel which they called a *Kulturroman;* actually every great novel deserves that name, for it is hard to think of one that is not precisely a romance of culture. By culture we must mean not merely the general social condition to which the novel responds but also a particular congeries of formulated ideas. The great novels, far more often than we remember, deal explicitly with developed ideas, and although they vary greatly in the degree of their explicitness they tend to be more explicit rather than less—in addition to the works already mentioned one can adduce such diverse examples as *Lost Illusions, The Sentimental Education, War and Peace, Jude the Obscure,* and *The Brothers Karamazov.* Nowadays the criticism which descends from Eliot puts explicit ideas in literature at a discount, which is one reason why it is exactly this criticism that is most certain of the death of the novel, and it has led many of us to forget how in the novel ideas may be as important as character and as essential to the given dramatic situation.

This then as I understand it is the nature of the novel as defined by the work it does. Of these defining conditions how many are in force today?

I think it is true to say that money and class do not

have the same place in our social and mental life that they once had. They have certainly not ceased to exist, but certainly they do not exist as they did in the nineteenth century or even in our own youth. Money of itself no longer can engage the imagination as it once did; it has lost some of its impulse, and certainly it is on the defensive; it must compete on the one hand with the ideal of security and on the other hand with the ideal of a kind of power which may be more directly applied. And for many to whom the ideal of mere security is too low and to whom the ideal of direct political power is beyond the reach of their imagination, money, in order to be justified, must be involved with virtue and with the virtuous cultivation of good taste in politics, culture, and the appointments of the home—money is terribly ashamed of itself. As for class, in Europe the bourgeoisie together with its foil the aristocracy has been weakening for decades. It ceased some time ago to be the chief source of political leaders; its nineteenth-century position as ideologue of the world has vanished before the ideological strength of totalitarian communism; the wars have brought it to the point of economic ruin. In England the middle class is in process of liquidating itself. In this country the real basis of the novel has never existed—that is, the tension between a middle class and an aristocracy which brings manners into observable relief as the living representation of ideals and the living comment on ideas. Our class structure has been extraordinarily fluid; our various upper classes have seldom been able or stable enough to establish their culture as authoritative. With the single exception of the Civil War, our political struggles have not had the kind of cultural implications which catch the imagination, and the extent to which this one conflict has engaged the American mind suggests how profoundly interesting conflicts of culture may be. (It is possible to say that the Cromwellian revolution appears in every English novel.) For the rest, the opposition between rural and urban ideals has always been rather factitious; and despite a brief attempt to insist on the opposite view, the conflict of capital and labor is at present a contest for the possession of the goods of a single way of life, and not a cultural struggle. Our most fervent interest in manners has been linguistic, and our pleasure in drawing distinctions between a presumably normal way of speech and an "accent" or a "dialect" may suggest how simple is our national notion of social difference.[3] And of recent years, although we grow more passionately desirous of status and are bitterly haunted by the ghost of every status-conferring ideal, including that of social class, we more and more incline to show our status-lust not by affirming but by denying the reality of social difference.

I think that if American novels of the past, whatever their merits of intensity and beauty, have given us very few substantial or memorable people, this is because one of the things which makes for substantiality of character in the novel is precisely the notation of manners, that is to say, of class traits modified by personality. It is impossible to imagine a Silas Wegg or a Smerdyakov or a Félicité (of *A Simple Heart*) or a Mrs. Proudie without the full documentation of their behavior in relation to their own class and to other classes. All great characters

[3] Lately our official egalitarianism has barred the exploitation of this interest by our official arts, the movies and the radio; there may be some social wisdom in this, yet it ignores the fact that at least certain forms and tones of the mockery of their speech habits are a means by which "extraneous" groups are accepted. Mention of this naturally leads to the question of whether the American attitude toward "minority" groups, particularly Negroes and Jews, is not the equivalent of class differentiation. I think it is not, except in a highly modified way. And for the purposes of the novel it is not the same thing at all, for two reasons: it involves no real cultural struggle, no significant conflict of ideals, for the excluded group has the same notion of life and the same aspirations as the excluding group, although the novelist who attempts the subject naturally uses the tactic of showing that the excluded group has a different and better ethos; and it is impossible to suppose that the novelist who chooses this particular subject will be able to muster the satirical ambivalence toward both groups which marks the good novel even when it has a social *parti pris*.

exist in part by reason of the ideas they represent. The great characters of American fiction, such, say, as Captain Ahab and Natty Bumppo, tend to be mythic because of the rare fineness and abstractness of the ideas they represent; and their very freedom from class gives them a large and glowing generality; for what I have called *substantiality* is not the only quality that makes a character great. They are few in number and special in kind; and American fiction has nothing to show like the huge, swarming, substantial population of the European novel, the substantiality of which is precisely a product of a class existence. In fiction, as perhaps in life, the conscious realization of social class, which is an idea of great power and complexity, easily and quickly produces intention, passion, thought, and what I am calling substantiality. The diminution of the reality of class, however socially desirable in many respects, seems to have the practical effect of diminishing our ability to see people in their difference and specialness.

Then we must be aware of how great has been the falling-off in the energy of ideas that once animated fiction. In the nineteenth century the novel followed the great lines of political thought, both the conservative and the radical, and it documented politics with an original and brilliant sociology. In addition, it developed its own line of psychological discovery, which had its issue in the monumental work of Freud. But now there is no conservative tradition and no radical tradition of political thought, and not even an eclecticism which is in the slightest degree touched by the imagination; we are in the hands of the commentator. On the continent of Europe political choice may be possible but political thought is not, and in a far more benign context the same may be said of England. And in the United States, although for different reasons, there is a similar lack of political intelligence: all over the world the political mind lies passive before action and the event. In psychological thought we find a strange concerted effort of regression from psychoanalysis, such as the reformulations of the analytical psychology which Dr. Horney and Dr. Sullivan make in the name of reason and society and progress, which are marked by the most astonishing weakness of mind, and which appeal to the liberal intellectual by an exploitation of the liberal intellectual's fond belief that he suspects "orthodoxy." Nor really can it be said that Freudian psychology itself has of late made any significant advances.

This weakness of our general intellectual life is reflected in our novels. So far as the novel touches social and political questions it permits itself to choose only between a cheery or a sour democratism; it is questionable whether any American novel since *Babbitt* has told us a new thing about our social life. In psychology the novel relies either on a mechanical or a clinical use of psychiatry or on the insights that were established by the novelists of fifty years ago.

It is not then unreasonable to suppose that we are at the close of a cultural cycle, that the historical circumstances which called forth the particular intellectual effort in which we once lived and moved and had our being is now at an end, and that the novel is part of that effort is as deciduous as the rest.

III

But there is an explanation of the death of the novel which is both corollary and alternative to this. Consider a main intellectual preoccupation of the period that ends with Freud and begins with Swift or with Shakespeare's middle period or with Montaigne—it does not matter just where we set the beginning so long as we start with some typical and impressive representation, secular and not religious, of man's depravity and weakness. Freud said of his own theories that they appealed to him as acting, like the theories of Darwin and Copernicus, to diminish man's pride, and this intention, carried out by means of the discovery and demonstration of man's depravity, has been one of the chief works of the human mind for some four hundred years. What the mind was likely to discover in this period was by and large much the sam thing, yet mind was always active in the enterprise of discovery; discovery itself was a kind of joy and sometimes a hope, no matter how great the depravity that was turned up; the activity of the mind was a kind of fortitude. Then too there was reassurance in the resistance that was offered to the assaults of mind upon the strong texture of the social façade of humanity. That part of the mind which delights in discovery was permitted its delight by the margin that existed between speculation and proof; had the mind been able fully to prove what it believed, it would have fainted and failed before its own demonstration, but so strongly entrenched were the forces of respectable optimism and the belief in human and social goodness that the demonstration could never be finally established but had to be attempted over and over again. Now, however, the old margin no longer exists; the façade is down; society's resistance to the discovery of depravity has ceased; now everyone knows that Thackeray was wrong, Swift right. The world and the soul have split open of themselves and are all agape for our revolted inspection. The simple eye of the camera shows us, at Belsen and Buchenwald, horrors that quite surpass Swift's powers, a vision of life turned back to its corrupted elements which is more disgusting than any that Shakespeare could contrive, a cannibalism more literal and fantastic than that which Montaigne ascribed to organized society. A characteristic activity of mind is therefore no longer needed. Indeed, before what we now know the mind stops; the great psychological fact of our time which we all observe with baffled wonder and shame is that there is no possible way of responding to Belsen and Buchenwald. The activity of mind fails before the incommunicability of man's suffering.

This may help to explain the general deterioration of our intellectual life. It may also help to explain an attitude to our life in general. Twenty-five years ago Ortega spoke of the "dehumanization" of modern art. Much of what he said about the nature of modern art has, by modern art, been proved wrong, or was wrong even when he said it. But Ortega was right in observing

of modern art that it expresses a dislike of holding in
the mind the human fact and the human condition, that
it shows "a real loathing of living forms and living
beings," a disgust with the "rounded and soft forms of
living bodies"; and that together with this revulsion, or
expressed by it, we find a disgust with history and
society and the state. Human life as an aesthetic object
can perhaps no longer command our best attention; the
day seems to have gone when the artist who dealt in
representation could catch our interest almost by the
mere listing of the ordinary details of human existence;
and the most extreme and complex of human dilemmas
now surely seem to many to have lost their power to
engage us. This seems to be supported by evidence
from those arts for which a conscious exaltation of hu-
manistic values is stock-in-trade—I mean advertising and
our middling novels, which, almost in the degree that
they celebrate the human, falsify and abstract it; in the
very business of expressing adoration of the rounded and
soft forms of living bodies they expose the disgust which
they really feel.

IV

At this point we are in the full tide of those desperate
perceptions of our life which are current nowadays
among thinking and talking people, which even when
we are not thinking and talking haunt and control our
minds with visions of losses worse than that of existence—
losses of civilization, personality, humanness. They sink
our spirits not merely because they are terrible and
possible but because they have become so obvious and
cliché that they seem to close for us the possibility of
thought and imagination.

And at this point too we must see that if the novel is
dead or dying, it is not alone in its mortality. The novel
is a kind of summary and paradigm of our cultural life,
which is perhaps why we speak sooner of its death than
of the death of any other form of thought. It has been
of all literary forms the most devoted to the celebration

and investigation of the human will; and the will of our society is dying of its own excess. The religious will, the political will, the sexual will, the artistic will—each is dying of its own excess. The novel at its greatest is the record of the will acting under the direction of an idea, often an idea of will itself. All else in the novel is but secondary, and those examples which do not deal with the will in action are but secondary in their genre. Sensibility in the novel is but notation and documentation of the will in action. Again *Don Quixote* gives us our first instance. In its hero we have the modern conception of the will in a kind of wry ideality. Flaubert said that Emma Bovary was Quixote's sister, and in her we have the modern will in a kind of corruption. Elizabeth Bennet and Emma Woodhouse and Jane Eyre are similarly related to all the Karamazovs, to Stavrogin, and to that Kirillov who was led by awareness of the will to assert it ultimately by destroying it in himself with a pistol shot.

Surely the great work of our time is the restoration and the reconstitution of the will. I know that with some the opinion prevails that, apart from what very well *may* happen by way of Apocalypse, what *should* happen is that we advance farther and farther into the darkness, seeing to it that the will finally exhausts and expends itself to the end that we purge our minds of all the old ways of thought and feeling, giving up all hope of ever reconstituting the great former will of humanism, which, as they imply, has brought us to this pass. One must always listen when this opinion is offered in true passion. But for the vision and ideal of apocalyptic renovation one must be either a particular kind of moral genius with an attachment to life that goes beyond attachment to any particular form of life—D. H. Lawrence was such a genius—or a person deficient in attachment to life in any of its forms. Most of us are neither one nor the other, and our notions of renovation and reconstitution are social and pragmatic and in the literal sense of the word conservative. To the restoration and reconstitution of the will thus understood the novelistic intelligence is most apt.

When I try to say on what grounds I hold this belief, my mind turns to a passage in Henry James's preface to *The American*. James has raised the question of "reality" and "romance," and he remarks that "of the men of largest resounding imagination before the human scene, of Scott, of Balzac, even of the coarse, comprehensive, prodigious Zola, we feel, I think, that the reflection toward either quarter has never taken place"; they have never, that is, exclusively committed themselves either to "reality" or to "romance" but have maintained an equal commerce with both. And this, James goes on to say, is the secret of their power with us. Then follows an attempt to distinguish between "reality" and "romance," which defines "reality" as "the things we cannot possibly not know," and then gives us this sentence: "The romantic stands . . . for the things that, with all the facilities in the world, all the wealth and all the courage and all the wit and all the adventure, we never *can* directly know; the things that can reach us only through the beautiful circuit of thought and desire."

The sentence is perhaps not wholly perspicuous, yet, if I understand it at all, it points to the essential moral nature of the novel. Julien Sorel eventually acquired all the facilities in the world; he used "all the wealth and all the courage and all the wit and all the adventure" to gain the things that are to be gained by their means; what he gained was ashes in his mouth. But what in the end he gained came to him in prison not by means of the "facilities" but through the beautiful circuit of thought and desire, and it impelled him to make his great speech to the Besançon jury in which he threw away his life; his happiness and his heroism came, I think, from his will having exhausted all that part of itself which naturally turns to the inferior objects offered by the social world and from its having learned to exist in the strength of its own knowledge of its thought and desire. I have said that awareness of the will in its beautiful circuit of thought and desire was the peculiar property of the novel, yet in point of fact we find it long before the novel came into existence and in a place where it always surprises us, in the *Inferno*, at the meetings of Dante with Paolo and Francesca, with Brunetto Latini and with Ulysses, the souls who keep the energy of thought and desire alive and who are therefore forever loved however damned. For James the objects of this peculiarly human energy go by the name of "romance." The word is a risky one and therefore it is necessary to say that it does not stand for the unknowable, for what is vulgarly called "the ideal," let alone for that which is pleasant and charming because far off. It stands for the world of unfolding possibility, for that which, when brought to actuality, is powerfully operative. It is thus a synonym for the will in its creative aspect, especially in its aspect of *moral* creativeness, as it subjects itself to criticism and conceives for itself new states of being. The novel has had a long dream of virtue in which the will, while never abating its strength and activity, learns to refuse to exercise itself upon the unworthy objects with which the social world tempts it, and either conceives its own right objects or becomes content with its own sense of its potential force—which is why so many novels give us, before their end, some representation, often crude enough, of the will unbroken but in stasis.

It is the element of what James calls "romance," this operative reality of thought and desire, which, in the novel, exists side by side with the things "we cannot possibly not know," that suggests to me the novel's reconstitutive and renovating power.

V

If there is any ground for my belief that the novel can, by reason of one of its traditional elements, do something in the work of reconstituting and renovating the will, there may be some point in trying to say under what particular circumstances of its own nature and action it may best succeed.

I think it will not succeed if it accepts the latest-advanced theory of the novel, Jean-Paul Sartre's theory of "dogmatic realism." According to the method of this theory, the novel is to be written as if without an author and without a personal voice and "without the foolish business of storytelling." The reader is to be subjected to situations as nearly equivalent as possible to those of life itself; he is to be prevented from falling out of the book, kept as strictly as possible within its confines and power by every possible means, even by so literal a means as the closest approximation of fictional to historical time, for the introduction of large periods of time would permit the reader to remember that he is involved in an illusion; he is, in short, to be made to forget that he is reading a book. We all know the devices by which the sensations of actual life, such as claustrophobia and fatigue, are generated in the reader; and although the novels which succeed in the use of these devices have had certain good effects, they have had bad effects too. By good and bad effects I mean, as Sartre means, good and bad social effects. The banishment of the author from his books, the stilling of his voice, have but reinforced the faceless hostility of the world and have tended to teach us that we ourselves are not creative agents and that we have no voice, no tone, no style, no significant existence. Surely what we need is the opposite of this, the opportunity to identify ourselves with a mind that willingly admits that it is a mind and does not pretend that it is History or Events or the World but only a mind thinking and planning—possibly planning our escape.

There is not very much that is actually original in Sartre's theory, which seems to derive from Flaubert at a not very great remove. Flaubert himself never could, despite his own theory, keep himself out of his books; we always know who is there by guessing who it is that is kept out—it makes a great difference just which author is kept out of a novel, and Flaubert's absence occupies more room than Sartre's, and is a much more various and impressive thing. And Flaubert's mind, in or out of his novels, presents itself to us as an ally—although, as I more and more come to think, the alliance it offers is dangerous.

As for what Sartre calls "the foolish business of story-telling," I believe that, so far from giving it up, the novel will have to insist on it more and more. It is exactly the story that carries what James calls "romance," which is what the theologians call "faith," and in the engaged and working literature which Sartre rightly asks for this is an essential element. To know a story when we see one, to know it *for* a story, to know that it is not reality itself but that it has clear and effective relations with reality—this is one of the great disciplines of the mind.

In speaking against the ideal of the authorless novel I am not, of course, speaking in behalf of the "personality" of the author consciously displayed—nothing could be more frivolous—but only in behalf of the liberating effects that may be achieved when literature understands itself to be literature and does not identify itself with what it surveys. (This is as intellectually necessary as for science not to represent itself as a literal picture of the universe.) The authorial minds that in *Tom Jones* and *Tristram Shandy* play with events and the reader in so nearly divine a way become the great and strangely effective symbols of liberty operating in the world of necessity, and this is more or less true of all the novelists who *contrive* and *invent*.

Yet when I speak in defense of the salutary play of the mind in the controlled fantasy of storytelling I am not defending the works of consciously literary, elaborately styled fantasy in the manner of, let us say, *Nightwood*, which in their own way subscribed to the principles of Sartre's dogmatic realism, for although the conscious literary intention of the author is always before us, yet style itself achieves the claustral effect which Sartre would manage by the representation of events.

Mr. Eliot praises the prose of *Nightwood* for having so much affinity with poetry. This is not a virtue, and I believe that it will not be mistaken for a virtue by any novel of the near future which will interest us. The loss of a natural prose, one which has at least a seeming affinity with good common speech, has often been noted. It seems to me that the observation of the loss has been too complacently made and that its explanations, while ingenious, have had the intention of preventing it from being repaired in kind. A prose which approaches poetry has no doubt its own value, but it cannot serve to repair the loss of a straightforward prose, rapid, masculine, and committed to events, making its effects not by the single word or by the phrase but by words properly and naturally massed. I conceive that the creation of such a prose should be one of the conscious intentions of any novelist.[4]

And as a corollary to my rejection of poetic prose for the novel, I would suggest that the novelist of the next decades will not occupy himself with questions of form. The admitted weakness of the contemporary novel, the far greater strength of poetry, the current strong interest in the theory of poetry, have created a situation in which the canons of poetical perfection are quite naturally but too literally applied to the novel. These canons have not so much reinforced as displaced the formal considerations of Flaubert and James, which have their own dangers but which were at least conceived for the novel itself. I make every expectable disclaimer of wishing to depreciate form and then go on to say that a conscious preoccupation with form at the present time is almost certain to lead the novelist, particularly the young novelist, into limitation. The notions of form which are at present current among even those who are highly trained in

[4] The question of prose is as important as that of prosody and we never pay enough attention to it in criticism. I am far from thinking that my brief paragraph even opens the subject adequately. The example of Joyce has been urged against the little I have just said. It seems to me that whenever the prose of *A Portrait of the Artist* becomes what we call poetic, it is in a very false taste; this has been defended as being a dramatic device, an irony against the hero. *Ulysses* may be taken as making a strong case against my own preference, yet I think that its basic prose, which is variously manipulated, is not without its affinities with the prose I ask for. The medium of *Finnegans Wake* may, without prejudice, be said to be something other than prose in any traditional sense; if it should establish a tradition it will also establish new criteria and problems.

literature—let alone among the semi-literary, who are always very strict about enforcing the advanced ideas of forty years ago—are all too simple and often seem to come down to nothing more than the form of the sonata, the return on the circle with appropriate repetitions of theme. For the modern highly trained literary sensibility, form suggests completeness and the ends tucked in; resolution is seen only as all contradictions equated, and although form thus understood has its manifest charm, it will not adequately serve the modern experience. A story, like the natural course of an emotion, has its own form, and I take it as the sign of our inadequate trust of story and of our exaggerated interest in sensibility that we have begun to insist on the precise ordering of the novel.

Then I venture the prediction that the novel of the next decades will deal in a very explicit way with ideas. The objections to this will be immediate. Everybody quotes Mr. Eliot's remark about Henry James having a mind so fine that no idea could violate it, which suggests an odd, violent notion of the relation of minds and ideas, not at all the notion that James himself held; and everybody knows the passage in which Mr. Eliot insists on the indifferent connection which Dante and Shakespeare had with the intellectual formulations of their respective times. I think I can understand—and sympathetically as well as sociologically—Mr. Eliot's feeling for a mode of being in which the act and tone of ideation are not dominant, just as I can understand something of the admiration which may be felt for a society such as Yeats celebrated, which expresses its sense of life not by means of words but by means of houses and horses and by means of violence, manners, courage, and death. But I do not understand what Mr. Eliot means when he makes a sharp distinction between ideas and emotions in literature; I think that Plato was right when in *The Symposium* he represented ideas as continuous with emotions, both springing from the appetites.

It is a prevailing notion that a novel which contains or deals with ideas is bound to be pallid and abstract and intellectual. As against this belief here is an opinion from the great day of the novel: "There are active souls who like rapidity, movement, conciseness, sudden shocks, action, drama, who avoid discussion, who have little fondness for meditation and take pleasure in results. From such people comes what I should call the Literature of Ideas." This odd definition, whose seeming contradictions we will not pause over, was made by Balzac in the course of his long review of *The Charterhouse of Parma,* and it is Stendhal whom Balzac mentions as the great exemplar of the literature of ideas. And we know what ideas are at work in *The Charterhouse* and *The Red and the Black:* they are the ideas of Rousseau and they are named as such. These ideas are not to be separated from the passions of Julien and Fabrice; they are reciprocally expressive of each other. To us it is strange that ideas should be expressed so, and also in terms of prisons and rope ladders, pistols and daggers. It should not seem strange, for it is in the nature of ideas to be so expressed.

Yet although these two great examples support much of my view of the place of ideas in the novel, they do not support all of it. They make for me the point of the continuity of ideas and emotions, which in our literary context is forgotten. And they remind us forcibly of the ideological nature of institutions and classes. But in Stendhal's novels the ideas, although precisely identified, are chiefly represented by character and dramatic action, and although this form of representation has of course very high aesthetic advantages, yet I would claim for the novel the right and the necessity to deal with ideas by means other than that of the "objective correlative," to deal with them as directly as it deals with people or terrain or social setting.

There is an obvious social fact which supports this claim. No one who is in the least aware of our social life today can miss seeing that ideas have acquired a new kind of place in society. Nowadays everyone is involved in ideas—or, to be more accurate, in ideology. The impulse of novelists, which has been much decried, to make their heroes intellectuals of some sort was, however dull it became, perfectly sound: they wanted people of whom it was clear that ideas were an important condition of their lives. But this limitation to avowed intellectuals is no longer needed; in our society the simplest person is involved with ideas. Every person we meet in the course of our daily life, no matter how unlettered he may be, is groping with sentences toward a sense of his life and his position in it; and he has what almost always goes with an impulse to ideology, a good deal of animus and anger. What would so much have pleased the social philosophers of an earlier time has come to pass—ideological organization has cut across class organization, generating loyalties and animosities which are perhaps even more intense than those of class. The increase of conscious formulation, the increase of a certain kind of consciousness by formulation, makes a fact of modern life which is never sufficiently estimated. This is a condition which has been long in developing, for it began with the movements of religious separatism; now politics, and not only politics but the requirements of a whole culture, make verbal and articulate the motive of every human act: we eat by reason, copulate by statistics, rear children by rule, and the one impulse we do not regard with critical caution is that toward ideation, which increasingly becomes a basis of prestige.

This presents the novel with both an opportunity and a duty. The opportunity is a subject matter. Social class and the conflicts it produces may not be any longer a compelling subject to the novelist, but the organization of society into ideological groups presents a subject scarcely less absorbing. Ideological society has, it seems to me, nearly as full a range of passion and nearly as complex a system of manners as a society based on social class. Its promise of comedy and tragedy is enormous; its assurance of relevance is perfect. Dostoevski adequately demonstrated this for us, but we never had in this country a sufficiently complex ideological situation to support it in our own practice of the novel. We have it now.

This opportunity of the novel clearly leads to its duty. Ideology is not ideas; ideology is not acquired by thought but by breathing the haunted air. The life in ideology, from which none of us can wholly escape, is a strange submerged life of habit and semihabit in which to ideas we attach strong passions but no very clear awareness of the concrete reality of their consequences. To live the life of ideology with its special form of unconsciousness is to expose oneself to the risk of becoming an agent of what Kant called "the Radical Evil," which is "man's inclination to corrupt the imperatives of morality so that they may become a screen for the expression of self-love."[5] But the novel is a genre with a very close and really a very simple relation to actuality, to the things we cannot possibly not know—not if they are pointed out to us; it is the form in which the things we cannot possibly not know live side by side with thought and desire, both in their true and beautiful state and in their corrupt state; it is the form which provides the perfect criticism of ideas by attaching them to their appropriate actuality. No less than in its infancy, and now perhaps with a greater urgency and relevance, the novel passionately concerns itself with reality, with appearance and reality.

VI

But I must not end on a note so high—it would falsify my present intention and my whole feeling about the novel. To speak now of "duty" and, as I earlier did, of the work the novel may do in the reconstitution and renovation of the will, to formulate a function and a destiny for the novel, is to put it into a compromised position where it has been far too long already. The novel was better off when it was more humbly conceived than it is now; the novelist was in a far more advantageous position when

[5] Reinhold Niebuhr, *The Nature and Destiny of Man*, vol. I, p. 120: "'This evil is radical,' [Kant] declares, 'because it corrupts the very basis of all maxims.' In analyzing the human capacity for self-deception and its ability to make the worse appear the better reason for the sake of providing a moral façade for selfish actions, Kant penetrates into spiritual intricacies and mysteries to which he seems to remain completely blind in his *Critique of Practical Reason*."

his occupation was misprized, or when it was estimated by simpler minds than his own, when he was nearly alone in his sense of wonder at the possibilities of his genre, at the great effects it might be made to yield. The novel was luckier when it had to compete with the sermon, with works of history, with philosophy and poetry and with the ancient classics, when its social position was in question and like one of its own poor or foundling or simple heroes it had to make its way against odds. Whatever high intentions it may have had, it was permitted to stay close to its own primitive elements from which it drew power. Believing this, I do not wish to join in the concerted effort of contemporary criticism to increase the superego of the novel, to conspire with our sense of cultural crisis to heap responsibilities upon it, to hedge it about with prescribed functions and spiked criteria; as things are, the novel feels quite guilty enough.

A sentence in Aristotle's *Ethics* has always been memorable, perhaps because I have never wholly understood it. Aristotle says, "There is a sense in which Chance and Art have the same sphere; as Agathon says, 'Art fosters Fortune; Fortune fosters Art.'" Taken out of its context, and merely as a gnomic sentence, this says much. It says something about the reciprocation which in the act of composition exists between form and free invention, each making the other, which even the most considerate criticism can never really be aware of and often belies. *Fortune fosters Art:* there is indeed something fortuitous in all art, and in the novel the element of the fortuitous is especially large. The novel achieves its best effects of art often when it has no concern with them, when it is fixed upon effects in morality, or when it is simply reporting what it conceives to be objective fact. The converse is of course also true, that the novel makes some of its best moral discoveries or presentations of fact when it is concerned with form, when it manipulates its material merely in accordance with some notion of order or beauty, although it must be stipulated that this is likely to occur only when what is manipulated resists enough, the novel being the form whose aesthetic must pay an unusually large and simple respect to its chosen material. This predominance of fortuitousness in the novel accounts for the roughness of grain, even the coarseness of grain as compared with other arts, that runs through it. The novel is, as many have said of it, the least "artistic" of genres. For this it pays its penalty and it has become in part the grave as well as the monument of many great spirits who too carelessly have entrusted their talents to it. Yet the headlong, profuse, often careless quality of the novel, though no doubt wasteful, is an aspect of its bold and immediate grasp on life.

But from this very sense of its immediacy to life we have come to overvalue the novel. We have, for example, out of awareness of its power, demanded that it change the world; no genre has ever had so great a burden of social requirement put upon it (which, incidentally, it has very effectively discharged), or has been so strictly ordered to give up, in the fulfillment of its assigned function, all that was unconscious and ambivalent and playful in itself. Our sense of its comprehensiveness and effectiveness have led us to make a legend of it: one of the dreams of a younger America, continuing until recently, was of *the* Great American Novel, which was always imagined to be as solitary and omniseminous as the Great White Whale. Then we have subjected it to criteria which are irrelevant to its nature—how many of us happily share the horror which John Gould Fletcher expressed at the discovery that Trollope thought of novel-writing as a trade. The overvaluation of love is the beginning of the end of love; the overvaluation of art is the beginning of the end of art.

What I have called the roughness of grain of the novel, and praised as such, corresponds with something in the nature of the novelists themselves. Of all practitioners of literature, novelists as a class have made the most aggressive assault upon the world, the most personal demand upon it, and no matter how obediently they have listened to their daemons they have kept an ear cocked at the crowd and have denounced its dullness in not responding with gifts of power and fame. This personal demand the haughtiest reserve of Flaubert and James did not try to hide. The novelists have wanted much and very openly; and with great simplicity and naïveté they have mixed what they personally desired with what they desired for the world and have mingled their mundane needs with their largest judgments. Then, great as their mental force has been, they have been touched with something like stupidity, resembling the holy stupidity which Pascal recommends: its effects appear in their ability to maintain ambivalence toward their society, which is not an acquired attitude of mind, or a weakness of mind, but rather the translation of a biological datum, an extension of the pleasure-pain with which, in a healthy state, we respond to tension and effort; the novelist expresses this in his coexistent hatred and love of the life he observes. His inconsistency of intellectual judgment is biological wisdom.

It is at this point that I must deal with a lapse in my argument of which I am aware. My statement of belief that the novel is not dead, together with what I have said about what the novel should or should not do, very likely does not weigh against those circumstances in our civilization which I have adduced as accounting for the hypothetical death of the novel. To me certainly the circumstances are very real. And as I describe the character of the novelist they inevitably occur to me again. For it is exactly that character and what it suggests in a culture that the terrible circumstances of our time destroy. The novelist's assertion of personal demand and his frank mingling of the mundane and personal with the high and general, his holy stupidity, or as Keats called it, "negative capability," which is his animal faith—can these persist against the assaults which the world now makes on them? If the novel cannot indeed survive without ambivalence, does what the world presents us with any longer permit ambivalence? The novelist could once speak of the beautiful circuit of thought and desire which exists beside the daily reality, but the question is now whether thought and desire have any longer a field of possibility. No answer can soon be forthcoming. Yet, "as Agathon says, 'Art fosters Fortune; Fortune fosters Art.'" There is both an affirmation and an abdication in that sentence; the abdication is as courageous as the affirmation, and the two together make up a good deal of wisdom. If anything of the old novelistic character survives into our day, the novelist will be sufficiently aware of Fortune, of Conditions, of History, for he is, as Fielding said, the historian's heir; but he will also be indifferent to History, sharing the vital stupidity of the World-Historical Figure, who of course is not in the least interested in History but only in his own demands upon life and thus does not succumb to History's most malign and subtle trick, which is to fix and fascinate the mind of men with the pride of their foreknowledge of doom. There are times when, as the method of Perseus with the Medusa suggests, you do well not to look straight at what you are dealing with but rather to see it in the mirror-shield that the hero carried. Which is to say, "Art fosters Fortune."

But the shrug which is implied by the other half of the sentence is no less courageous. It does not suggest that we compare our position with what appears to be the more favored situation of the past, or keep in mind how History has robbed the novelist of a great role. What a demand upon the guarantees of History this would imply! What an overvaluation of security, and of success and the career, and of art, and of life itself, which must always be a little undervalued if it is to be lived. Rather should the phrase suggest both the fortuitous and the gratuitous nature of art, how it exists beyond the reach of the will alone, how it is freely given and not always for good reason, and for as little reason taken away. It is not to be demanded or prescribed or provided for. The understanding of this cannot of itself assure the existence of the novel but it helps toward establishing the state of the soul in which the novel becomes possible.

The Meaning of a
Literary Idea

> . . . Though no great minist'ring reason sorts
> Out the dark mysteries of human souls
> To clear conceiving: yet there ever rolls
> A vast idea before me, and I glean
> Therefrom my liberty . . .
>
> Keats: "Sleep and Poetry"

I

The question of the relation which should properly obtain between what we call creative literature and what we call ideas is a matter of insistent importance for modern criticism. It did not always make difficulties for the critic, and that it now makes so many is a fact which tells us much about our present relation to literature.

Ever since men began to think about poetry, they have conceived that there is a difference between the poet and the philosopher, a difference in method and in intention and in result. These differences I have no wish to deny. But a solidly established difference inevitably draws the fire of our question; it tempts us to inquire whether it is really essential or whether it is quite so settled and extreme as at first it seems. To this temptation I yield perhaps too easily, and very possibly as the result of an impercipience on my part—it may be that I see the difference with insufficient sharpness because I do not have a proper notion either of the matter of poetry or of the matter of philosophy. But whatever the reason, when I consider the respective products of the poetic and of the philosophic mind, although I see that they are by no means the same and although I can conceive that different processes, even different mental faculties, were at work to make them and to make them different, I cannot resist the impulse to put stress on their similarity and on their easy assimilation to each other.

Let me suggest some of the ways in which literature, by its very nature, is involved with ideas. I can be quite brief because what I say will not be new to you.

The most elementary thing to observe is that literature is of its nature involved with ideas because it deals with man in society, which is to say that it deals with formulations, valuations, and decisions, some of them implicit, others explicit. Every sentient organism *acts* on the principle that pleasure is to be preferred to pain, but man is the sole creature who formulates or exemplifies this as an idea and causes it to lead to other ideas. His consciousness of self abstracts this principle of action from his behavior and makes it the beginning of a process of intellection or a matter for tears and laughter. And this is but one of the innumerable assumptions or ideas that are the very stuff of literature.

This is self-evident and no one ever thinks of denying it. All that is ever denied is that literature is within its proper function in bringing these ideas to explicit consciousness, or ever gains by doing so. Thus, one of the matters of assumption in any society is the worth of men as compared with the worth of women; upon just such an assumption, more or less settled, much of the action of the *Oresteia* is based, and we don't in the least question the propriety of this—or not until it becomes the subject of open debate between Apollo and Athene, who, on the basis of an elaborate biological speculation, try to decide which is the less culpable, to kill your father or to kill your mother. At this point we, in our modern way, feel that in permitting the debate Aeschylus has made a great and rather silly mistake, that he has for the moment ceased to be *literary*. Yet what drama does not consist of the opposition of formulable ideas, what drama, indeed, is not likely to break into the explicit exposition and debate of these ideas?

This, as I say, is elementary. And scarcely less elementary is the observation that whenever we put two emotions into juxtaposition we have what we can properly call an idea. When Keats brings together, as he so often does, his emotions about love and his emotions about death, we have a very powerful idea and the source of consequent ideas. The force of such an idea depends upon the force of the two emotions which are brought to confront each other, and also, of course, upon the way the confrontation is contrived.

Then it can be said that the very form of a literary work, considered apart from its content, so far as that is possible, is in itself an idea. Whether we deal with syllogisms or poems, we deal with dialectic—with, that is, a developing series of statements. Or if the word "statements" seems to pre-judge the question so far as literature is concerned, let us say merely that we deal with a developing series—the important word is "developing." We judge the value of the development by judging the interest of its several stages and the propriety and the relevance of their connection among themselves. We make the judgment in terms of the implied purpose of the developing series.

Dialectic, in this sense, is just another word for form, and has for its purpose, in philosophy or in art, the leading of the mind to some conclusion. Greek drama, for example, is an arrangement of moral and emotional elements in such a way as to conduct the mind—"inevitably," as we like to say—to a certain affective condition. This condition is a quality of personal being which may be judged by the action it can be thought ultimately to lead to.

We take Aristotle to be a better critic of the drama than Plato because we perceive that Aristotle understood and Plato did not understand that the form of the drama was of itself an idea which controlled and brought to a particular issue the subordinate ideas it contained. The form of the drama *is* its idea, and its idea *is* its form. And form in those arts which we call abstract is no less an idea than is form in the representational arts. Govern ments nowadays are very simple and accurate in their perception of this—much more simple and accurate than are academic critics and aestheticians—and they are as quick to deal with the arts of "pure" form as they are to deal with ideas stated in discourse: it is as if totalitarian governments kept in mind what the rest of us tend to forget, that "idea" in one of its early significations exactly means form and was so used by many philosophers.

It is helpful to have this meaning before us when we come to consider that particular connection between literature and ideas which presents us with the greatest difficulty, the connection that involves highly elaborated ideas, or ideas as we have them in highly elaborated systems such as philosophy, or theology, or science. The modern feeling about this relationship is defined by two texts, both provided by T. S. Eliot. In his essay on Shakespeare Mr. Eliot says, "I can see no reason for believing that either Dante or Shakespeare did any thinking on his own. The people who think that Shakespeare thought are always people who are not engaged in writing poetry, but who are engaged in thinking, and we all like to think that great men were like ourselves." And in his essay on Henry James, Mr. Eliot makes the well-known remark that James had a mind so fine that no idea could violate it.

In both statements, as I believe, Mr. Eliot permits his impulse to spirited phrase to run away with him, yielding too much to what he conceives to be the didactic necessities of the moment, for he has it in mind to offer resistance to the nineteenth-century way of looking at poetry as a heuristic medium, as a communication of knowledge. This is a view which is well exemplified in a sentence of Carlyle's: "If called to define Shakespeare's faculty, I should say superiority of Intellect, and think I had included all in that." As between the two statements about Shakespeare's mental processes, I give my suffrage to Carlyle's as representing a more intelligible and a more available notion of intellect than Mr. Eliot's, but I think I understand what Mr. Eliot is trying to do with his—he is trying to rescue poetry from the kind of misinterpretation of Carlyle's view which was once more common than it is now; he is trying to save for poetry what is peculiar to it, and for systematic thought what is peculiar to it.

As for Mr. Eliot's statement about James and ideas, it is useful to us because it gives us a clue to what might be called the sociology of our question. "Henry James had a mind so fine that no idea could violate it." In the context "violate" is a strong word, yet we can grant that the mind of the poet is a sort of Clarissa Harlowe and that an idea is a sort of Colonel Lovelace, for it is a truism of contemporary thought that the whole nature of man stands in danger of being brutalized by the intellect, or at least by some one of its apparently accredited surrogates. A specter haunts our culture—it is that people will eventually be unable to say, "They fell in love and married," let alone understand the language of *Romeo and Juliet*, but will as a matter of course say, "Their libidinal impulses being reciprocal, they activated their individual erotic drives and integrated them within the same frame of reference."

Now this is not the language of abstract thought or of any kind of thought. It is the language of non-thought. But it is the language which is developing from the peculiar status which we in our culture have given to abstract thought. There can be no doubt whatever that it constitutes a threat to the emotions and thus to life itself.

The specter of what this sort of language suggests has haunted us since the end of the eighteenth century. When he speaks of the mind being violated by an idea, Mr. Eliot, like the Romantics, is simply voicing his horror at the prospect of life being intellectualized out of all spontaneity and reality.

We are the people of the idea, and we rightly fear that the intellect will dry up the blood in our veins and wholly check the emotional and creative part of the mind. And although I said that the fear of the total sovereignty of the abstract intellect began in the Romantic period, we are of course touching here upon Pascal's opposition between two faculties of the mind, of which *l'esprit de finesse* has its heuristic powers no less than *l'esprit de géométrie*, powers of discovery and knowledge which have a particular value for the establishment of man in society and the universe.

But to call ourselves the people of the idea is to flatter ourselves. We are rather the people of ideology, which is a very different thing. Ideology is not the product of thought; it is the habit or the ritual of showing respect for certain formulas to which, for various reasons having to do with emotional safety, we have very strong ties of whose meaning and consequences in actuality we have no clear understanding. The nature of ideology may in part be understood from its tendency to develop the sort of language I parodied, and scarcely parodied, a moment ago.

It is therefore no wonder that any critical theory that conceives itself to be at the service of the emotions, and of life itself, should turn a very strict and jealous gaze upon an intimate relationship between literature and ideas, for in our culture ideas tend to deteriorate into ideology. And indeed it is scarcely surprising that criticism, in its zeal to protect literature and life from the tyranny of the rational intellect, should misinterpret the relationship. Mr. Eliot, if we take him literally, does indeed misinterpret the relationship when he conceives of "thinking" in such a way that it must be denied to Shakespeare and Dante. It must puzzle us to know what thinking is if Shakespeare and Dante did not do it.

And it puzzles us to know what René Wellek and Austin Warren mean when in their admirable *Theory of Literature* they say that literature can make use of ideas only when ideas "cease to be ideas in the ordinary sense of concepts and become symbols, or even myths." I am not sure that the ordinary sense of *ideas* actually is *concepts*, or at any rate concepts of such abstractness that they do not arouse in us feelings and attitudes. And I take it that when we speak of the relationship of literature and ideas, the ideas we refer to are not those of mathematics or of symbolic logic, but only such ideas as can arouse and traditionally have aroused the feelings—

the ideas, for example, of men's relation to one another
and to the world. A poet's simple statement of a psychological fact recalls us to a proper simplicity about the
nature of ideas. "Our continued influxes of feeling,"
said Wordsworth, "are modified and directed by our
thoughts, which are indeed the representatives of all our
past feelings." The interflow between emotion and idea is
a psychological fact which we do well to keep clearly in
mind, together with the part that is played by desire,
will, and imagination in philosophy as well as in literature. Mr. Eliot, and Mr. Wellek and Mr. Warren—and
in general those critics who are zealous in the defense of
the autonomy of poetry—prefer to forget the ground
which is common to both emotion and thought; they
presume ideas to be only the product of formal systems
of philosophy, not remembering, at least on the occasion
of their argument, that poets too have their effect in the
world of thought. *L'esprit de finesse* is certainly not to be
confused with *l'esprit de géométrie*, but neither—which
is precisely the point of Pascal's having distinguished and
named the two different qualities of mind—is it to be
denied its powers of comprehension and formulation.

Mr. Wellek and Mr. Warren tell us that "the artist
will be hampered by too much ideology[1] if it remains
unassimilated." We note the tautology of the statement
—for what else is "too much" ideology except ideology
that *is* unassimilated?—not because we wish to take a
disputatious advantage over authors to whom we have
reason to be grateful, but because the tautology suggests
the uneasiness of the position it defends. We are speaking of art, which is an activity which defines itself exactly
by its powers of assimilation and of which the essence
is the just amount of any of its qualities or elements; of
course too much or unassimilated ideology will "hamper"
the artist, but so will too much of anything, so will too
much metaphor: Coleridge tells us that in a long poem
there can be too much *poetry*. The theoretical question

[1] The word is used by Mr. Wellek and Mr. Warren, not in
the pejorative sense in which I have earlier used it, but
to mean simply a body of ideas.

is simply being begged, out of an undue anxiety over the "purity" of literature, over its perfect literariness.

The authors of *Theory of Literature* are certainly right to question the "intellectualist misunderstanding of art" and the "confusions of the functions of art and philosophy" and to look for the flaws in the scholarly procedures which organize works of art according to their ideas and their affinities with philosophical systems. Yet on their own showing there has always been a conscious commerce between the poet and the philosopher, and not every poet has been violated by the ideas that have attracted him. The sexual metaphor is forced upon us, not only explicitly by Mr. Eliot but also implicitly by Mr. Wellek and Mr. Warren, who seem to think of ideas as masculine and gross and of art as feminine and pure, and who permit a union of the two sexes only when ideas give up their masculine, effective nature and "cease to be ideas in the ordinary sense and become symbols, or even myths." We naturally ask: symbols of what, myths about what? No anxious exercise of aesthetic theory can make the ideas of, say, Blake and Lawrence other than what they are intended to be—ideas relating to action and to moral judgment.

This anxiety lest the work of art be other than totally self-contained, this fear lest the reader make reference to something beyond the work itself, has its origin, as I have previously suggested, in the reaction from the earlier impulse—it goes far back beyond the nineteenth century—to show that art is justified in comparison with the effective activity of the systematic disciplines. It arises too from the strong contemporary wish to establish, in a world of unremitting action and effectiveness, the legitimacy of contemplation, which it is now no longer convenient to associate with the exercises of religion but which may be associated with the experiences of art. We will all do well to advance the cause of contemplation, to insist on the right to a haven from perpetual action and effectiveness. But we must not enforce our insistence by dealing with art as if it were a unitary thing, and by making reference only to its "purely" aesthetic element, requiring that every work of art serve our contemplation by being wholly self-contained and without relation to action. No doubt there is a large body of literature to which ideas, with their tendency to refer to action and effectiveness, are alien and inappropriate. But also much of literature wishes to give the sensations and to win the responses that are given and won by ideas, and it makes use of ideas to gain its effects, considering ideas—like people, sentiments, things, and scenes —to be indispensable elements of human life. Nor is the intention of this part of literature always an aesthetic one in the strict sense that Mr. Wellek and Mr. Warren have in mind; there is abundant evidence that the aesthetic upon which the critic sets primary store is to the poet himself frequently of only secondary importance.

We can grant that the province of poetry is one thing and the province of intellection another. But keeping the difference well in mind, we must yet see that systems of ideas have a particular quality which is much coveted as their chief effect—let us even say as their chief aesthetic effect—by at least certain kinds of literary works. Say what we will as critics and teachers trying to defend the province of art from the dogged tendency of our time to ideologize all things into grayness, say what we will about the "purely" literary, the purely aesthetic values, we as readers know that we demand of our literature some of the virtues which define a successful work of systematic thought. We want it to have—at least when it is appropriate for it to have, which is by no means infrequently—the authority, the cogency, the completeness, the brilliance, the *hardness* of systematic thought.[2]

---

[2] Mr. Wellek and Mr. Warren say something of the same sort, but only, as it were, in a concessive way: "Philosophy, ideological content, in its proper context, seems to enhance artistic value because it corroborates several important artistic values: those of complexity and coherence. . . . But it need not be so. The artist will be hampered by too much ideology if it remains unassimilated" (p. 122). Earlier (p. 27) they say: "Serious art implies a view of life which can be stated in philosophical terms, even in terms of systems. Between artistic coherence . . . and philosophic co-

Of late years criticism has been much concerned to insist on the indirection and the symbolism of the language of poetry. I do not doubt that the language of poetry is very largely that of indirection and symbolism. But it is not only that. Poetry is closer to rhetoric than we today are willing to admit; syntax plays a greater part in it than our current theory grants, and syntax connects poetry with rational thought, for, as Hegel says, "grammar, in its extended and consistent form"—by which he means syntax—"is the work of thought, which makes its categories distinctly visible therein." And those poets of our time who make the greatest impress upon us are those who are most aware of rhetoric, which is to say, of the intellectual content of their work. Nor is the intellectual content of their work simply the inevitable effect produced by good intelligence turned to poetry; many of these poets—Yeats and Eliot himself come most immediately to mind—have been at great pains to develop consistent intellectual positions along with, and consonant with, their work in poetry.

The aesthetic effect of intellectual cogency, I am convinced, is not to be slighted. Let me give an example for what it is worth. Of recent weeks my mind has been much engaged by two statements, disparate in length and in genre, although as it happens they have related themes. One is a couplet of Yeats:

> We had fed the heart on fantasies,
> The heart's grown brutal from the fare.

I am hard put to account for the force of the statement. It certainly does not lie in any metaphor, for only the dimmest sort of metaphor is to be detected. Nor does it lie in any special power of the verse. The statement has for me the pleasure of relevance and cogency, in part conveyed to me by the content, in part by the rhetoric. The other statement is Freud's short book, his last, *An*

---

herence there is some kind of correlation." They then hasten to distinguish between emotion and thinking, sensibility and intellection, etc., and to tell us that art is more complex than "propaganda."

Outline of Psychoanalysis, which gives me a pleasure which is no doubt different from that given by Yeats's couplet, but which is also similar; it is the pleasure of listening to a strong, decisive, self-limiting voice uttering statements to which I can give assent. The pleasure I have in responding to Freud I find very difficult to distinguish from the pleasure which is involved in responding to a satisfactory work of art.

Intellectual assent in literature is not quite the same thing as agreement. We can take pleasure in literature where we do not agree, responding to the power or grace of a mind without admitting the rightness of its intention or conclusion—we can take our pleasure from an intellect's *cogency*, without making a final judgment on the correctness or adaptability of what it says.

II

And now I leave these general theoretical matters for a more particular concern—the relation of contemporary American literature to ideas. In order to come at this as directly as possible we might compare modern American prose literature—for American poetry is a different thing —with modern European literature. European literature of, say, the last thirty or forty years seems to me to be, in the sense in which I shall use the word, essentially an active literature. It does not, at its best, consent to be merely comprehended. It refuses to be understood as a "symptom" of its society, although of course it may be that, among other things. It does not submit to being taped. We as scholars and critics try to discover the source of its effective energy and of course we succeed in some degree. But inevitably we become aware that it happily exists beyond our powers of explanation, although not, certainly, beyond our powers of response. Proust, Joyce, Lawrence, Kafka, Yeats and Eliot himself do not allow us to finish with them; and the refusal is repeated by a great many European writers less large than these. With exceptions that I shall note, the same thing cannot be said of modern American literature.

American literature seems to me essentially passive: our minds tend always to be made up about this or that American author, and we incline to speak of him, not merely incidentally but conclusively, in terms of his moment in history, of the conditions of the culture that "produced" him. Thus American literature as an academic subject is not so much a *subject* as an *object* of study: it does not, as a literature should, put the scrutinizer of it under scrutiny but, instead, leaves its students with a too comfortable sense of complete comprehension.

When we try to discover the root of this difference between European and American literature, we are led to the conclusion that it is the difference between the number and weight or force of the ideas which the two literatures embody or suggest. I do not mean that European literature makes use of, as American literature does not, the ideas of philosophy or theology or science. Kafka does not exemplify Kierkegaard, Proust does not dramatize Bergson. One way of putting the relationship of this literature to ideas is to say that the literature of contemporary Europe is in competition with philosophy, theology, and science, that it seeks to match them in comprehensiveness and power and seriousness.

This is not to say that the best of contemporary European literature makes upon us the effect of a rational system of thought. Quite the contrary, indeed; it is precisely its artistic power that we respond to, which I take in part to be its power of absorbing and disturbing us in secret ways. But this power it surely derives from its commerce, according to its own rules, with systematic ideas.

For in the great issues with which the mind has traditionally been concerned there is, I would submit, something *primitive* which is of the highest value to the literary artist. I know that it must seem a strange thing to say, for we are in the habit of thinking of systematic ideas as being of the very essence of the not-primitive, of the highly developed. No doubt they are: but they are at the same time the means by which a complex civilization keeps the primitive in mind and refers to it.

Whence and whither, birth and death, fate, free will, and immortality—these are never far from systematic thought; and Freud's belief that the child's first inquiry—beyond which, really, the adult does not go in kind—is in effect a sexual one seems to me to have an empirical support from literature. The ultimate questions of conscious and rational thought about the nature of man and his destiny match easily in the literary mind with the dark *un*conscious and with the most primitive human relationships. Love, parenthood, incest, patricide: these are what the great ideas suggest to literature, these are the means by which they express themselves. I need but mention three great works of different ages to suggest how true this is: *Oedipus, Hamlet, The Brothers Karamazov.*

Ideas, if they are large enough and of a certain kind, are not only not hostile to the creative process, as some think, but are virtually inevitable to it. Intellectual power and emotional power go together. And if we can say, as I think we can, that contemporary American prose literature in general lacks emotional power, it is possible to explain the deficiency by reference to the intellectual weakness of American prose literature.

The situation in verse is different. Perhaps this is to be accounted for by the fact that the best of our poets are, as good poets usually are, scholars of their tradition. There is present to their minds the degree of intellectual power which poetry is traditionally expected to exert. Questions of form and questions of language seem of themselves to demand, or to create, an adequate subject matter; and a highly developed aesthetic implies a matter strong enough to support its energy. We have not a few poets who are subjects and not objects, who are active and not passive. One does not finish quickly, if at all, with the best work of, say, Cummings, Stevens, and Marianne Moore. This work is not exempt from our judgment, even from adverse judgment, but it is able to stay with a mature reader as a continuing element of his spiritual life. Of how many writers of prose fiction can we say anything like the same thing?

The topic which was originally proposed to me for this occasion and which I have taken the liberty of generalizing was the debt of four American writers to Freud and Spengler. The four writers were O'Neill, Dos Passos, Wolfe, and Faulkner. Of the first three how many can be continuing effective elements of our mental lives? I hope I shall never read Mr. Dos Passos without interest nor ever lose the warm though qualified respect that I feel for his work. But it is impossible for me to feel of this work that it is autonomous, that it goes on existing beyond our powers of explanation. As for Eugene O'Neill and Thomas Wolfe, I can respect the earnestness of their dedication, but I cannot think of having a living, reciprocal relation with what they have written. And I believe that is because these men, without intellectual capital of their own, don't owe a sufficient debt of ideas to anyone. Spengler is certainly not a great mind; at best he is but a considerable dramatist of the idea of world history and of, as it were, the natural history of cultures; and we can find him useful as a critic who summarizes the adverse views of our urban, naturalistic culture which many have held. Freud is a very great mind indeed. Without stopping to specify what actual influence of ideas was exerted by Spengler and Freud on O'Neill, Dos Passos, or Wolfe, or even to consider whether there was any influence at all, we can fairly assume that all are in something of the same ambiance. But if, in that ambiance, we want the sense of the actuality of doom—actuality being one of the qualities we expect of literature—surely we do better to seek it in Spengler himself than in any of the three literary artists, just as, if we want the sense of the human mystery, of tragedy truly conceived in the great terms of free will, necessity, and hope, surely we do far better to seek it directly in Freud himself than in these three literary men.

In any extended work of literature, the aesthetic effect, as I have said, depends in large degree upon intellectual power, upon the amount and recalcitrance of the material the mind works on, and upon the mind's success in mastering the large material. And it is exactly the lack of intellectual power that makes our three writers, after our first response of interest, so inadequate aesthetically. We have only to compare, say, Dos Passos's *USA* to a work of similar kind and intention, Flaubert's *L'Education Sentimentale,* to see that in Dos Passos's novel the matter encompassed is both less in amount and less in resistance than in Flaubert's; the energy of the encompassing mind is also less. Or we consider O'Neill's crude, dull notion of the unconscious and his merely elementary grasp of Freud's ideas about sex and we recognize the lamentable signs of a general inadequacy of mind. Or we ask what it is about Thomas Wolfe that always makes us uncomfortable with his talent, so that even his admirers deal with him not as a subject but as an object —an object which must be explained and accounted for—and we are forced to answer that it is the disproportion between the energy of his utterance and his power of mind. It is customary to say of Thomas Wolfe that he is an emotional writer. Perhaps: although it is probably not the most accurate way to describe a writer who could deal with but one single emotion; and we feel that it is a function of his unrelenting, tortured egoism that he could not submit his mind to the ideas that might have brought the variety and interest of order to the single, dull chaos of his powerful self-regard, for it is true that the intellect makes many emotions out of the primary egoistic one.

At this point it may be well to recall what our subject is. It is not merely the part that is played in literature by those ideas which may be derived from the study of systematic, theoretical works; it is the part that is played in literature by ideas in general. To be sure, the extreme and most difficult instance of the general relation of literature to ideas is the relation of literature to highly developed and formulated ideas; and because this is indeed so difficult a matter, and one so often misconceived, I have put a special emphasis upon it. But we do not present our subject adequately—we do not, indeed, represent the mind adequately—if we think of ideas only as being highly formulated. It will bring us back to the proper generality of our subject if I say that the two contemporary writers who hold out to me the possibility of a living reciprocal relationship with their work are Ernest Hemingway and William Faulkner—it will bring us back the more dramatically because Hemingway and Faulkner have insisted on their indifference to the conscious intellectual tradition of our time and have acquired the reputation of achieving their effects by means that have the least possible connection with any sort of intellectuality or even with intelligence.

In trying to explain a certain commendable quality which is to be found in the work of Hemingway and Faulkner—and a certain quality only, not a total and unquestionable literary virtue—we are not called upon by our subject to show that particular recognizable ideas of a certain force or weight are "used" in the work. Nor are we called upon to show that new ideas of a certain force and weight are "produced" by the work. All that we need to do is account for a certain aesthetic effect as being in some important part achieved by a mental process which is not different from the process by which discursive ideas are conceived, and which is to be judged by some of the criteria by which an idea is judged.

The aesthetic effect which I have in mind can be suggested by a word that I have used before—activity. We feel that Hemingway and Faulkner are intensely at work upon the recalcitrant stuff of life; when they are at their best they give us the sense that the amount and intensity of their activity are in a satisfying proportion to the recalcitrance of the material. And our pleasure in their activity is made the more secure because we have the distinct impression that the two novelists are not under any illusion that they have conquered the material upon which they direct their activity. The opposite is true of Dos Passos, O'Neill, and Wolfe; at each point of conclusion in their work we feel that *they* feel that they have said the last word, and we feel this even when they represent themselves, as O'Neill and Wolfe so often do, as puzzled and baffled by life. But of Hemingway and Faulkner we seldom have the sense that they have deceived themselves, that they have misrepresented to themselves the nature and the difficulty of the matter they work on. And we go on to make another intellectual judgment: we say that the matter they present, together with the degree of difficulty which they assume it to have, seems to be very cogent. This, we say, is to the point; this really has something to do with life as we live it; we cannot ignore it.

There is a traditional and aggressive rationalism that can understand thought only in its conscious, developed form and believes that the phrase "unconscious mind" is a meaningless contradiction in terms. Such a view, wrong as I think it is, has at least the usefulness of warning us that we must not call by the name of thought or idea all responses of the human organism whatever. But the extreme rationalist position ignores the simple fact that the life of reason, at least in its most extensive part, begins in the emotions. What comes into being when two contradictory emotions are made to confront each other and are required to have a relationship with each other is, as I have said, quite properly called an idea. Ideas may also be said to be generated in the opposition of ideals, and in the felt awareness of the impact of new circumstances upon old forms of feeling and estimation, in the response to the conflict between new exigencies and old pieties. And it can be said that a work will have what I have been calling cogency in the degree that the confronting emotions go deep, or in the degree that the old pieties are firmly held and the new exigencies strongly apprehended. In Hemingway's stories[3] a strongly charged piety toward the ideals and attachments of boyhood and the lusts of maturity is in conflict not only with the imagination of death but also with that imagination as it is peculiarly modified by the dark negation of the modern world. Faulkner as a Southerner of today, a man deeply implicated in the pieties of his tradition, is of course at the very heart of an exigent historical event which thrusts upon him the awareness of the inadequacy

[3] It is in the stories rather than in the novels that Hemingway is characteristic and at his best.

and wrongness of the very tradition he loves. In the work of both men the cogency is a function not of their conscious but of their unconscious minds. We can, if we admire Tolstoi and Dostoevski, regret the deficiency of consciousness, blaming it for the inadequacy in both our American writers of the talent for generalization.[4] Yet it is to be remarked that the unconscious minds of both men have wisdom and humility about themselves. They seldom make the attempt at formulated solution, they rest content with the "negative capability." And this negative capability, this willingness to remain in uncertainties, mysteries, and doubts, is not, as one tendency of modern feeling would suppose, an abdication of intellectual activity. Quite to the contrary, it is precisely an aspect of their intelligence, of their seeing the full force and complexity of their subject matter. And this we can understand the better when we observe how the unconscious minds of Dos Passos, O'Neill, and Wolfe do not possess humility and wisdom; nor are they fully active, as the intellectual histories of all three men show. A passivity on the part of Dos Passos before the idea of the total corruption of American civilization has issued in his later denial of the possibility of economic and social reform and in his virtually unqualified acceptance of the American status quo. A passivity on the part of O'Neill before the clichés of economic and metaphysical materialism issued in his later simplistic Catholicism. The passivity of Thomas Wolfe before all his experience led him to that characteristic *malice* toward the objects or partners of his experience which no admirer of his ever takes account of, and eventually to that simple affirmation, recorded in *You Can't Go Home Again,* that literature must become the agent of the immediate solution of all social problems and undertake the prompt eradication of human pain; and because his closest friend did not agree

[4] Although there is more impulse to generalization than is usually supposed. This is especially true of Faulkner, who has never subscribed to the contemporary belief that only concrete words have power and that only the representation of things and actions is dramatic.

that this was a possible thing for literature to do, Wolfe terminated the friendship. These are men of whom it is proper to speak of their having been violated by ideas; but we must observe that it was an excess of intellectual passivity that invited the violence.

In speaking of Hemingway and Faulkner I have used the word "piety." It is a word that I have chosen with some care and despite the pejorative meanings that nowadays adhere to it, for I wished to avoid the word "religion," and piety is not religion, yet I wished too to have religion come to mind as it inevitably must when piety is mentioned. Carlyle says of Shakespeare that he was the product of medieval Catholicism, and implies that Catholicism *at the distance at which Shakespeare stood from it* had much to do with the power of Shakespeare's intellect. Allen Tate has developed in a more particular way an idea that has much in common with what Carlyle here implies. Loosely put, the idea is that religion in its decline leaves a detritus of pieties, of strong assumptions, which afford a particularly fortunate condition for certain kinds of literature; these pieties carry a strong charge of intellect, or perhaps it would be more accurate to say that they tend to stimulate the mind in a powerful way.

Religious emotions are singularly absent from Shakespeare and it does not seem possible to say of him that he was a religious man. Nor does it seem possible to say of the men of the great period of American literature in the nineteenth century that they were religious men. Hawthorne and Melville, for example, lived at a time when religion was in decline and they were not drawn to support it. But from religion they inherited a body of pieties, a body of issues, if you will, which engaged their hearts and their minds to the very bottom. Henry James was not a religious man and there is not the least point in the world in trying to make him out one. But you need not accept all the implications of Quentin Anderson's thesis that James allegorized his father's religious system to see that Mr. Anderson is right when he says that James was dealing, in his own way, with the questions that his father's system propounded. This will indicate something of why James so catches our imagination today, and why we turn so eagerly again to Hawthorne and Melville.

The piety which descends from religion is not the only possible piety, as the case of Faulkner reminds us, and perhaps also the case of Hemingway. But we naturally mention first that piety which does descend from religion because it is most likely to have in it the quality of transcendence which, whether we admit it or no, we expect literature at its best to have.

The subject is extremely delicate and complex and I do no more than state it barely and crudely. But no matter how I state it, I am sure that you will see that what I am talking about leads us to the crucial issue of our literary culture.

I know that I will not be wrong if I assume that most of us here are in our social and political beliefs consciously liberal and democratic. And I know that I will not be wrong if I say that most of us, and in the degree of our commitment to literature and our familiarity with it, find that the contemporary authors we most wish to read and most wish to admire for their literary qualities demand of us a great agility and ingenuity in coping with their antagonism to our social and political ideals. For it is in general true that the modern European literature to which we can have an active, reciprocal relationship, which is the right relationship to have, has been written by men who are indifferent to, or even hostile to, the tradition of democratic liberalism as we know it. Yeats and Eliot, Proust and Joyce, Lawrence and Gide—these men do not seem to confirm us in the social and political ideals which we hold.

If we now turn and consider the contemporary literature of America, we see that wherever we can describe it as patently liberal and democratic, we must say that it is not of lasting interest. I do not say that the work which is written to conform to the liberal democratic tradition is of no value but only that we do not incline to return to it, we do not establish it in our minds and affections. Very likely we learn from it as citizens; and as citizen-scholars and citizen-critics we understand and explain it. But we do not live in an active reciprocal relation with it. The sense of largeness, of cogency, of the transcendence which largeness and cogency can give, the sense of being reached in our secret and primitive minds—this we virtually never get from the writers of the liberal democratic tradition at the present time.

And since liberal democracy inevitably generates a body of ideas, it must necessarily occur to us to ask why it is that these particular ideas have not infused with force and cogency the literature that embodies them. This question is the most important, the most fully challenging question in culture that at this moment we can ask.

The answer to it cannot of course even be begun here, and I shall be more than content if now it is merely accepted as a legitimate question. But there are one or two things that may be said about the answer, about the direction we must take to reach it in its proper form. We will not find it if we come to facile conclusions about the absence from our culture of the impressive ideas of traditional religion. I have myself referred to the historical fact that religion has been an effective means of transmitting or of generating ideas of a sort which I feel are necessary for the literary qualities we want, and to some this will no doubt mean that I believe religion to be a necessary condition of great literature. I do not believe that; and what is more, I consider it from many points of view an impropriety to try to guarantee literature by religious belief.

Nor will we find our answer if we look for it in the weakness of the liberal democratic ideas in themselves. It is by no means true that the inadequacy of the literature that connects itself with a body of ideas is the sign of the inadequacy of those ideas, although it is no doubt true that some ideas have less affinity with literature than others.

Our answer, I believe, will rather be found in a cultural fact—in the kind of relationship which we, or the writers who represent us, maintain toward the ideas we claim as ours, and in our habit of conceiving the nature of ideas in general. If we find that it is true of ourselves that we conceive ideas to be pellets of intellection or crystallizations of thought, precise and completed, and defined by their coherence and their procedural recommendations, then we shall have accounted for the kind of prose literature we have. And if we find that we do indeed have this habit, and if we continue in it, we can predict that our literature will continue much as it is. But if we are drawn to revise our habit of conceiving ideas in this way and learn instead to think of ideas as living things, inescapably connected with our wills and desires, as susceptible of growth and development by their very nature, as showing their life by their tendency to change, as being liable, by this very tendency, to deteriorate and become corrupt and to work harm, then we shall stand in a relation to ideas which makes an active literature possible.